D1569083

CÉSAR VALLEJO

CÉSAR VALLEJO

THE DIALECTICS OF POETRY
AND SILENCE

Jean Franco

Professor of Spanish
Stanford University, California

CAMBRIDGE UNIVERSITY PRESS

CAMBRIDGE

LONDON · NEW YORK · MELBOURNE

Published by the Syndics of the Cambridge University Press
The Pitt Building, Trumpington Street, Cambridge CB2 1RP
Bentley House, 200 Euston Road, London NW1 2DB
32 East 57th Street, New York, NY 10022, USA
296 Beaconsfield Parade, Middle Park, Melbourne 3206, Australia

First published 1976

Printed in the United States of America
Typeset, printed and bound by Vail-Ballou Press, Inc.,
Binghamton, New York

Library of Congress Cataloguing in Publication Data
Franco, Jean.
    César Vallejo: the dialectics of poetry and silence.
Includes bibliographical references and index.
1. Vallejo, César Abraham, 1892–1938.
PQ8497.V35Z687   861 [B]   75–39393
ISBN 0 521 21063 1

CONTENTS

PREFACE

A strange fate, that of Vallejo. A poet for whom the notion of the individual was problematic, he was surrounded after his death by a personality cult so effective that his poems have usually been thought of as 'spiritual radiographies'.[1] 'The legend begins' wrote one of his acquaintances when he died in 1938. Legend already dominated the act of homage held at his graveside in Montrouge Cemetery at which Louis Aragon read a prescient message. 'He was not only a poet', said Aragon, 'but a fighter for socialism'. Yet for Aragon and most of the others present on the occasion, Vallejo was an unknown poet; his *Poemas humanos* and *España, aparta di mí este cáliz* had still to be published. Few of them suspected that his poetry responded to questions they had not begun to ask.

When he began to write, poetry was an act of transgression against the ecumenical faith of his fathers, a demonic religion whose practice took him away from his roots in the Peruvian *sierra*. In this period, before the publication in 1919 of his first collection of poems *Los heraldos negros,* he lived out the myth of the *poète maudit,* discovering in the process not a new Logos but a superstructure raised by false consciousness itself. The vatic role which, for his contemporaries, put the poet above society and absolved him from its norms was not even viable since, for the Peruvian establishment, poetry scarcely existed except as tradition or adornment; it was something intended to enhance civilized life, not to shake its foundations. Vallejo's destruction of musicality, his focusing on semantic contradictions, his sense of parody, could only bring him into conflict with society.

From *Trilce* (1922) onwards, Vallejo is the ruthless destroyer of hierarchies and values; fragments of ancient belief, the vestiges of Christian faith and of humanist *hubris* accumulate in his

---

[1] The term comes from Leo Spitzer's 'Linguistics and Literary History', *Linguistics and Literary History* (Princeton, 1948), pp. 1–40.

poems, expressed in synecdoche which no longer refers parts to a whole, in figures which no longer serve as analogies for another reality. Against the clamour of words, Vallejo sets the silent document of the body as a living text in which (after Haeckel), he saw the history of the species inscribed. For him, arms signal the fact that they have refused to become wings, the feet as columns on which *homo erectus* has raised himself over the rest of nature, his eyes are 'fatal pilots', nails are vestigial claws. Each woman's sex is the silent mouth of the species, each mouth a cry for individual survival. These are the scriptures on which each life is a gloss. The liberal thinkers of the nineteenth century had equated progress with evolution, believing that the species in its struggle for life would develop morally as well as physically and they saw the domination of nature as a necessary condition for the sovereignty of the 'I'. Though Marx separated natural evolution from the progress of social man, even he underestimated the price paid for mastery and the sinister side of enlightenment.[2] Vallejo's originality is to have related language to domination of nature as well as to civil society. It is a perception particularly interesting in Latin America where the alphabet was introduced through conquest and where script was conspicuously the tool of authority. Nevertheless, to generations of writers after Independence, the printed word was a kind of magic, the *grimoire* which would bring about liberation. The haunting ambivalence of writing fascinates contemporary novelists and the best-known of modern Latin American poets, Pablo Neruda, threw much of his energy into restoring the communion and the sense of presence which is the advantage of the spoken over the written word. When Vallejo grew up in Santiago de Chuco, literacy was still a mark of status and for the rest of his life, the sound of the first syllables a child hears and the sight of the first letters on the page are moments charged with significance. If, as Walter Ong, has suggested, script destroys the sense of presence experienced in spoken communication by giving priority to the sense of sight, then Vallejo's poetry is a desperate battle waged on two fronts –

2 The concept of enlightenment has been criticised by Max Horkheimer and Theodore W. Adorno. Their essay, 'The Concept of Enlightenment' is included in Max Horkheimer and Theodore W. Adorno, *Dialectic of Enlightenment* (New York, 1972).

against the illusion of presence and the spurious authority of script.[3]

During his long stay in Europe, from 1923 until his death, Vallejo was drawn towards committed art and active left-wing politics. He joined the Communist party and experimented in different genres – especially theatre and the narrative – which, he believed, lent themselves more readily than poetry to the socialist cause. Never as centrally involved as Brecht and many others in polemics of revolutionary art, he was, nevertheless in the Soviet Union during the critical period in which socialist realism was formulated. In the early 1930s, he even wrote materialist poems which were included in his posthumous collection, *Poemas humanos*, though these by no means dislodged his central obsessions. The poetry of the 30s records the attempt to inscribe his 'being of smoke' in a text which will outlive the silent, mortal body. The poetic subject loses all connection with a structured world, living as a stranger among reified objects he has produced but which no longer reflect a human image. Written from the vantage-point of Utopia or Apocalypse, the poems focus on the present as if it were a grotesque error. When the Spanish Civil War broke out in 1936, he fleetingly envisaged the possibility of a new scripture inscribed by the collective sacrifice in the book of humanity.

It is this analogy of the text which the present study traces. My work owes much to the considerable body of Vallejo criticism mentioned in the Guide to texts and criticism. Because of the textual problems, particularly those presented by the posthumously published poems and because of the controversy which has surrounded successive readings of his works, I have included a short guide to different critical approaches which have been applied to his work and a brief explanation of my own method.[4]

---

3 Walter Ong S.J., *The Presence of the Word* (New York, 1967). As against his defence of oral communication, see Jacques Derrida, *De la grammatologie* (Paris, 1967).

4 The term 'foregrounding' which I frequently use is derived from Jan Mukarovský, 'Standard Language and Poetic Language', trans. Paul L. Garvin, *A Prague School Reader on Esthetics, Literary Structure, and Style* (Washington, D.C., 1964). Mukarovský refers to the potential relationship between intonation and meaning, syntax, word order, or the relationship of the word as a meaningful

Though I have concentrated on those aspects of his work which I have mentioned in this introduction, I have tried to write a book that will also be useful as a general introduction to readers encountering Vallejo's poetry for the first time. The difficulty of translation cannot entirely account for the eclipse of this poet in the Anglo-Saxon world in which there is always resistance to those Latin American writers who can neither be readily incorporated into the literary system or categorized as exotic. Happily the number of translations is increasing. Those already published are listed at the end of this book and there are besides new translations of some poems. For these, I am grateful to Reginald Gibbons, who gracefully faced the obvious difficulties of making a selection from a manifold of connotations which could not possibly always match the original. A poet who uses puns as frequently as Vallejo inevitably offers a formidable task to the translator and the final versions cannot offer more than a selection among possible readings. I am also grateful to Madame Georgette de Vallejo for giving me permission to quote from her late husband's work both in the original and in translation. I should like to thank, in addition, the many people who have helped me by discussing my work, and in particular Reginald Gibbons who worked on the bibliography as well as the translating; Joseph Sommers who read part of the manuscript; the many helpful people in Peru and especially José Miguel Oviedo who gave me generous help when he was director of the Instituto de Cultura. In addition, I thank the University of Essex for enabling me to visit Peru in the summer of 1971 and the University of Stanford for a grant to complete this manuscript.

JEAN FRANCO

University of Stanford
March 1976

unit to the phonetic structure of the text, to the lexical selection found in the text, to other words as units of meaning in the context of the same sentence etc. as interlinking phenomena which in poetry are organized according to principles of subordination and superordination. Foregrounding is the process by which the dominant component which might be intonation, rhyme or the semantic properties of words energizes the poem.

ABBREVIATIONS

AO. Luis Alberto Sánchez (ed.), *Artículos olvidados de CV* (Lima, 1960).

Aproximaciones. Angel Flores (ed.), *Aproximaciones a CV,* 2 vols. (New York, 1971).

Aula Vallejo, no. 1 (1959); no. 2 corresponds to 2–3–4 (Córdoba, Argentina, 1962); no. 3 to numbers 5–6–7 (1967).

LA. CV, Literatura y Arte (Buenos Aires, 1966).

NCC. CV, Novelas y cuentos completos (Lima, 1970).

OC. Obras completas de CV (Lima, 1973–4). Vol. I: *Contra el secreto professional;* vol. II: *El arte y la revolución;* vol. III: *Obra poética completa.*

OPC. Obra poética completa (Lima, 1968).

VP. Visión del Peru, no. 4 (July 1969). This was entirely devoted to César Vallejo and is 'Homenaje internacional a CV'. Some overflow material is included in no. 5 (June 1970).

1

POETRY AS A MODE OF EXISTENCE

> When early youth had past, he left his cold
> Fireside and alienated home to seek strange
> Truths in undiscovered lands.
>
> Shelley

Human fields

The geography of Vallejo's poetry is that of anachronism: time measured in arduous distance along mountain roads, towns nestling in the past, protected by the screen of provincialism from the rude awakening into the twentieth century, villages sunk in an even remoter time, sugar-estates and mines forming brutal links in the chain of Peru's dependency. The landscape unfolds in a series of shocks quite unlike the homogeneous contemporaneity of North America. The grandeur of the past, the commonplaces of the present, traces of religious faith and sorties into bohemia – a whole archaeology of human experience is expressed in the poet's rasping, uneven poetry.

He had first of all envisaged poetry as something else, as the eagle's-eye-view of a terrain that others trudged on foot, as some rapid transit into the utmost reaches of modernity. What ensued was different. Vallejo found that to step outside the province was, in itself, to constitute a challenge to its ideology, to become subversive; yet, of itself, this challenge did not give him a passport into the modern world. Anachronism was both his curse and his hidden weapon. It stigmatized him as a provincial, but it prevented him from accepting the contemporary world as a given or as a glory. There would be no Futurist celebration of the machine, just as there would be no sentimentalization of the past. When he began his journey in Santiago de Chuco he wanted to become a poet in the Romantic manner, to be above and beyond the reach of ordinary men. He quickly found that to become a poet in this sense, he would have to falsify poetry; that to write would take him where he had not originally wanted to go.

1

When Vallejo was born, on 16 March 1892, Santiago de Chuco was a *sierra* town of about 14,000 inhabitants, situated in the district of *La Libertad*. The journey to the provincial capital of Trujillo was difficult enough – four days' horse-ride to the nearest rail-head on the Menocucho estate and then a train journey to Trujillo. To get to Lima meant taking the boat at the port of Salaverry near Trujillo and a three-day voyage down the Pacific coast. The length of the journey gives a measure of the anachronism, which as Vallejo said in one of his stories made the hill town a Shangri-La, forgotten by the rest of Peru.[1] The region had, in pre-colonial times, formed part of the empire of the Chimu-Mojica desert peoples and both the coast plains and the mountains were rich in archaeology. It was, like most of the rest of Peru, a region of large estates, peon labour and feudal paternalism, where the introduction of industry had served to strengthen the landowning oligarchy. Mining, the main form of industrial production, was particularly well-served by the feudal structure since it gave the mine-owners access to forced labour.[2] The base of the pyramidal social structure was formed by an exploited labour-force of Indians and *cholos* (those of mixed Indian and Hispanic blood). In between were the lawyers, teachers and artisans who formed the middle sector of Santiago de Chuco and who, whatever standing they might have locally, could never hope to make a mark outside the province. The family was the most important social unit. As in mediaeval Europe, feast days had great ritual importance in the life of the town, and that of Santiago el Apóstol held between July 13th and early August was the highpoint of the liturgical year.[3]

A friend of Vallejo's student days was to describe him sentimentally as a 'humble mountain boy' with 'modest ambitions to graduate just like so many poor Indians pitilessly engulfed by the University'.[4] But though modest by Trujillo or Lima standards, in Santiago de Chuco the Vallejo family were certainly not considered either Indian or particularly humble. The two grandmothers of Vallejo, Justa Benites and Natividad Gurrionero were Chimu women who must have been assimilated into *mestizo* culture and had probably entered the priest's house as housekeepers or servants. When César was born, the youngest son in a family of eleven children, his father (born in 1840) was already fifty-two and his mother forty-two.[5] Vallejo's father became a local dignitary who served as one of the governors of Santiago de Chuco, that is, as a district official directly responsible to the sub-prefect. Photographs of the family show strong faces, immense pride, a certain care – even elegance – in their manner of dress which reflects a sense of their own worth. This sense was fortified by the moral rectitude of the father and mother, the religious upbringing of the children and the daily family prayers. The structure and stability of social and private life were positive aspects of provincialism and gave a strong sense of identity. Lines were clearly drawn, duties clearly defined, behaviour governed by a generally accepted code. Because the family was a micro-model of the holy family, these structures did not appear arbitrary but constant and universal.

In the restricted environment of Santiago de Chuco, there was probably little open conflict between the public and private domains. God's book was interpreted by the Church, man's civic state by laws. Vallejo's father had, so to speak, one foot in both camps, being a deeply religious man who worked as a notary and undertook minor legal business and litigation. It was a profession of importance, since the high level of illiteracy gave the clerk a privileged position in the community. It is no exaggeration to see the notary's relation to the law as analogous to that of the priest. Both the Church and the state operated through a hier-archy of mediators who interpreted the texts for the layman; for both, the 'word' was the source of truth but also of error. So Vallejo grew up in an environment in which words had extra-ordinary power; the acquisition of language marked the begin-ning of consciousness and also of a sense of alienation. This is borne out by a vivid anecdote; as a child, he would watch the bellringer Santiago coming and going from the belfry at vespers. Though blind, Santiago was afraid of the dark, and used to walk back from the belfry muttering the magic formula, 'Don't be afraid, Santiago'.[6] Vallejo's fascination with this anecdote sprang from his sense of both the power and the inefficacy of words. In poem 20, of *Trilce*, learning to spell, letter by letter, becomes a significant part of the child's rite of passage into the confusion of adulthood:

> La niña en tanto pónese el índice
> en la lengua que empieza a deletrear
> los enredos de enredos de los enredos.

While the little girl puts her finger
On her tongue, that's beginning to spell out
The tangles of the tangles of the tangles.

In 1905, when he was thirteen, Vallejo went to secondary
school in the city of Huamachuco, where he boarded throughout
his studies. His stay was intermittent: in 1907, because of family
financial difficulties, he was at home in Santiago, but he returned
to Huamachuco to complete his secondary schooling in 1908. The
novelist Ciro Alegría, who came from this region, gives a description of the dramatic landscape 'filled with solitude and silence',
with its great rocks and dizzying ravines.[7] Vallejo was to remember the journey on horseback to the town he later referred
to (perhaps ironically) as the 'Athens of the Andes' and speaks
humorously of 'trotting away on my chestnut pony, my hair awry,
like a nomadic tent lost in the desert'.[8] And the return journey to
Santiago was as unforgettable, with the ride across grain fields
and the town in the distance on its low table-land.

The journeys grew longer. In 1910 he registered at the Faculty
of Letters at Trujillo University, and in 1911 he was in Lima,
where he studied briefly as a medical student before being forced
to withdraw for economic reasons. Between leaving secondary
school and the short periods of university life, he also tried his
hand at a series of jobs. He helped his father with his legal
documents, and worked in the offices of mines in Tambores and
Quiruvilca,[9] an experience he later used in his novel El tungsteno
(1931). In 1911 he became tutor to the son of a wealthy mine-
owner in the province of Pasco in Central Peru and in 1912 held
a job in the accounts department of a large sugar estate, the
hacienda 'Roma' in the Chicama valley. So, before completing a
degree at the University, and before any of his poetry was published, Vallejo had tried most of the careers open to someone in
his position. His brothers, Víctor, Nestor and Manuel, were to
settle for what they could get. Víctor became the administrator
of an estate, Nestor a judge in Huamachuco. Only the poet César
escaped from the conditions of his social class.

The period 1908–13 is one of the least documented in Vallejo's
life and it is only from his later writing that we can judge its
significance. The mines and the sugar estates on which he worked
for a short time were places of brutal repression, in which the
class to which he belonged acted as willing or unwilling instru-

ments of the owners. In his depiction of Benites (the surname of his paternal grandmother) in the novel *El tungsteno,* he must have drawn on his own early experience. Benites has to work at the mine (like Vallejo) to earn money to continue his studies. He finds that the Christian morality he has brought to the job is inadequate in the brutal conditions in which he now finds himself. Christian love conflicts with the Samuel Smiles' philosophy of the petty bourgeois, and both are totally irrelevant to the cruel and naked repression inherent in the system. Vallejo's actual experience could not have been much different; on the sugar plantations and in the mines around Santiago de Chuco, the regimentation of unorganized and helpless workers and their slave-like condition threw into relief the pathetic irrelevancy of Christian teaching, which, at its simplest level, stated that it was better to give than to receive and that the rich man would not find it easy to enter the kingdom of Heaven. Vallejo's society was one in which a brash, merciless capitalism (mostly of foreign origin) co-existed with traditional Christian ideology, which supported the status quo; there was no bourgeois class prepared to challenge the oligarchy or demand elementary rights for the whole of society. Apart from isolated intellectuals, like Manuel González Prada, who derived their reputation from their polemical writings rather than from any broadly based social movement, there were few willing to combat the obvious injustices of society.

The sugar estate where Vallejo worked in 1912 was another stage of his education in the nature of Peruvian society. The 'Roma' was owned by the Larco Herreras, one of two big families (the other being the Gildemeisters) who had come to monopolize the sugar industry after the end of the war of the Pacific in 1883. The Larco Herreras and the Gildemeisters were immigrant families who had acquired vast estates in the Chicama valley between the *sierra* and the Pacific, estates which recruited an army of labourers, mainly from the surrounding rural areas, and converted them into a proletariat.[10] Life on the sugar plantations was highly regimented. Even the clerks like Vallejo, who worked in the administration building, lived lives of stark simplicity, isolated from all but their co-workers. They were forced to spend long hours in the office, especially when pay-packets were being prepared, and Larco Herrera's puritanical and paternalistic ré-

gime made life even harder for them, since they were not allowed to buy alcohol and had to go to bed early. The estates
were virtually self-sufficient enclaves. Workers bought their sup-
plies from a company store, and after the Gildemeisters' successful campaign to open their own port, which finally started
functioning in 1918, the sugar plantations became independent
even of the Trujillo merchants. This isolation, and the conditions
under which the workers lived, encouraged the organization of
labour; some of the active militants in the strikes of 1921 (at
least one of whom, like Vallejo, came from Santiago de Chuco)
were first introduced to the works of Lenin, Trotsky, Kropotkin
and Gorky on the 'Roma' estate.[11] Even before the days of union
organization, there were spontaneous riots, when machete-
wielding workers shouted threats against the bosses and the
administration. During the year that Vallejo worked on the
'Roma', the nearby Gildemeister estate was looted and burned
by angry workers, some of whom were shot by troops brought
in to quell the riot. At the very least, it must have made Vallejo
aware of his perilous situation as middleman between boss and
workers. Certainly in his novel and short stories written many
years after, he invariably expresses repugnance for estate life. In
El tungsteno, the protagonist recalls an estate-owner 'famous for
his bloody tyranny over the workers', and in a short story 'Viaje
alrededor del porvenir',[12] written towards the end of his life, a
brutal owner has injected material incentives even into the private relations of his estate-manager, offering him a money re-
ward if and when his wife conceives a son.

   To be a poet in this kind of society is, unless one is content
to be the local poetaster, to declare oneself dangerously nonconformist.[13] Vallejo, who was early in life labelled a poet, found
that transgression of the social norm quickly turned into defiance
of a society which tolerated only those who were prepared to
support its ideological assumptions, and that what was tolerated
as an aberration in Santiago de Chuco was considered wild
eccentricity in Trujillo.

Modernism and anachronism

Vallejo's years as a student at the University really began in 1913,
when he registered at Trujillo for a degree in literature. While
studying, he taught first at the Centro Escolar de Varones and

later as a primary school teacher in the Colegio Nacional de San Juan.[14] The poets he had read at this time were mostly Spanish – the great poets of the Golden Age, especially Quevedo – and the Romantic poetry that was still popular in the provinces.[15] This very popularity, especially for the sentimental verse written by the Mexicans Juan de Dios Pieza and Manuel Acuña was, of course, an indication that it was 'safe', a respectable literary outlet for 'feeling'. And Trujillo, hopelessly in the wake of literary innovation, scarcely seemed a promising place in which to begin an education as a poet. It was a city that still preserved the atmosphere of colonial times with little social life outside the family. The painter, Macedonio de la Torre, has left a vivid description of its tedium:

The children of the rich did not dirty their hands; they never dreamed of work or a profession. They were all hunters, card-players and cock-fighters. They had great packs of dogs, and guns, rifles, game-cocks and they believed themselves infallible in everything. They knew everything. The city was like a monastery. There were no meetings or parties and no days off except on the 28th July and at Christmas. When the 28th July celebrations were over, I used to feel sad, thinking that I should have to spend another year without being able to meet my fellow-men. Everybody shut themselves up inside their houses. The whole of life went on behind closed doors and behind the barred windows of the silent city. Falling in love was, of course, a problem. To meet a woman, we had to stand on guard at street-corners, day after day, and when the beauty showed herself from behind a blind or at a half-open door, we had to take advantage of this to throw her a note written on paper that had yellowed with the waiting.[16]

In this anachronistic environment, Vallejo discovered the Romantic movement as if it were newly proclaimed. Writing his dissertation on the subject of 'Romanticism in Castilian poetry', he shows himself well aware of contemporary positivist theories of literature and ideas such as those of Taine, Le Bon and Fouillée who had accounted for national characteristics in literature and intellectual life. But when he deals with a poet he really likes, such as the Spanish poet, José Espronceda, his prose becomes more fervent, imitating the lofty flights of the Cuban writer, José Martí. For Vallejo, the poet is already a hero who seizes the 'standard of rebellion and rising up with it to heights never before scaled by man, he plants it there before flying off to his Glory'.[17] These lofty claims for poetry, made among others by his compatriot, Manuel González Prada, encouraged dizzying ambitions in the young writers of Latin America, most of whom had not yet understood that public poetry was not, however noble its tone, 'beyond ideology' and so must be either an adornment for the system or in conflict with it. Nor did anyone question the poet's authority to assume a prophetic or public tone. For Manuel González Prada, for instance, it was simply a matter of choice: 'He who speaks of himself, his family or nation,' he wrote, 'deserves a narrow public: but he who speaks for Humanity has the right to be heard by all men'.[18]

When Vallejo was writing his first poetry in Trujillo, the enormously popular essay *Ariel* by the Uruguayan José Enrique Rodó was circulating in Latin America. Published in 1900, the essay influenced several generations of Latin Americans, giving a picture of the nobility of the life of the spirit: indeed, 'nobility' was a word much used at the time to refer to the 'aristocracy of the best' as against those who were possessed of mere material power and possessions. Poets like Rubén Darío, José Santos Chocano, Ricardo Jaimes Freyre considered themselves spokesmen of their race or nation precisely because they belonged to this aristocracy of the spirit and believed their motives to be 'disinterested'. Certainly there was some validity in their claims: poets were appointed consuls, became arbiters of frontier disputes, and were called upon to celebrate important civic occasions in their poetry. All this strengthened their conviction that they were 'above the battle' when in fact they sometimes found themselves under the patronage of the oligarchs. Both Darío and Santos Chocano enjoyed writing ornamental rhetorical verse which was not at all in conflict with the tastes of elegant oligarchs who knew what was fashionable in Paris. It is too simple to see these poets as the voices of a class; on the other hand their contempt for 'materialism' and the bourgeois hardly went deep enough to disturb the wealthy landowners and elegant cattle-barons who, no doubt, also felt above 'materialism'. However, the Modernists were a dazzling success at giving prestige and dignity to the practice of letters and, as a result, poetry was one clear light for someone like Vallejo who wished to find his way out of the provincialism of Trujillo.

The first poem Vallejo published under his own name belongs to the tradition of civic poetry with which the Modernists had never completely broken. He declaimed it at a student parade, reciting his verse from a balcony overlooking O'Donovan square.[19]

The poem, 'Primaveral', is a celebration of youth (hardly surprisingly). It ended in an abrupt anti-climax, as the poet appears suddenly to realize that he is in danger of becoming blasphemous:

> ¡Juventud! Patria en flor. Trueno. Armonía
> y suspiro de amor . . . La Primavera
> renovando tus ímpetus podría
> convertirte en un Dios . . . si Dios no hubiera.[20]

> Youth! Nation in flower. Thunder. Harmony
> And sighs of love. Spring
> Which renews your powers might
> Turn you into a God . . . if God did not exist.

Vallejo also wrote didactic poems for children, published in the magazine *Cultura Infantil*. Pedagogy through poetry was not unusual in a period when the ideal of the 'teacher' as enlightener was held by many intellectuals who believed that a better society would only be achieved through education. Two contemporaries of Vallejo, Gabriela Mistral of Chile and the Venezuelan novelist Rómulo Gallegos, were dedicated teachers who regarded their profession as a mission. Even so, there is something incongruous about Vallejo's attempts to versify the laws of condensation, exmosis and the scientific explanation of phosphorescence in churchyards.

If nothing else, these 'scientific' poems reflect his belief in the power of education and the demystifying virtues of scientific knowledge, which in turn suggests that his childhood faith must at some moment have come into shattering conflict with the theories of science. His interest in the latter is borne out by books he received as University prizes during the years 1913 and 14. Whether he chose them himself or whether they were chosen for him is not clear but they show a strong bias towards positivism and evolutionism. They included Taine's *Twentieth Century Philosophy*, Max Müller's *History of Religion*, Gumplowitz's *Sociology and Politics* and Gérard's *Attic Eloquence*. Perhaps most significant of all, he received Ernst Haeckel's *The Riddle of the Universe*.[21]

A parenthesis on Haeckel, Müller and the natural history of 'Trilce' and 'Poemas Humanos'

Haeckel was a discovery. A great popularizer of evolutionary theories, his book introduced Vallejo to a monistic, materialist interpretation of creation and the universe, the vocabulary of which left deep impressions on his poetry. Phrases like '*ciliado arrecife*', '*arácnidas* cuestas', 'grupo *dicotiledón*', '999 calorías' stand out in the poems not merely because they belong to 'scientific language' but because they denote a scientific explanation of the creation of the universe and the descent of man from simpler forms of life. Haeckel was by no means a dull pedant; his *History of Creation* (at least in the English translation)[22] is delightful, even picturesque reading, with its graphic account of 'tangle forests of algae' and 'plant souls' and the dramatic story of the formation of mountains, lakes and oceans. *The Riddle of the Universe* (Vallejo's prize) speedily disposed of notions such as the immortality of the soul, and the dogmas which put man at the centre of the universe and created a god in man's image as an apotheosis of the human organism. Man is now given a far more modest role. As Haeckel put it: 'This boundless presumption of vainglorious man has misled him into making himself "the image of God", claiming an "eternal life" for his ephemeral personality and imagining that he possesses unlimited freedom of will'.[23]

The poetic space of *Trilce* becomes the battle-ground between the privileged individual of Christianity and this cosmic speck, who can now be considered as a complex of functions – feet, spinal column, teeth, hair, nails – each of which has its evolutionary history. To a young man brought up in the most orthodox faith, the impact of theories which dismissed the Middle Ages as 'insane' and refused to see in Christ anyone more interesting than an illegitimate child, was obviously profound. 'Los caynas', a short story that Vallejo included in his collection, *Escalas melografiadas* (published in 1923) suggests the shattering effect which evolutionist theory had on him.[24] It is the story of a young man who returns to his home in a mountain village so remote that for long periods it has no contact with the outside world, to find that his family and the entire village have turned into monkeys. It was as if his introduction to theories of the descent of man from earlier primates had suddenly made even the warmest of family relationships appear a grotesque caricature. In Vallejo's poetry, however, the impact is most of all on language; a seismological upheaval was caused by this change of status of man. The upheaval was all the more devastating in that Vallejo's religious beliefs were destroyed without his sharing the optimistic faith of Haeckel and others in human enlightenment. He did not believe that 'upon the vast fields of ruins, rises, majestic and brilliant, the new sun of our realistic monism, which reveals to us the wonderful temple of nature in all its beauty. In the sincere cult of the true, the good and the beautiful which is the heart of our new monistic religion, we find ample compensation for the anthropistic ideals of God, freedom and immortality which we have lost'.[25]

Max Müller's *History of Religion* carried evolutionism even further by showing how religious ideas derived from nature, from man's family chain which leads back to the great-great-grandfather of all men and all things and from a study of our own nature. Müller found in language the key to understanding ancient religions; gods were, for him, the personifications of causal phenomena. By comparing religions from all parts of the globe, and the names given to deities, he suggested a common pattern of religious belief. Müller's theories helped to provide Vallejo with the tools he used in *Trilce* for conceptualizing the infinite.

The Trujillo Bohemians

Vallejo's education as a poet began in 1915, when a group of students and writers began to meet together to read their own poems and those of the Modernists, Whitman and others in order to escape the tedium of provincial life. At this time, their only hope of publication was in the Trujillo newspapers – *La Industria* (founded in 1895), *La Reforma, La Razón* and *El Federal*[26] – which published poems and articles on literature. The only literary magazine seems to have been *Iris*, founded in 1914 by José Eulogio Garrido,[27] a member of the Trujillo circle who introduced Vallejo to the poetry of Whitman, Verlaine and Maeterlinck. The group included Antenor Orrego Espinoza, a young man with philosophical leanings who was well acquainted with the work of Emerson, Unamuno and Rodó and who wrote articles on a wide variety of topics for *La Reforma* and *La Libertad*. Orrego was one of Vallejo's first serious critics, and in later years a member of the *Apra* (*Alianza Popular Revolucionaria Americana*) movement; there was also Alcides Spelucín, son of a merchant whose business had been ruined by the competition of the Gildemeisters, and who with Orrego became co-founder of the important newspaper *El Norte* in 1923. Finally, there was

Víctor Raúl Haya de la Torre who soon left Trujillo to become one of the leaders of the University Reform Movement in Peru and then a founder of the *Apra* movement.[28] In 1915, however, the nonconformity of these young men was mainly literary and social. The writer Juan Parra del Riego, who named the group the 'Trujillo Bohemia', had interviewed Garrido who offered him an account of their harmless activities. There were 'meetings on Wednesdays and Saturdays for poetry-readings, excursions to the ruins of Chan Chan and moonlight picnics on the beach'.[29] The participants gave one another nicknames, Vallejo's being Korris-cosso, the name of a character from Eça de Queiroz's story, 'A Lyric Poet'. The name was appropriate, for Eça's Korriscosso was a Greek with a passion for poetry employed as a waiter in the mundane Charing Cross Hotel. The incompatibility of poetry and mutton gave Eça a fine opportunity to poke fun at the Romantic ideal, though perhaps it was not the irony that impressed Vallejo's friends but the isolation of the poet writing in Greek with no hope of ever finding a public. Certainly Vallejo seems to have assumed the role of Romantic poet even in his love affairs. The two girls he courted during his Trujillo days, María Rosa Sandoval (known as Maria Bashkirtseff) and Zoila Rosa Cuadro (addressed as Mirtho in his poems) were made to fit into a Romantic ideal which soon came to seem incongruous.[30] The adoption of these anachronistic Romantic attitudes is scarcely surprising. Even today, it is not hard to find groups of young men in provincial Latin American towns for whom literature has come to be the main expression of rebellion against family and tradition. Many of them later become solid citizens and Sunday poets; a few, like Vallejo, finally accept their vocation and dedicate their lives to poetry. Most of the members of the Trujillo Bohemia turned to politics, transforming what was, at first, only a literary revolt into a direct confrontation with the burghers of Trujillo. Antenor Orrego described how this initial nonconformity led to a more openly radical position:

We did not want to resign ourselves to an ivory tower or to a coterie existence. This seemed mean, selfish and sterile. We had to get out of our little world and we did so. As we were not and could not be con-formists because that would have been to deny our very natures – we had to come into conflict with everything and everybody – with insti-tutions, political power, social conventions, the university, an exploiting and insolent plutocracy, its sacred falsehoods, class etiquette, its lack of honesty and honour, its base servility, its exploitation of the worker, its bureaucracy, professional politics, presumptuous ignorance . . . all these had to endure our attacks.[31]

In 1915, 'épater le bourgeois' implied flouting the moral code, which was hardly an easy thing to do, especially for a student who was earning his living in the respectable profession of teaching. Vallejo was registered as a law student as well as being a student of literature, in order, as he wrote to his brother Manuel, to labour for the future of the family.[32] He had not yet irrevocably broken with Trujillo, though he was already stereotyped as a poet, largely because of his long hair as one of his pupils, Ciro Alegría, was later to remember.[33] Alegría recalls too that his poems excited controversy, being praised by some and attacked by others.[34] His defence came largely from his own small literary circle. It was they who encouraged his writing, they who wrote favourable criticism, praising the 'air of modernity and innovation' in his poetry.[35] Outside this friendly circle, he was subject to merciless attacks. One critic of the newspaper *La Industria* berated him for his hymns 'to green alfalfa', and speculated as to whether his appetite for alfalfa were not a throw-back. With great literal-mindedness, the same critic declared that the poet wanted to be a baker and 'to have an oven in his heart' (a reference to a line in the title poem of *Los heraldos negros*) and that 'he would like to knock on everybody's door, and his bones feel alien and he is a thief'.[36] A poem sent to the Lima periodical *Variedades* was even more cruelly received, the critic recommending that it be put in the wastepaper basket.[37] On the other hand, José María Eguren, a fellow-poet to whom Vallejo sent some of his verses in 1917, wrote of the 'musical and imaginative wealth' of his poetry, of its 'depth'.[38]

The hostility of the Trujillo merchants was expressed more directly in the slights and daily insults. He was reportedly attacked on one occasion. His early poems refer insistently to the hostility of a materialist society identified, as was common at the period, with the Jews, a society which was in total contrast to the ideal world of the poet.

Afilados judíos cruzan por estos años
al lado de insolencias parásitas y vacuas!
¡Y aquel que sueña y canta, sin pan y abandonado
va recamando harapos de un hilo azul de lágrimas!

Sharp jews cross through the years
Along with parasitic, empty insolence
And he who dreams and sings, abandoned and without bread
Embroiders rags with a blue thread of tears.[39]

Despite the self-pity, the lines show how readily the pain inflicted by the Trujillo bourgeoisie could be sublimated into the
myth of the poet's superiority. Occasionally the allusions are
veiled, though still obvious enough:

> ¡En los mares fenicios beben todos los labios
> y la fuente Castalia se queda sola y calla!

> In the Phoenician seas all lips drink
> And the Castalian fount remains silent and alone.

His own loneliness was solaced by poetry in that cultural desert.
And poetry also enabled him to launch a counter-attack very
much in the lofty disdainful tone of Asunción Silva or Rubén
Darío:

> ¡Yo me quedo tan frío ante esos odios!
> ¡Canto siempre en desdén mayor mi verso!
> ¡Y ante la boca abierta de los charcos
> llevo en mi mano, como un gran jilguero,
> el propio corazón del Universo![40]

> Thus hatred leaves me unmoved.
> I always sing my verse in Disdain Major
> And over the gaping mouths of muddy pools
> Like a great thrush I carry
> The very heart of the Universe.

The antagonism turned Vallejo into something of a poet-martyr,
facing the Philistines, or the 'Zoilos' as the enemy were called
after a particularly unpleasant Greek who had dared to criticize
Homer. The play *Vanity Triumphant*, which Haya de la Torre
wrote under the (apt) pseudonym 'Juan Amateur', sums up the
mythology of the group; it dramatizes the tale of a poor poet in
love with a rich girl whose father only consents to the marriage
after the poet has won fame and glory. Vallejo wrote a poem on
the theme in which he talks of the 'hollow Jewish laughter' of the
merchant classes.[41] Later, in Lima, he was still to recall 'Those
unhealthy stupid September days, full of boredom; the vulgar

idiotic examinations, my eyes heavy with insomnia and anointed with ether and pain – and the Vegas Zanabrias, the Chavarrys, horrors!' Yet he is also curious to know how those 'imbecile citizens of Trujillo' had reacted to the news of his departure from their midst.[42]

There was, then, a real conflict of values between Vallejo as a poet and the society in which he lived, a conflict sublimated into literature. His earliest poems, however, were skilful imitations. Antenor Orrego, one of his first literary mentors, recalls having seen between twenty and thirty compositions which were influenced by the Spanish literature of the Golden Age and by mediaeval poets like Gonzalo de Berceo and the Arcipreste de Hita. Vallejo came to Trujillo steeped in tradition, and in that quiet, boring town rapidly began to read everything he could lay his hands on – Shakespeare, Fenimore Cooper, Dickens and Dostoievsky (serialized in newspapers), Romain Rolland, Barbusse and even Kierkegaard.[43] It was about this time that Víctor Raúl Haya de la Torre was also receiving his political education from reading books he found in a workers' library in Trujillo,[44] so Vallejo was by no means an isolated case. One stroke of luck was coming across an anthology of French poetry edited by Fernando Fortún and Enrique Diez-Canedo which included a comprehensive selection of modern poems translated into Spanish. Among the authors translated were Nerval, Baudelaire, Gautier, Banville and the Parnassians, Corbière, Laforgue, Rimbaud, Verlaine, Mallarmé, Samain, Jammes, Maeterlinck and Claudel as well as a host of now relatively forgotten poets such as René Arcos, Charles Vildrac, Georges Duhamel and Jules Romains.[45] From these and the prose writings of the Uruguayan poet Julio Herrera y Reissig, Vallejo derived an aesthetic more sophisticated than Romanticism. Art, for many of these writers, was a timeless text, 'a Holy of Holies, the very heart of the Enigma which is Iris, which is Nature, the only God and the only Life. First Cause and Absolute Science': a Book of Books, with pages of dazzling whiteness; 'a white poem like a veiled vision, snow of the first mystic springtime which falls upon the blessed state of ecstasies and then dissolves in sighs' . . .[46] In this anthology, he read Verlaine's 'Art poétique', Gautier's 'Tout passe – L'art robuste/ Seule a l'éternité;/Le buste/Survit à la cité'. And here he must

have come across an image that later haunted him, that dizzying
fall into space which Mallarmé had evoked in 'Les fenêtres':

> Est-il moyen, ô Moi qui connais l'amertume,
> D'enfoncer le cristal par le monstre insulté
> Et de m'enfuir, avec mes deux ailes sans plume
> – Au risque de tomber pendant l'éternité?

Reading this anthology, Vallejo compressed a hundred years of
French culture from Romanticism to the latest avant-garde writing into a few months. At the same time, he was able to keep up
with even newer developments, thanks to a few literary magazines which arrived after some delay in Trujillo, the most important of which was *Cervantes*, a Spanish magazine edited by
Rafael Cansinos Assens. *Cervantes* acted as an antenna of the
literary movements of the time – Symbolism, Dada and Futurism
– publishing avant-garde manifestos whose strident tone must
have made odd reading in cloistered Trujillo. In addition, the
magazine published some avant-garde poetry – Mallarmé's 'Coup
de dès', for instance, in a translation by Rafael Cansinos Assens,
and poems by Apollinaire, Valéry, Aragon, Cendrars, Jacob,
Tzara and the Chilean creationist Vicente Huidobro.[47]
Provincial as the city was, however, living there had not meant
total isolation. Thanks to the magazines and the literary pages of
newspapers, the great wave of innovation coming from Europe
in the grip of war sent its eddies to these distant, anachronistic
backwaters. But like Haya de la Torre, Vallejo found the atmosphere increasingly intolerable and perhaps, had he stayed, it
would have even been impossible for him to become the poet of
Trilce. As soon as he could after taking the law degree that was
necessary if he were to embark on a career (but he never used
it), Vallejo set sail for Lima and arrived there in the very last
days of 1917.

Lima at the end of la belle époque

Vallejo was to spend two and a half years in Lima, and during
much of the time he worked as a teacher. His arrival coincided
with the end of what Luis Alberto Sánchez termed 'la belle
époque', the years of the presidency of José Pardo during which
the small but elegant and snobbish Lima aristocracy held sway
quite undeterred by the first murmurings of social unrest. Change,

however, was in the air, a change that for a time threatened the traditional structures of Peruvian society; and two individuals, Raúl Haya de la Torre who had arrived in Lima earlier in 1917, and José Carlos Mariátegui, then editor of *El Tiempo* and later founder of *Nuestra Época,* were to have a decisive influence on the political history of the next decades. Whether by accident or choice, Vallejo was drawn first into the literary circles of the Lima bohemia which gathered in the Palais Concert, a vast Paris-style café in which Abraham Valdelomar, among others, held court.[48] Vallejo found work in May 1918 as a teacher in the Colegio Barrós, and led a dual life, at night devoting himself to café life or even to excursions into the opium dens of Chinatown. Most important, however, were his first meetings with Lima writers and intellectuals and especially with Abraham Valdelomar, then the most avant-garde of the Lima writers. Like the Modernists before him, Valdelomar had assumed an aristocratic pseudonym, the 'Conde de Lemos', which reflected his self-proclaimed membership of the aristocracy of art. As a poet, his characteristic tone was of nostalgia, as in the poem which may have been the initial stimulus for Vallejo's 'La cena miserable', though Valdelomar hardly rises above the sentimental in his evocation of the absent brother:

> pero no hay la alegría ni el afán de reír
> que animaron antaño la cena familiar;
> y mi madre que acaso algo quiere decir
> ve el lugar del ausente y se pone a llorar.

('But there is not the happiness nor merriment / which once enlivened the family repast / and my mother who perhaps would like to speak / sees the empty place and begins to weep.')

Valdelomar, was, however, best known for a charming regional story 'El Caballero Carmelo', the tale of an heroic cock-fight in the town of Pisco, where he had spent his youth. He was also editor of the literary magazine *Colónida,* founded in 1916. Mariátegui was to describe *Colónida* accurately enough as the project of a diverse group of people whose only common concern was their dislike of the pedantic. 'They were united by the spirit of protest, not by any positive programme' he wrote.[49] The contributors to *Colónida* held firmly to the myth of the artist as Christ, saviour and enemy of the money-changers, and Valdelomar himself buttressed his beliefs with an elaborate neo-Pythagoreanism. On a

lecture tour through northern Peru in 1918, he made aesthetics
the highest pinnacle of human endeavour (somewhat in the
manner of the Mexican thinker Vasconcelos, who had visited
Peru and had met Valdelomar in 1916). His lecture-notes list
headings such as 'Christ, the sublime, the greatest artist of
humanity', 'The supreme ideal of Modern Aesthetics' (which is
to reach God); and under these headings, there fitted an entire
scheme of psychology, sociology and history, even of bullfighting.
(A treatise he wrote on the then popular bullfighter Belmonte,
applied his general rhythmic principle to the art of bullfighting).
A firm believer in geniuses, Valdelomar gave lectures to school-
children in which he spoke of the 'great artists' of humanity –
Moses, St. Francis and Christ, claiming that 'they have many
disciples on earth and some are poets and sing with divine music
of all that ennobles and strengthens'.[50]

In *Trilce*, Vallejo turns Valdelomar's theory of rhythm into
something comico-grotesque, but this did not prevent him from
valuing Valdelomar's friendship highly, especially just after his
own arrival in Lima. To his friend Oscar Imaña he wrote, 'I am
with him often and feel better with him.'[51] Valdelomar not only
promised to write the introduction for *Los heraldos negros* but
addressed Vallejo as 'brother in suffering and beauty, brother in
God':

> There is in your spirit the divine spark of the elect. You are a great
> artist, a sincere and good man, a child full of suffering, sadness, con-
> cern, darkness and hope. You can undergo all the pain in the world,
> the canine teeth of envy will attack you; you will perhaps see your
> dreams dissipated, and men may not believe in you; slaves will not
> kneel as you pass by; however, your spirit in which there is the spark
> of God will be immortal, it will inspire other souls and will live radiant
> in glory for centuries. Amen.[52]

This is the complete myth of the poet, a myth that in Lima in
1918 was particularly appealing, promising immortality and glory,
the exaltation of those of low degree and the removal of the
mighty of Trujillo from their seats.[53] Vallejo only gradually realized that this myth had élitist implications, though, in an interview with Valdelomar soon after his arrival in Lima, he records
that the latter held views about the 'aristocracy of the best' which
would give the artist a political role. 'We have to form a group',
the Count maintained, 'a group of the best in the country which

will bring together the best national energies and set a new, healthier intellectual goal that will shed light on the present state of artistic immorality, created and maintained by those evil men'.[54] His purpose in touring Peru in 1918 was to form an 'intellectual federation' of these elements in the nation. What intellectual in modern times has not had this kind of dream? Moreover Valdelomar had enough energy and conviction to have formed a movement. His absurd death, as a result of a fall just after he had attended the first session of a regional congress in Ayacucho to which he had been elected deputy, occurred at the very moment when he had become politically committed. He died without writing the promised preface to *Los heraldos negros* but his influence on the younger poet was deep, and in a note written after his death Vallejo affirmed that he had brought 'rebellion, freedom, breadth of horizons and more fresh air of feeling' to the national scene.[55] It was, however, an ambiguous influence and the Romantic notion of 'genius' was to appear increasingly problematic in the turbulent aftermath of the First World War.

Vallejo interviewed another poet, José María Eguren, in the months after leaving Trujillo. Eguren, a Symbolist who wrote somewhat precious poetry, was probably the most talented Peruvian poet of the time, though his style was too different from Vallejo's own to touch him very deeply. There was mutual admiration but no real convergence of interests. Far more important was his meeting with Manuel González Prada, director of the National Library and Peru's leading intellectual, an exemplary figure who despite his aristocratic birth had always been nonconformist, a perpetual rebel to whom Vallejo would dedicate his poem, 'The Eternal Dice'. Whilst the contact with Valdelomar had assured Vallejo of his place in the brotherhood of poetry, his interview with González Prada gave him much needed assurance that iconoclasm was not mere licence. González Prada's own political opposition had begun during the Peruvian-Chilean war and more specifically with his movement of national regeneration, inaugurated with a famous speech in 1888 at which he had proclaimed 'Old men to the tomb, young men to their labours'. Neither years spent abroad in Paris nor middle-age had dampened his revolutionary ardour, rather they increased it. Not only was he a skilful, if limited, poet, he also took an active part in the young workers' movements, writing for journals such as *Los Parias*.[56] He exemplified the best qualities of the nineteenth-century intellectual in Latin America. The very isolation of such men, their uniqueness, often stimulated them to push their convictions to the utmost limits. Indeed there was nothing for them to compromise with except the unacceptable status quo. Nearing the end of his life when Vallejo interviewed him, González Prada was still able to give generous encouragement, telling the young visitor that he loved audacity and did not care about breaches of grammatical correctness. Vallejo was delighted at what seemed to him the validation of his own work. 'I think of all those hostile hands now distant', he wrote, 'and I think there will be a new dawn tomorrow'.[57] He was referring, of course, to Trujillo which was not quite so distant as he would have liked to think.

Given the intense political involvement of all those around him at this time (including Valdelomar), it seems surprising that Vallejo was not drawn more speedily into politics. The arrival in Lima of the Argentine socialist leader Alfredo Palacios, the foundation of the newspaper *La Razón* in 1919 edited by César Falcón and José Carlos Mariátegui, the beginning of the University Reform Movement in Córdoba Argentina in June 1918, whence it extended to other Latin American countries including Peru made this an exciting period. The economic prosperity of the 1914–18 war period had changed the composition of Peruvian society. The labour movement had emerged as a new and powerful force and in 1919 a general strike was organized. At the same time, an influx of the middle classes into the university not only increased student numbers but also student unrest, culminating in the Reform Movement in which Haya de la Torre gradually came to play a significant part as president of the Peruvian Student Federation. The Reform Movement called for a change in the university structure and courses and for the foundation of people's universities. At the same time, the return of General Leguía from abroad and his campaign for a *Patria Nueva* encouraged hopes for the end of oligarchic government and the beginning of a new era. For a brief year or two, life seemed to be breathed into the rigid Peruvian political scene. The alliance of workers and students, which put Leguía and his *Patria Nueva* in power was, however, speedily broken up. Powerful interests who were well aware of the Bolshevik Revolution in Russia were soon at work to prevent the 'new fatherland' from becoming a reality. The labour movement met with repression, and certain dangerous intellectuals like Mariátegui were sent abroad on scholarships. And Haya de la Torre, who led demonstrations against Leguía when he decided to dedicate the country to the Sacred Heart of Jesus, was soon in exile.[58]

Vallejo, undoubtedly sympathetic to the University Reform Movement, seems to have remained on the margin of all this, for in 1918 and 1919 he was mainly concerned with the appearance of his first collection of poetry. *Los heraldos negros* had been printed in 1918 but was only distributed in June 1919 after Vallejo had waited for months for Valdelomar to write the promised introduction. He paid for the edition himself but once it appeared, the collection received several long, favourable reviews, and not only in the Trujillo press but also in two Lima papers, *La Crónica* and *La Prensa*.[59] His friend Antenor Orrego contributed the most glowing article in *La Reforma*. This critical reception was his final initiation ritual; from now on, he could truly consider himself a poet.

But Vallejo's acceptance into the ranks of promising poets soon turned to ashes. It was one thing to proclaim the poet's alienation from society and quite another to practise bohemianism within the rigid social *mores* of Lima which, if less staid than Trujillo, was still a very orthodox place as far as moral norms were concerned. Vallejo was involved in a banal affair with a girl known as Otilia, whose brother-in-law taught in the Colegio Barrós. On the death of the school's owner, Vallejo became headmaster and it evidently became increasingly difficult to carry on the affair without ceding to family pressure to marry the girl. Whatever his own opinion of marriage and children (and there is abundant evidence of what he thought in *Los heraldos negros* and *Trilce*), they were certainly not shared by Otilia's brother-in-law. The poet, his head filled with the example of Hugo and D'Annunzio, found himself treated like Mr Kipps. In the middle of the tribulations of his private life, his mother died in Santiago, leaving him, he declared, with no desire to go on living. To his brother, Manuel, he wrote, 'In this world there is now nothing left. Except our father's well-being. And when his (life) comes to an end, I shall also have died to life and to the future; my road will go downhill.'[60] He refusal to marry Otilia, even though it cost him his job in May 1919, certainly rose out of a deep conviction of the futility of reproducing human life. His final break with the girl in August 1919 together with the death of his mother were two deep experiences which confirmed in him the feeling of the pathos and the futility of human love.

He lost a second teaching job in Lima early in 1920, and in April returned to Santiago de Chuco to a house haunted by the loss of his mother and of a brother, Miguel, who had died in 1915. But he had at any rate his reputation as a poet and on a visit to his old school town of Huamachuco, he assumed the arrogance of a prophet, surprised to find himself not acclaimed in his own country.[61] What followed reveals the desperate hopelessness of Peruvian provincial life at this time, its domination by conservative landowning interests terrified by what they considered to be the dangerous liberalism of the Leguía government. When Vallejo arrived in Santiago, he found that Carlos Santa María, a local storekeeper and governor of one of the districts of the town had become acting sub-prefect and hence the person chiefly responsible for law and order.[62] A supporter of Prado, Santa María seized the opportunity to settle a few scores against political opponents among whom was Nestor Vallejo, César's brother. The tension in the area was probably increased by labour troubles in the Chicama valley which eventually resulted in the closing down of the 'Roma' and the formation of the first farmworkers' union in Trujillo. But in Santiago de Chuco, the struggle was on a more petty level. Nestor had found himself under arrest in March, and a constant stream of telegrams was received by *La Reforma* of Trujillo, complaining of the abuses of the acting sub-prefect. The appointment of a new sub-prefect in June 1920 polarized the forces, in which the Vallejo family plainly stood on the side of progress. Manuel had signed a telegram in January 1920 as a Leguía supporter and César in June spoke at a meeting which called for a new railway line to link Santiago with Cajamarca. In response, the opposition promised 'sinister things' for the August festivities.

Many years later, in his farce, *Colacho Hermanos*[63] and in the novel, *El tungsteno*, Vallejo painted a scathing portrait of these small-town oppressors who committed petty abuses from behind the counter of the village store. Meanwhile in 1920, he was the victim of the system. The Santa Marías, unhappy at the appointment of a new sub-prefect who did not represent their interests, encouraged a police strike at the height of the August festivities. Several gendarmes left the barracks without leave, got drunk and, complaining that they had not been paid, set some of the prisoners in the jail free. Vallejo remained with the sub-prefect during the night, in the course of which some of the striking gendarmes fired shots from the barrack roof, killed one of the sub-prefect's aides, and then escaped to take refuge in the Santa María shop which was burned down some time later. The sub-prefect at the height of the uprising was unable even to send a telegram or to telephone Trujillo because the machine had been hidden and the telephone disconnected by one of Santa María's men. The whole is a classic illustration of the miseries of provincial life – a nervous shopkeeper heavily committed to maintain the status quo, the panic fear of mass violence (of which there had been precedents in the nearby Chicama valley) and above all, suspicion of the 'intellectual instigator' – for this is what Vallejo became in the weeks that followed. As soon as Vallejo knew that he was in danger of arrest, he left for Huamachuco where he hid for some weeks in a country house owned by Antenor Orrego. In November, he decided to move to Trujillo and here was arrested on 6 November 1920. Astonishingly, despite protest telegrams from intellectuals and newspaper editors as well as from the Federation of Peruvian Students, Vallejo was not released until 26 February. He himself later described his imprisonment as 'the most serious moment' of his life and, writing to a friend during this period, he said 'I am in a rage not exactly because of my *honour* but because of the material, the entirely material deprivation of my animal freedom.'[64] Nevertheless he was not idle. He evidently worked on some of the *Trilce* poems and entered the poem 'Fabla de gesta' for a Trujillo prize under his nickname Korriscosso. No first prize was given, but Vallejo won second place.

The protest movement, the intercession of the prominent Arequipa poet, Percy Gibson, and 'irregularities' discovered in the procedure for his arrest brought about Vallejo's provisional release, though he was not free of the charges until 1926. The threat of return to prison certainly contributed to his decision to leave the country in 1923, and probably accounts for the fact that he stayed abroad even during the first difficult winters in Europe.

The incident illustrates how limited was the power of the intellectual, especially when powerful local interests were at work. We can be sure that the Santa María faction were not one whit affected by the intelligentsia's support of the poet.

Vallejo's release was celebrated by his Trujillo friends at a banquet at which the poet recited some of his latest poems, the revolutionary nature of which was in astonishing contrast to 'Fabla de gesta', with which Vallejo had won the poetry prize. Addressed to the 'epic' foundation of Trujillo, 'Fabla de gesta' was written in the tradition of Modernist civic poetry;[65] it was the last 'public' poem that Vallejo wrote before the Spanish Civil War and even as he submitted it for the prize, he must have been conscious that the civic poem was no longer an authentic project in a society where the 'civic' also meant the Santa Marías or others like them.

Vallejo's last two years in Peru were spent in Lima where, after a period without work, he became a teacher in the Colegio Guadalupe. He now began to enjoy a modest success, winning a literary prize with a short story for Entre Nous. The proceeds went towards the payment for an edition of Trilce.

Now established as a writer, his home became a meeting-place for the young intelligentsia, especially the Trujillo group; once again, there were café discussions and excursions to Chinatown. But when his second collection of poems with its strange title Trilce appeared in 1922, the reception was disconcertingly hostile. Just before its publication, he had rather pretentiously thought of adopting the name César Perú after the example of Anatole France (in Chile, Neftalí Reyes was soon to become Pablo Neruda). The notion reflects a certain aspiration to be the national voice, and the reception of the poems must have shattered it, if he had not already abandoned the idea. Only Antenor Orrego's 'prefatory words' to the edition offered him the assurance that he was a poet and that he had written a 'great book'. Orrego saw correctly that in Trilce Vallejo had 'disembowelled the rhetorical puppets of poetry and had sought to give a more direct and immediate representation of life'. But the inevitable comparison with Whitman rings false as does his Emersonian description of the poet as one who 'reconstructs what is dispersed within us'. Orrego continues, 'He takes the anatomical part and places it in a functional position. He restores to its origin the essence of being, which has been obscured, crushed, devitalized by the intellectual weight of tradition. In this manner, his art comes to express eternal man and the eternity of man despite the local or national characteristics of his emotions.'[66]

The publication of *Trilce* had coincided with the arrival in Lima of a more colourful 'Whitman of America' – José Santos Chocano, the Modernist poet who had proclaimed himself the 'voice of native America'. On his return to Lima after seventeen years of absence, he was received with acclaim. His immediate past as poet laureate of Estrada Cabrera (a grotesque Guatemalan prototype for Miguel Angel Asturias's sinister 'Señor Presidente') was forgotten, though he had narrowly escaped execution at the hands of the vengeful opposition when Estrada Cabrera fell. Now released from prison after a protest campaign, he enjoyed a new role as prodigal son, received by crowds (among them, Vallejo) and appearing on the balcony of his house to embrace his aged mother. Newspapers described him as 'the greatest poet of America' and there was a public act of homage.[67] The contrast between this flamboyant theatrical bard and the young poet in the crowd could hardly have been greater. Neither of them could foresee that to become a national or continental poet in the style of Santos Chocano was already a tarnished dream, that the notoriety of the older man's public life would not rescue his poetry or convert it into more than elegant adornment. For the moment, though, it was Santos Chocano's hour. *Trilce*, on the other hand, was ignored or received with dismay and hostility. In *Mundial*, Luis Alberto Sánchez, who was later to modify his opinion, described Vallejo's new collection as 'incomprehensible' and 'weird' (estrambótico) and failed to understand how it had come to be written.[68] In the school where Vallejo taught, the poems were publicly ridiculed by colleagues.[69] In Trujillo, there was a chorus of protest against the free style of the verse.

Vallejo had long been thinking of leaving Peru. The last months of his stay in Lima must have confirmed that any further poetic adventures would meet with frustration. The modest drinking parties and the visits to a literary bookshop, La Aurora Literaria, the increasing repressiveness of the Leguía regime, all pointed to a narrow and unpromising future. He stayed long enough in Lima to have his stories *Escalas melografiadas* and his short novel *Fabla salvaje* published, and on 17 June 1923 he took the steamship *Oroya* and left Peru forever.

Europe! Those Latin American writers who could not make the pilgrimage would not be freed from its grip. In his years in Peru, Vallejo lived the contradictions of the writer, experiencing at first hand the impossibility of being the poet-prophet that the Modernists had celebrated. The absurd prison incident marked the gulf between the poet's proclamation of civic authority and the true situation. Europe was to be a different kind of lesson, the lesson that revolutions are not brought about by pen and ink, and perhaps even more profoundly, the lesson that we cannot live the revolution of others.

2

THE ALIENATED ROMANTIC: *LOS HERALDOS NEGROS*

> To end that eternal conflict between our self and the world, to restore the peace that passeth all understanding, to unite ourselves with nature so as to form one endless whole – that is the goal of all our strivings.
>
> Hölderlin

In *Los heraldos negros,* Vallejo discovers that what he had taken to be Romantic defiance of convention was also a problem of language and poetics. To shake his fist at the burghers of Trujillo, he had to abandon his family gods and with them the Christian Logos. His experience in the mines and on the sugar estates showed him that the moral teachings of Christianity were a dead letter; the one counter-ideology available to him was that of poet–demon, the literary rebel who takes on the whole of material creation. *Los heraldos negros* is imbued with the Romantic myth of man's fall into division and separation, his yearning for wholeness and the circular journey back to the peace of death[1] though it is a myth that the poet accepts only to destroy it. Those vast billowy syntheses, God, Humanity, Love were, he found, no longer useful as cohesive myths. It is not Vallejo who rendered them absurd but society around him which converted love into a business contract, the Word into words and humanity into an élite. Vallejo lays hands on them as substitutes for the Christian Logos but destroys his own Romantic base by behaving as if these abstractions still had meaning, by taking the poetic logic to its *reductio ad absurdum* so that at times he seems on the verge of discovering the delights of parody. Love is a passion? Very well then, the lover's lips are of wood like the cross. God is immanent? Why then he is in time and as mortal as ourselves. This strategy makes it important for us to attend to the *gestus* that goes with the poems as well as the words on the page, and to the inflections which signal the presence of irony.

Los heraldos negros (Black Heralds) is a collection of seventy-two poems arranged in thematic clusters to which Vallejo gave vague though allusive titles. The principle that unites the poems in each cluster is not easy to detect, and there is little point in trying to establish spurious connections. Roughly speaking, 'Plafones ágiles' (Agile ceilings) and 'De la tierra' (Earth) are about profane love; 'Nostalgias imperiales' (Imperial longings) have Peruvian Indian motifs; 'Buzos' (Soundings) and 'Truenos' (Thunderclaps) are concerned with metaphysical explorations and 'Canciones de hogar' (Songs of home) are addressed to his own family. However, neither this grouping nor the order in which the poems were written necessarily implies a consistent strategy.[2] For instance, in a three-month period between June and the end of August 1917, he published 'Comunión' and 'La cena miserable' (The wretched supper)[3] both of which use the analogy of communion feast and sacrifice. Yet where the first borrows the language of religion in order to dignify profane love in the Romantic and Modernist tradition, 'The wretched supper', a savagely ironic poem, lays bare the impossibility of giving the act of eating sacred connotations in a world without God. Both poems are forms of blasphemy, but their strategy and language differ profoundly.

This inconsistency is hardly surprising in apprentice poetry, though there is a more interesting explanation for the vacillation between strategies than lack of confidence. Vallejo was aware that his poetry explored experiences that would seem outrageous to his contemporaries had he not masked rather than revealed their import. The death of God and its consequences for moral and social life was, outside intellectual circles at least, still a taboo subject and to have argued it out openly would certainly have separated him from his family.[4] In 1922, President Leguía tried to win popular support by dedicating Peru to the Sacred Heart of Jesus, an event that indicated the persistent power of religious rhetoric. But Vallejo must also have known that what excites the most hostile reaction is transgression of linguistic taboos. More people remembered Shaw's *Pygmalion* for the word 'bloody' than for the 'message.' Vallejo's contorted metaphors may have hidden his deeper purpose but they certainly excited the ridicule of his contemporaries. In order to foreground the degradation of sacred language in the modern world, he would have to transgress rules of grammar and versification in ways which were bound to excite criticism, for every schoolboy

'knows' the rules of grammar and can recognize a rhyme. Furthermore, most of the poems of this collection were written in the
benighted atmosphere of Trujillo, a town where even in declaring
himself a poet he had announced his rebellion against convention.

From early on, Vallejo's innovations showed a different character from those of the Modernists who, even when they thought
of themselves as political revolutionaries (as González Prada
did), clung to a certain poetic decorum. Whilst inventing or
reviving verse forms, most Modernists prized virtuosity and poetic
skill, believing that poetic form was a reflection of deeper har-
monies. Poetry suggested resolutions and coherencies not apparent in the phenomenal world, and the very elegance and
balance of the verse became the visible manifestation of art's
superiority to life. That is why Ricardo Jaimes Freyre, even while
he revolutionized the theory of Castilian prosody, suggesting
rhythmic principles instead of the syllabic count as a metrical
basis, still deplored those devices which destroy the harmony of
the poem.[5] Darío's delight in the ornamental and the musical
stemmed, similarly, from a view of poetry as the privileged area
of *structured* experience. It is true that the people with whom
Vallejo had to contend were not practising poets so much as
critics who had vulgarized Modernism into technical virtuosity,
but in any case he was plainly not interested in pleasing them by
producing conventional verse forms. Even when in the earlier
poetry he adopts the sonnet or the silva, he was unconventional
in his use of imagery. For instance, the opening lines of a sonnet
in alexandrines was an incongruous analogy:

> Amada, en esta noche tú te has crucificado
> sobre los dos maderos curvados de mi beso.[6]

> Beloved, on this night, you have been crucified
> On the two curved branches of my kiss.

Though the form does not violate prosodic decorum, the metaphor which turns the poet's embrace into the arms of the cross
produces a bizarre image. The very incongruity reminds us, however, that the one word, 'passion' refers to two totally disparate
experiences, that of divine love and that of profane love. The
less perceptive of Vallejo's contemporaries were outraged by the
image without appreciating that it was the ambivalence of language which Vallejo wished to foreground.[7]

Vallejo's poetics did, of course, derive largely from the Modernists; the very freedom with which they played with traditional analogies tended to increase the instability of language. And it was precisely the discovery of the 'elasticity' of language which fascinated Vallejo when he encountered it in the French Symbolists. Perhaps too he had read an article in *Colónida* on Symbolist theory which had explained that 'the word is not simply the vehicle for a single idea. The word is important too for its sound and its associations with other sounds, for the ideas or symbols which that sound and that association of sounds evoke, and even for its very configuration'.[8]

What Vallejo foregrounds in *Los heraldos negros* is the incongruity of a whole series of metaphors and analogies which had structured man's moral and affective life. One of his University prizes (p. 9) had been the *History of Religion,* where Max Müller had studied the historical origins of religions, using language as an important source of evidence. This approach discouraged the student of religion from seeing Christianity or any other religion as a privileged set of beliefs, and insisted on relating the names of deities to the human actions and the natural world which are the source of religious belief.[9] From whatever source, Vallejo had, by the time he came to write the earliest poems of *Los heraldos negros,* a sense that certain metaphors were not anchored to a stable set of referents but were fraught with ambiguities. For instance, metaphors of journey and return, of sickness and of health, of fall and redemption are common both to Christianity and Romantic 'natural supernaturalism'.[10] It is this punning relationship between the language of disparate beliefs that came to exercise Vallejo. In 'El poeta a su amada', the beloved is *crucified,* and the unmentioned word 'passion' unites the experience of profane and sacred love. Yet the reader cannot identify the two experiences for if he is to take crucifixion seriously it is outrageous to use the word to refer to the kiss of passion. On the other hand, the very use of the word 'crucified' in a profane sense undermines its religious significance.

Poet as demon

The title of Vallejo's first collection, *Los heraldos negros,* belongs to the vocabulary of Romantic alienation, with the poet as dark voice of destruction and negation instead of the herald of light and order. We find an apprehension of this demonic role in his dissertation on Romanticism in which he quotes a striking passage by José Martí.[11] Martí had accounted for the dearth of epic poetry and the importance of lyric poetry on the ground that there was no better subject in the modern world than the individual himself. But the individual is dogged by uncertainty and lack of faith. In a dramatic passage, Martí speaks of the spectre that haunts the modern world: 'a huge pale man, his face withered, his eyes filled with tears, his mouth dry. He is dressed in black and walks with heavy steps, without rest or sleep. He has entered every home, laid a tremulous hand on every pillow. What hammer-blows upon the brain! what longing for what we cannot have! what ignorance of our true significance! what feelings of pleasure and disgust in our minds! – disgust at the day that is fading, delight in the morning.'[12]

In that 'huge pale man' we have Romantic despair personified. We are reminded of the spectres who haunted Shelley, those gaunt figures at the nineteenth-century feast. He is certainly one of Vallejo's 'black heralds', the dark muse of modern poetry and in the first poem of Vallejo's collection *Los heraldos negros,* the hammer-blows that had sounded for Martí rain down on the Peruvian poet:

> Hay golpes en la vida, tan fuertes . . . Yo no sé!
> Golpes como del odio de Dios; como si ante ellos,
> la resaca de todo lo sufrido
> se empozara en el alma . . . Yo no sé!
>
> Son pocos; pero son . . . Abren zanjas oscuras
> en el rostro más fiero y en el lomo más fuerte.
> Serán talvez los potros de bárbaros atilas;
> o los heraldos negros que nos manda la Muerte.
>
> There are blows in life so brutal . . . I just don't know!
> Blows as if from God's own hatred; as if, faced with them,
> The backsurge of everything endured
> Sank in the well of the soul . . . I just don't know!
>
> There aren't many, but . . . they crack open
> The most ferocious face, and the strongest back,
> Perhaps they're the young steeds of barbarous Attilas,
> Or the black heralds sent by Death.

The motive of the poem arises out of the gratuitous nature of evil, and the conclusion that suffering without apparent cause can only come from the hatred of God. Yet even to suppose a hating God destroys the notion of a creator and hence removes any prospect of salvation. What distinguishes Vallejo's poem from dozens of similar statements of despair and death is the manner in which he builds the uncertainty-principle into language itself, and makes the poetic voice the voice of ignorance and negation. The Orphic role of the poet has been destroyed by those blows, so that he can no longer claim to be a secular priest with a vision of unity unperceived by ordinary men. The poet's 'I do not know' casts him into the common pit, a victim of destruction, as impotent as any other person to make a whole out of the fragment. Instead of channelling the goodness and the grace of creation, the waters of human suffering have stagnated in the soul without possibility of issue. The sense of stagnation is important, for it eventually threw Vallejo back on to the domain of the given; and even in this comparatively early poem, the verb 'to open' refers not to escape or transcendence but to the furrows made by suffering on man's own body, on which Vallejo will eventually rewrite the Holy Scriptures. In *Los heraldos negros* man's attempt to get beyond the divided self is thwarted, and his gaze turns backward as if to try and identify the source of his alienation rather than looking forward into a future in which his state might be changed.

Son las caídas hondas de los Cristos del alma,
de alguna fe adorable que el Destino blasfema.
Esos golpes sangrientos son las crepitaciones
de algún pan que en la puerta del horno se nos quema.

Y el hombre . . . Pobre . . . pobre! Vuelve los ojos, como
cuando por sobre el hombro nos llama una palmada;
vuelve los ojos locos, y todo lo vivido
se empoza, como charco de culpa, en la mirada.

Hay golpes en la vida, tan fuertes . . . Yo no sé!

They're the profound falls of the soul's Christs
From some worshipful faith that fate has blasphemed.
Those bloody blows are the crackling
Of some loaf of bread we've left burning at the oven door.

And man . . . miserable wretch. He turns his eyes, as
When someone's hand claps us on the back;
He turns his crazed eyes, and all he's lived through
Sinks like a pool of guilt in the well of his glance.

There are blows in life so brutal . . . I just don't know!

The fall of 'the soul's Christs' introduces a plurality of saviours which destroys the belief in a unique Creator. If human destiny is blasphemous then the notion of grace or redemption is ruled out. The crackling and burning of 'a loaf of bread' at the oven door not only refers to destroyed hope but, more powerfully, to the burning of the bread of salvation. In each of the comparisons of the poem, words with Christian connotations – Christ, bread – are deliberately trivialized, foregrounded as similes without the power of magic to transform the human condition. The guilt and suffering of the poet and of man in general are without issue outside human life, the only possible virtue being the sense of compassion they feel for one another because of their common condition. Yet even this is vitiated by separation and guilt, for man's 'mad eyes' look backwards towards the oblivion of the past, his gaze is a pool of guilt, though a stagnant pool. Consciousness has become a guilt-ridden parenthesis between a forgotten past and future oblivion.

José Carlos Mariátegui, a most perceptive critic who had himself experienced a deep religious crisis as a young man, was later to deny that Vallejo's pessimism had any 'relationship or affinity with the intellectual nihilism and scepticism of the West', adding that 'Vallejo's pessimism, like that of the Indian, is not a concept but a feeling'.[13] The then fashionable distinction between 'conceptualizing' and 'feeling' peoples now has an archaic ring, but apart from this, Mariátegui, here at least, is shooting wide of the mark. Vallejo had read Haeckel, Müller, Schopenhauer (at least he mentions Schopenhauer in his dissertation), as well as Manuel González Prada's essay, 'Death and life', which was profoundly influenced by Western European thought.[14] His poems are often a direct response to other writers and thinkers, and the separation of conceptualization from feeling is particularly misleading when applied to his poetry because he responds emotionally to concepts and tries to give body to abstract ideas. We have only to read his own description of his poem 'La araña' (The spider) to understand how deeply he was influenced by European Romanticism. The spider is very similar to the divided man described by Hugo as soaring towards the Heavens while part of him remains chained to the earth.[15] The spider, explained Vallejo, 'with its head divided from its abdomen, symbolizes man on the stone's edge of life. The head struggles to rise towards

the ideal whilst the belly, on the other hand, pulls towards the
earth.'[16] The division in the human soul which he personifies in
the poem 'En las tiendas griegas' (In the Greek tents) has more
to do with Aristotle than with Indian attitudes. Heart and Soul
are divided from 'Thought' a general who like Achilles reads
auguries of destruction.

> Y el General escruta volar siniestras penas
> allá......................
> en el desfiladero de mis nervios!

> And the General watches sinister pain hovering
> there............................
> over the precipice of my nerves.

No one could doubt that this is the divided consciousness of the
Western world which Vallejo inherited in common with other
poets of his time.

Vallejo's poetry, then, is in part a comment on other texts
which are important for an understanding of his poems, not as
'influences' or 'sources' but because they represent what has been
said and not what he wants to say. This 'given' does not simply
include the poems in Modernist style but many other varieties of
discourse. Critics have often assumed, for instance, that poems
in which Vallejo uses a homely or colloquial set of terms are more
typical of his 'style' than those in which he derives a vocabulary
from Modernism. But poetry which gave the impression of homely
intimacy was already a convention at the time when he was
writing,[17] so his use of colloquial or childish language is not his
personal invention. What is significant, however, is the way he
brings into question both literary and colloquial language, showing how loaded they are with contradictory significance. When
the poem which had begun so grandly with the line 'Amada, en
esta noche tú te has crucificado' ends 'Y en una sepultura /los
dos nos dormiremos, como dos hermanitos' ('And in a tomb /the
two of us will sleep like little brother and sister'), the very childishness of hoping to prolong a pure and yet profane love beyond
the tomb brings the poet into direct conflict with Christian belief.
The childishness of the hope is emphasized by the diminutive
'hermanitos', so that the homeliness of the language is a function
of an ironic viewpoint. It is not that Vallejo is wavering between
a grand style and a colloquial style, but rather that the juxta-

position of the lofty and the childish isolates the inconsistencies of man's traditional views of the afterlife.

Logos and words

It is above all the disparity between the promise of the sacred book and the insignificance of modern man that bursts through traditional systems of analogies in Vallejo's poems. The Romantics had already contributed to the instability of language by extending notions such as 'God' or 'love' greatly beyond a Christian significance; and Vallejo now pushes the consequences of this over-extension to the limits of absurdity. There is hardly an act of daily life – travelling, eating, sleeping, hardly a common object – water, bread, rivers, mountains, cities, which has not been used to suggest the supernatural and the infinite.[18] Vallejo is concerned with the loss of the spiritual power that formerly attached to these, and the loss too of that divine magic he had felt in childhood and which contrasted so brutally with the trivialization of language in the modern world. In the absence of Logos, man is left with words, with a language which can no longer refer to the infinite. The immediate consequence is that the Passion of Christ is no longer a single unique event which bestows meaning on the multiplicity of passions upon earth. Once pluralized, the notion of Christ loses all meaning. To refer, as Vallejo does, to 'Los Cristos del alma' (the soul's Christs), to 'Marías que se van' (Marias who go away) devirtualizes Christian myth and, by association, all other metaphors related to the Passion. 'The red crown of Jesus' becomes a term of comparison for the moon, though the very notion of Christ's sacrifice is inconsistent with the planetary circle. The poems speak of '*one* Palm Sunday', '*a* host in red blood', '*a* sinning Christ', '*a* Baptist' instead of John the Baptist, 'one eternal morning' instead of eternity, '*a* Good Friday', instead of Good Friday, '*this* bohemian god' instead of God. When, in a love poem, Vallejo declares that 'the child Jesus of your love was born', the trivialization is complete. The profane world has taken over. But though Christ and the Passion are rendered insignificant, other nouns – *Vida* (Life), *Luz* (Light), *Sombra* (Shadow), *Razón* (Reason), *Muerte* (Death), *Verano* (Summer) are capitalized, a typographical device which puts them into the same category of substantives as God or Christ.

And this is not simply a device but represents a re-evaluation of categories and shows how universal categories are created out of human experience.

Nietzsche makes a similar point in an essay he wrote on 'Truth and falsehood in their extra-moral sense', an essay that sheds some light on Vallejo's own reorganization of hierarchies. Nietzsche showed that our vocabulary has its origins in sense-impressions which have gradually acquired abstract meanings from which men have constructed schemata and hierarchies of values. They have built up a 'pyramidal order with castes and grades', have created 'a new world of laws, privileges, sub-orders, delimitations, which now stands opposite the other perceptual world of first impressions and assumes the appearance of being the more fixed, general, known, human of the two and therefore the regulating and imperative one'.[19] Vallejo's poetry, however, also lays bare the devaluation of words like 'communion', 'passion' and 'pilgrimage' rather than using them to inflate the importance of his personal emotions as the Modernists often did.

The Symbolists and some of the Modernists had believed that by bringing words into the poetic system and emphasizing musicality or ideal connotations, they put the reader in touch with a more enduring reality beyond the phenomenal world, – with 'everything in humanity that may have begun before the world and may outlast it', according to Arthur Symons,[20] with rhythm according to Abraham Valdelomar,[21] with beauty according to Herrera y Reissig.[22] Yet the very project was fraught with contradictions. When Herrera y Reissig writes a poem like 'La reconciliación' which is 'musical', the very musicality undermines the force of certain traditional connotations. The poem deals with a lover's quarrel smoothed over when the woman plays the piano:

> Una profética efluxión de miedos,
> entre el menudo aprisco de tus dedos
> como un David, el piano interpretaba.

> A prophetic shiver of fear
> Within the tiny fold of your fingers,
> Like a David, the piano interpreted.

We are not intended of course to take the comparison between David's harp and the piano too seriously. The lady who plays the piano is envisaged in terms of voluptuous anticipation; meanwhile something drastic happens to the Biblical prophet. The very name David, coming as it does just before the caesura, adds gravity and importance to the line. But what Herrera expresses is his own virtuosity rather than that of David, and this in turn profanes the religious connotations so that a word like 'prophetic', for instance, now comes to mean any thrill of anticipation.

'Oh ideal, holy elasticity of Symbolism. Oh modern French lyric poetry', Vallejo had once written; but he was aware of the price of this elasticity.[23] His response was to see where it took him, to jump into the dizzying space. And the way he did this is to make language perform its own downfall. So poems which begin as prayers reduce the Lord Almighty to a ghostly *voyeur* or the creation of man himself:

> Señor! Estabas tras los cristales
> humano y triste de atardecer.[24]

> Lord, beyond the window-panes you were
> Human and sad of dusk.

We are not sure where to put that phrase 'de atardecer', whether to attach it to the window-panes or to the sadness. Perhaps to both. For as soon as we imagine a God at twilight behind the 'cristales', we recognize him as our invention, condemned like us to mortality. In another of his poems, 'Retablo', Vallejo speaks of the 'suicide of God', and, in the final poem of the collection, 'Espergesia', he has a God who fell sick on his own birth-day:

> Yo nací un día
> que Dios estuvo enfermo,
> grave.

> The day I was born
> God was ill,
> Seriously.

The order of words gives force to the cliché, 'seriously ill'; and the Spanish word for serious, *grave,* like the English 'gravely' comes from the same root as gravity or weight so that the lines literally draw God down to earth.

Schopenhauer's withering description of a Jehovah who created the world 'out of misery and woe, out of pure caprice and because he enjoyed doing it'[25] is not far removed from the God of many of Vallejo's poems. Schopenhauer had disposed succinctly of the supposition that the world was created by an 'all-wise, all-

good and, at the same time, all-powerful being', arguing that
there are two reasons which make this belief impossible: 'firstly,
the misery which abounds in it everywhere; and secondly, the
obvious imperfections of its highest product man, who is the
burlesque of what he should be'.[26] Vallejo later carried this logic
to a further extreme, drawing an analogy between God and the
doctor who can diagnose but not cure the sick. In the poem,
'Dios' God is like a friar attending the dying, 'como un hospital-
ario bueno y triste'. In *Trilce*, God like a healthy doctor operates
on his own creation, extracting hope:

> Y Dios sobresaltado nos oprime
> el pulso, grave, mudo,
> y como padre a su pequeña,
>   apenas,
> pero apenas, entreabre los sangrientos algodones
> y entre sus dedos toma a la esperanza.

> God anxiously takes
> Our pulse, seriously and silent
> And like a father treating his child,
>   gently,
> But gently, opens the blood-stained cotton-wool
> And with his fingers extracts hope.   (Poem 31)

The 'healthy doctor', fleetingly referred to in poem 58 of *Trilce*
becomes that helpless surgeon of the *Poemas en prosa* who ex-
amines his patients for hours; 'and I have seen those patients die
precisely because of the reflected love of the surgeon, from those
long diagnoses, from the correct dose, from the thorough analysis
of urine and faeces'.[27]

Already in *Los heraldos negros* Vallejo allows us to feel the
absurdity of speaking of the infinite in words which constantly
betray their human origins. Whatever images we make of God
simply reflect, as Feuerbach had pointed out, our own desires,
and also our limitations. But Vallejo depicts the image with such
literal fervour that it turns into parody as if he were an over-
zealous priest whose exaggerated responses attract attention to
himself rather than the object of his worship. So, for instance, if
man conceives of an immanent God, Vallejo will logically suggest
his going down into the twilight of non-being:

> Siento a Dios que camina
> tan en mí, con la tarde y con el mar.
> Con él nos vamos juntos. Anochece.
> Con él anochecemos. Orfandad. . . .   ('Dios')

I sense that God travels
So in me, with dusk and the sea.
We go together with him. It grows dark.
We go down in dusk with him. Orphanhood . . .

Because the poet situates himself firmly in the physical world,
weighing creation in the 'false balance' of a woman's breasts, he
can only create a God in his own imperfect and alienated image:

> Yo te consagro Dios, porque amas tanto;
> porque jamás sonríes; porque siempre
> debe dolerte mucho el corazón.

> I consecrate you God because you love so much
> Because you never smile; because forever
> Your heart must pain you so much.

These 'metaphysical' poems cannot, then, refer us to a 'beyond',
because our very manner of conceiving the absolute is charged
with its own destructive power. It is as if, in the manner of Frank-
enstein, we can only create monsters out of the imperfections of
the world.

There is an impressive example in a poem he called 'Absolute'
which builds up from the melancholy of seasonal change into a
cry for 'sublime unity' only to fall back again into the alienated
plurality of existence. But it is the opening of the poem that is
interesting, for it is not the seasons which encompass man in
their mood but rather the mustiness of second-hand clothes which
imbues the season:

> Color de ropa antigua. Un julio a sombra,
> y un agosto recién segado.

> The colour of old clothes. A shadowed July
> And a just-harvested August.

By juxtaposing the 'colour of old clothes' with the description of
the Peruvian winter months of July and August, Vallejo suggests
a process of ageing without renewal, a process that God appears
unable to prevent:

> Mas ¿no puedes, Señor, contra la muerte,
> contra el límite, contra lo que acaba?
> Ay! la llaga en color de ropa antigua,
> cómo se entreabre y huele a miel quemada!

> Can you not prevail, oh Lord, against death,
> Against limits, against that which ends?
> Ay, the wound the colour of old clothes,
> How it opens and smells of burnt honey.

What the stigmata of this helpless God open to reveal is not salvation or resurrection but burnt honey, the destroyed sweetness of religious faith. It throws into pathetic relief the poet's cry for 'sublime unity', for a love 'against space and against time' and the 'one rhythm . . . God'. While Valdelomar had found no difficulty in envisioning 'sublime unity' in the universal principle of rhythm, Vallejo perceives only repetition and staleness which stand in ironic contrast to the clamour for wholeness. Valdelomar had seen geniuses as peaks in this rhythmic pattern 'over which the spirit of man marches towards his perfect state, towards a supreme rhythm so that he may unite himself with the pre-existing rhythms and fully merge with the great rhythmic unity that is God'.[28] In 'Absoluta', the very voicing of the possibility in a temporal context underscores its unattainability, so that the poem ends with the reply of the very limits which he had wished to transcend.

> Y al encogerse de hombros los linderos
> en un bronco desdén irreductible,
> hay un riego de sierpes
> en la doncella plenitud del 1.
> ¡Una arruga, una sombra!

> And as the boundaries shrug their shoulders
> With rough irreducible disdain,
> A shower of serpents falls
> On the virgin plentitude of 1.
> A wrinkle. A shadow.

'A wrinkle. A shadow' bring us firmly back into the world of change and death. The Platonic ascent is reversed as the poem slips back into time and limitation, in which the original sin is the human condition itself. Instead of the unique temptation in Paradise, we have a multiplicity of evil, a 'shower of serpents'. And this very multiplicity denotes the nature of evil and the impossibility of a 'virgin plenitude'.

The loss of the Christian Logos (explicit in the poem 'Enereida') could not be compensated, then, by some vague Platonic Absolute. The effect of this would be a total disruption of the traditional hierarchies of values, a disruption which Vallejo already glimpsed in some of the poems of *Los heraldos negros*. In 'La de a mil', for instance, Divine Providence has turned into a lottery-ticket vendor, a ragged beggar who is a living mockery

of the fortune he peddles. In 'Los dados eternos' (The eternal
dice), the tables are turned, with man claiming God-like status
because he alone suffers. Though the poem is addressed to God
as a blasphemous prayer, we do not need to be too literal-minded
in reading the text, for the poet's reproach is directed against any
notion of an ethical principle (whether Christian or Romantic)
which does not derive from existence:

> Dios mío, si tú hubieras sido hombre,
> hoy supieras ser Dios;
> pero tú, que estuviste siempre bien,
> no sientes nada de tu creación.
> Y el hombre sí te sufre: el Dios es él!

> My God, if you had been a man
> You'd know how to be a God;
> But you, who always did all right,
> You don't feel any of your creation.
> And man suffers you indeed. He's God.

By dissociating the notion of a transcendent being from an ethical
principle, Vallejo lays bare the contradictions inherent in the
notion of a Creator. God cannot be *both* a perfect being *and* a
guide to everyday conduct, for man alone knows the suffering
and alienation of existence. The poem pushes the logic of this
even further by setting the Demiurge and man on an equal foot-
ing as opponents in a cosmic dice game.

> Hoy que en mis ojos brujos hay candelas,
> como en un condenado,
> Dios mío, prenderás todas tus velas,
> y jugaremos con el viejo dado . . .
> Talvez ¡oh jugador! al dar la suerte
> del universo todo,
> surgirán las ojeras de la Muerte,
> como dos ases fúnebres de lodo.

> Dios mío, y esta noche sorda, oscura,
> ya no podrás jugar, porque la Tierra
> es un dado roído y ya redondo
> a fuerza de rodar a la aventura,
> que no puede parar sino en un hueco,
> en el hueco de inmensa sepultura.

> Today in my demon eyes there are tapers,
> As in one condemned,
> My God, you'll light all your candles,
> And will throw the ancient die . . .

Maybe – O gambler – with the luck
Of the whole universe dealt,
The baggy eyes of Death will come up,
Like two lugubrious aces of mud.

My God, and on this dark, deaf night,
You can play no longer, for the Earth's
A worn die, gnawed down and round
From rolling so wildly,
That can only come to a stop in a hole,
In the hollow of a huge sepulchre.

The word *dado* (dice) in Spanish is also the word for 'given'. The poet cannot replicate God's creation of the world but he can challenge God to a game within the 'given', for the rules are now the same for both of them. In this cosmic game, the poet's witch-eyes are alight with candles as if he were a heretic whose 'light' is blasphemous knowledge. He is a condemned blasphemer, condemned because he has consciousness, and his perceptions (his eyes) tell him that the universe is on a downward path. God's illumination (the candles) light up the game which he can no longer control. The dice are worn down from rolling towards the window (a Mallarméan symbol of the ideal[29]) and now can only roll to a stop on a single number – the one, the 'unity' of non-being, the tomb. We have reached the term of Romantic alienation which is the journey back from alienated existence to the 'resolution' of death.

Platonism turned on its head

Rooted as this early poetry is in the tradition of Romanticism, it is understandable that Vallejo should have addressed himself to love and to idealized woman. Two sections of *Los heraldos negros* – 'Los plafones ágiles' and 'De la tierra', respond to the prescription he had himself put forward in his dissertation on Romanticism in which he had explained that 'love is the soul of the world and everything great is its work'; for this reason, poetry finds its highest motive in love, in other words in an aspect of life in which beat the greatest emotions, the holiest of raptures, the noblest and most selfless feelings; in short it is in love that humanity is seen in its greatest beauty, and in the deepest and most intimate responses of the heart. But as man's senses rebel against pure virtue and idealism, inner struggles arise, inner battles which have to be lived by the muse wherever they occur.'[30] The dualism between the ideal and the real gave way in the later poems to different types of paradox and dialectic opposition. In *Los heraldos negros*, Romantic dualism is frequently a motive of the poem, though occasionally there are suggestions of a triadic or dialectic pattern. This dualism suggests an unresolvable conflict between the purity of abstraction and the impurity of matter, between spirit and body. However, some of the poems also indicate that this demand for spiritual purity masks a social norm. We know that Vallejo found himself in conflict with social *mores* both in Trujillo and in Lima, a conflict that accounts for the bitter irony of many of the *Trilce* poems and their deliberate reduction of sex to the grossest possible terms. In *Los heraldos negros*, however, Vallejo was still attempting to match an ideal of purity against a real woman whose chastity was prescribed as much for social as for religious reasons. However, he is not ready to confront the ambiguity, and in many of the poems, the woman's chastity is upheld. For instance, in 'Nervazón de angustia', he speaks of the 'rock-like dignity' of his beloved's chastity and the 'Judith-like mercury' of her inner sweetness. In 'Ascuas' which he addresses to 'Tilia', he refers to the woman's 'invincible chastity'.

> Ya en la sombra, heroína, intacta y mártir,
> tendrás bajo tus plantas a la Vida.

> Now in the shadow, heroine, virgin, martyr,
> under your feet you will tread life.

Yet in both these poems, there is a disguised and perhaps a scarcely articulated feeling that chastity, even when heroic, is life-denying. The Biblical Judith was one of those ambiguous symbols of the late nineteenth century whose heroism was a pretext for the expression of masochistic or sadistic feeling.[31] Vallejo, for whom this was difficult terrain, sometimes follows the Modernist tradition of ennobling profane love through religious analogies, and of clothing it in an imagery drawn from the arts as if to civilize emotion. Yet the very thoroughness of this imitation of Modernism borders on parody. For instance, in a poem he called 'Nochebuena' (Christmas), the beloved's return is compared to the coming of the Messiah and the celebration of the Resurrection:

> Espero que ría la luz de tu vuelta;
> y en la epifanía de tu forma esbelta,
> cantará la fiesta en oro mayor.

> I wait for the laughing light of your return;
> and in the epiphany of your slender form,
> I will sing the feast in high gold.

The comparison that springs to mind is with the *Sonatas* of Valle-Inclán whose extravagant comparisons between sacred and profane love almost spill over into parody. When in the 'Sonata de Estío', he writes, 'we celebrated our wedding with seven copious sacrifices which we offered to the gods as the triumph of life', we are but one brief step from comic exaggeration. In some of Vallejo's early poems we have a similar impression, even though the poet did not intend parody but rather a new and daring religion of love. A good example of this is 'Comunión', a reworking of a poem first written in 1916 which expressed his infatuation for a Trujillo beauty he had glimpsed at a nocturnal 'rout'. She is described in the early version as both sensuous and pure, smiling but rejecting and is, in short, the incarnation of the Romantic ideal.[32] When Vallejo rewrote the poem in 1917, anecdote is buried in a series of metaphors in which the girl's body has become the finite symbol of the infinite. Carlyle had described the symbol as 'some embodiment and revelation of the Infinite; the Infinite is made to blend itself with the Finite, to stand visible, and as it were attainable there',[33] and in Vallejo's poem, each part of the girl's body is analogous to the intangible 'beyond'. The veins convey flux and duration, hair is the tree of knowledge and also signifies loss of innocence. There is nothing new in this, of course, not even the metaphors, and it represents the kind of writing that he was soon to put behind him.[34] What he came to see as impossible, however, was the very nature of the metaphor itself. Woman is not a substitute for the Saviour. However much he tries to read the signs of infinity in her body, he cannot convert flesh into a message of redemption. At best, she reminds him of the plenitude that might have preceded conscious existence:

> Tus pies son dos heráldicas alondras
> que eternamente llegan de mi ayer!

> Linda Regia! Tus pies son las dos lágrimas
> que al bajar del Espíritu ahogué,
> un Domingo de Ramos que entré al Mundo,
> ya lejos para siempre de Belén.

> Your feet are two heraldic larks
> Which arrive eternally from my yesterday!
> Lovely Regia! Your feet are the two tears
> That I smothered on descending from the Spirit,
> One Palm Sunday when I entered the World,
> Faraway, for all time, from Bethlehem.

The very notion that man has *descended* from the spirit is neo-Platonic for, according to Plotinus, 'gravity' and 'descent' marked man's initial fall and that of all the created world from the source of light, the godhead. 'The Fatherland to us is there *whence* we have come and there is the Father', Plotinus wrote, and echoing him Vallejo puts perfection back into the plenitude that preceded earthly existence. 'Without true repose no well being is possible'[35]: Vallejo had quoted Schopenhauer's phrase in his dissertation on Romanticism; in *Los heraldos negros* he finds that Romanticism offers repose only in the pre-conscious or in an ideal so abstract as to be meaningless. Yet for him, the poet's business will preferably be with *consciousness* and with its instrument – language; here, indeed, he finds a thicket of paradox. Whatever symbols he lays hands on seem to suggest opposing ideologies, which stand in the way of the perfect poetry. Even the lover's kiss transmits two contradictory messages:

> Mi beso es la punta chispeante del cuerno
> del diablo; mi beso que es *credo* sagrado.[36]

> My kiss is the sparking point of devil's
> horns; my kiss which is sacred creed.

For the Christian, the kiss heralds the fall and the mouth is the gateway to sin and temptation. For the neo-Platonist, it is the sacred *creed*, his token of ascent to the ideal. But the ambiguity suggests a relativity of reference which undermines the significance of the act; we cannot have it both ways, yet on what basis do we choose one significance over another? The poem from which these lines are taken, 'Amor Prohibido' (Forbidden love) makes the poet a blasphemer against the Christian notion of sin, proclaiming an alternative creed which, however, he cannot, despite the purity of intention, separate from physical reality:

Espíritu es el horópter que pasa
¡puro en su blasfemia!
¡el corazón que engendra al cerebro!
que pasa hacia el tuyo, por mi barro triste.
¡Platónico estambre
que existe en el cáliz donde tu alma existe!

The spirit is the eyebeam that penetrates
pure in its blasphemy!
The heart that engenders the head!
That passes through to yours, through my sad flesh.
Platonic fibre
That exists in the chalice where your soul exists!

Vallejo does not use the word 'Platonic' lightly: he shows how even 'pure' love cannot escape physical nature, since perception itself depends on physical organs. The 'horópter' is the line along which the vision of separate eyes comes together, suggesting a union (Cartesian optics held that it was the soul that sees and not the eye). Yet in Vallejo's poem, there is no way of getting around the 'barro triste' and significantly the adjective 'Platonic' is attached to the noun 'estambre' which suggests materialization.

So Vallejo comes very early on to the irreparable physical nature of man, and his cry for 'Platonic love' is answered by silence and negation.

¿Algún penitente silencio siniestro?
¿Tú acaso lo escuchas? Inocente flor!
. . . Y saber que donde no hay un Padrenuestro,
el Amor es un Cristo pecador!

Some sinister penitent silence.
Do you hear it, Innocent flower
. . . Know that where there is no Our Father
Love is a sinning Christ.

The conclusion is full of contradiction for everything depends on how seriously we take the Our Father. Obviously if we are Christians, sexual love separated from procreation is sinful. But why a sinning Christ? The lines suggest that there is *no* Our Father to address and that a human Christ who is not the Son of God cannot redeem or save us from suffering.

Many critics have mentioned Vallejo's youthful nostalgia for ideal love[37] but the love poems are by no means so straightforward. They lay bare the treachery of language we have traditionally used to refer to moral hierarchies; and by putting 'ideal' longings into physical contexts the poet increases the dubiousness of the categorization. These very contradictions which open up at the intensest moments of the poems suggest that the abstract values which had replaced the Christian Logos no longer cohered and that any generalization that went beyond the individual's empirical knowledge was meaningless.

Brotherly love

The impossibility of abstract ideals becomes particularly sub-versive when Vallejo is writing about moral conduct. Words such as 'good', 'high', 'low', actions such as 'giving' and 'taking' tradi-tionally have ethical connotations. Whether we attach such terms to the Augustinian notion of transcending the imperfections of the flesh or the Aquinian notion of transforming desires in order to serve God, the criterion for the morally good cannot be sepa-rated from the notion of God and eternity. Christian behaviour is directed to an other-worldly end. However, we also use words such as 'good', 'high', and 'low' in contexts which do not imply universal moral and religious categories, for 'good' may refer to 'what is done well according to socially acceptable standards' and high and low are spatial relationships. Furthermore, 'good' may be used phatically as when we say 'Good afternoon', a phrase in which the original value judgment is lost. Once we abandon the Christian view of life and accept Darwinism or a Schopen-hauerian ontology which makes the life force work for the good of the species with no regard for individual suffering, then terms such as 'good' or 'bad' acquire connotations which reverse the Christian moral code. Schopenhauer, for instance, believed malice to be an essential aspect of human nature and compassion only possible in the rare cases when man obliterates his self-will and no longer strives for his own existence.[38] There are many veiled references in *Los heraldos negros* which suggest that Vallejo saw human relationships as a conflict between individual and life force. In this conflict, what is good for the species may well be bad from a social or individual point of view. His frequent refer-ences to his own 'cruelty' seem to spring not from Christian guilt so much as from his frustration because of the impossibility of entering into a human relationship without causing suffering. In 'Setiembre', he writes:

Aquella noche sollozaste al verme
hermético y tirano, enfermo y triste.

That night, you wept seeing me
Cold and brutal, sick and sad.

And in the poem, 'Heces':

Y yo recuerdo
las cavernas crueles de mi ingratitud;
mi bloque de hielo sobre su amapola,
más fuerte que su 'No seas así!'

I remember
The cruel caverns of my ingratitude;
My block of ice upon your poppy flower
Stronger than your 'Don't be that way!'

The social situation that lies behind this can be guessed. The
male is traditionally the seducer and hence the demonic partner,
but he escapes the social censorship that is the woman's lot. But,
on the other hand, he is also convinced that 'purity' is an abstraction and the woman's insistence on her virtue life-denying. So
even while he ironically rails against purity, he feels the guilt of
having hurt another human being.

The moral consequences of abandoning Christian hope had
been examined by González Prada in his essay, 'Death and life',
in which he had warned against speculating on the possibilities
of an afterlife: 'A hundredfold wall of granite separates life from
death and for centuries we have tried to perforate the wall with
a needle's point', he wrote, inferring that 'if we escape from the
disaster of the tomb, nothing authorizes us to suppose that we
shall reach more hospitable shores than those of the earth'.[39] Describing the wasteful prodigality of nature which puts millions of
people into the world for no other purpose than the perpetuation
of the species, he goes on to derive from this a stoic philosophy
and a moral code based on the notion of human betterment. But
what struck Vallejo, many of whose poems seem to reflect González Prada's speculations, was a notion which gained in strength
as he grew older – that of the contingency of the individual and
the shadowy nature of any sense of identity. In a poem, 'Santoral',
which he addressed to Osiris, the Egyptian God who mediated
between life and death, he describes himself as a 'shade'. 'Everything passes beneath my eternal column's steps', he wrote, repre-

senting himself as a temple of the species yet as mere phantom. In a world where all men are individuals but all constitute the 'eternal column' of the species, then there is no reason why César Vallejo should exist rather than somebody else. So the poem turns into an ironic pardon for his God's failure to found being in anything more than contingency:

> Viejo Osiris! Perdónote! Que nada
> alcanzó a requirirme, nada, nada . . .

> Old Osiris, I forgive thee! For
> Nothing was required of me, nothing, nothing . . .

Precisely because Osiris asks 'nothing, nothing', the poet has no feeling of essentiality. Alone we are nothing, but in relations with others we must give of ourselves. This unhappy consciousness is developed in 'Agape', the title of which suggests the feast of brotherly love, though the substance of the poem is man's sense of loneliness and alienation from others:

> Hoy no ha venido nadie a preguntar;
> ni me han pedido en esta tarde nada.

> No he visto ni una flor de cementerio
> en tan alegre procesión de luces.
> Perdóname, Señor: qué poco he muerto!

> En esta tarde todos, todos pasan
> sin preguntarme ni pedirme nada.

> Y no sé qué se olvidan y se queda
> mal en mis manos, como cosa ajena.

> He salido a la puerta,
> y me da ganas de gritar a todos:
> Si echan de menos algo, aquí se queda!

> Porque en todas las tardes de esta vida,
> yo no sé con qué puertas dan a un rostro,
> y algo ajeno se toma el alma mía.

> Hoy no ha venido nadie;
> y hoy he muerto qué poco en esta tarde.

> No one's come to question, today;
> Nor asked me this afternoon for anything.

> I haven't seen even one graveyard flower
> In such a gay procession of lights.
> Forgive me, Lord: I have died so little!

> This afternoon everybody, everybody goes by
> Without asking or wanting anything of me.
>
> And I wonder what it is that's been forgotten, that remains
> Here, so badly, in my hands, like an alien thing.
>
> I have gone to the door
> And it makes me want to shout at everyone:
> If you're missing something, here it is!
>
> Because, in all the afternoons of this life,
> I can't figure out what doors will stand before one,
> And my soul is taken over by something alien.
>
> No one's come today;
> Today I have died so little this afternoon!

In 'Agape', the poet's identity in the here and now (the 'today' and 'this afternoon') is fixed within the parenthesis outside which is non-being. The poet stands in the house of his identity, intact, so to speak, as long as nothing is demanded of him; yet separation is the source of unease and guilt. His existence as an individual rests on this separation, on not being asked to give of himself; yet it is precisely this which creates his sense of alienation. The poem suggests ironies and ambiguities by means of a series of 'mobile' words – 'tarde' (in its senses of 'afternoon' and 'late'), 'preguntar' and 'pedir', 'quedar' and 'pasar' – all of which are susceptible to wide ranges of sense and function. It is precisely this fluidity which creates the mood of the poem, which is of an apparent well-being overlaying real guilt and alienation. The door to which the poet goes represents that limit between the self and the other which it is finally impossible to cross, since to cross the threshold would mean 'dying'. There could be no more vivid illustration of the Romantic paradox of alienated existence[40] and it is compounded by the insistence on the nouns of time – the 'hoy' and the 'esta tarde' – which indicate the source of his separation from others, so that the doors and streets are already, as they will be in later poems, the spatial configurations of time itself.

The walls of 'Santoral', the doors of 'Agape' represent the elaboration of a figurative system, a system in which poetic space becomes co-extensive with a self hedged in by 'limitaciones', 'bordas', 'desfiladeros', beyond which there is the hollow of the tomb, or the sea of undifferentiated matter. These limits, however, also determine the moral space of existence in which all men have in common a sense of alienation which prevents the communion they long for. In 'Agape', this gives rise to a feeling that individual life is an 'excess', something left over in an existential economy which functions for the species, not for the individual. But this will only be elaborated in *Trilce*.

The relation of individual to species in Vallejo's poems reverses the Christian emphasis on personal salvation for now it is the species which incarnates purpose and process but, in doing so, undermines the language and authority of the religion into which the poet had been born. Logocentrism turns into parody. Thus, for instance, though the voice in 'La cena miserable' (The wretched supper) echoes with the sound of the voice of Job or the psalmist,[41] the message is now transmitted to the empty space left by the death of God.

> Hasta cuándo estaremos esperando lo que
> no se nos debe . . . Y en qué recodo estiraremos
> nuestra pobre rodilla para siempre! Hasta cuándo
> la cruz que nos alienta no detendrá sus remos.
>
> Hasta cuándo la Duda nos brindará blasones
> por haber padecido . . .
>   Ya nos hemos sentado
> mucho a la mesa, con la amargura de un niño
> que a media noche, llora de hambre, desvelado . . .
>
> Y cuándo nos veremos con los demás, al borde
> de una mañana eterna, desayunados todos,
> Hasta cuándo este valle de lágrimas, a donde
> yo nunca dije que me trajeran.
>   De codos
> todo bañado en llanto, repito cabizbajo
> y vencido: hasta cuándo la cena durará.
>
> Hay alguien que ha bebido mucho, y se burla
> y acerca y aleja de nosotros, como negra cuchara
> de amarga esencia humana, la tumba . . .
>   Y menos sabe
> ese oscuro hasta cuándo la cena durará!
>
> How long will we wait for what
> Is owed to us . . . and in what corner
> Will we have bent our poor knees forever! How long
> Will the cross that nourishes us not ship its oars.

How long will Doubt drink to us with glory
For having suffered . . .
                   We have sat down
Often at the table, with the bitterness of a child
Who cries with hunger at midnight, wide awake . . .

And when will we be with the others, at the edge
Of an eternal morning, the fast broken for all,
How long in this vale of tears, where
I never asked them to bring me.
                   Beaten down
Bathed in lamentation, I repeat, head bowed
And defeated: how long will the supper last.

Someone has drunk a lot, and jeers,
And approaches and then leaves us, like a black ladle
Of bitter mortal essence, the tomb.
                   And that dark one
Knows even less how long the supper will last!

Vallejo's poem is addressed to God but answered by death. The
irony of the poem resides in the familiarity of the psalmist's outcry which arouses expectations in the reader but disconcertingly
there is no deity to respond. Vallejo's foregrounding of symbolic
language which had, in the past, signalled a 'beyond' – the knees
(traditionally bent in prayer), the vale of tears, the supper and
the cross – reveals that these images belong to logocentric discourse, and that they have received significance from man's
yearning for a more satisfactory existence rather than from any
reality. So the question 'hasta cuándo' is finally unanswerable because by asking when? or how long? the poet situates himself
within temporality.

The apparent futility of individual existence is compounded by
the linear nature of life. In 'El pan nuestro' (Our daily bread),
human beings cannot aspire to communion with the rest of
humanity when each existence implies the death of ancestors.
González Prada had shown that life involves 'killing others, as-
similating the corpses of many others. We are walking ceme-
teries in which myriads of beings are buried in order to give us
life with their deaths.'[42] 'El pan nuestro' begins with a vivid image
of life feeding on the blood of ancestors:

> Se bebe el desayuno . . . Húmeda tierra
> de cementerio huele a sangre amada.

One drinks breakfast . . . The wet
Grave earth smells of beloved blood.

As in 'La cena miserable', the poet responds by demanding an
impossible levelling of the rich and the poor, a justice that can
never be realized since it is impossible to restore the unjustly
dead to life. So the poem 'logically' concludes that it is better not
to wake into consciousness at all:

> Pestaña matinal, no os levantéis!
> ¡El pan nuestro de cada día dánoslo,
> Señor . . .!

> Early morning eyelashes, don't wake!
> Our daily bread give us,
> Lord!

The contradiction resides in the fact that the poem rejects consciousness but demands the daily bread of spiritual grace though
as in 'La cena miserable', there is no response from God. The
poet is left with guilt and not with grace:

> Todos mis huesos son ajenos;
> yo talvez los robé!
> Yo vine a darme lo que acaso estuvo
> asignado para otro;
> y pienso que, si no hubiera nacido,
> otro probre tomara este café!
> Yo soy un mal ladrón . . . A dónde iré?

> All my bones are alien;
> Maybe I stole them!
> I managed to give myself what was
> Meant perhaps for another;
> And I think that, if I had not been born,
> Another poor man would be drinking this coffee!
> I'm a rotten thief . . . Where will I end up?

The poem's logic reaches the silence of death and the only justice
which the poet can conceive is outside the conditions of human
existence:

> Y en esta hora fría, en que la tierra
> trasciende a polvo humano y es tan triste,
> quisiera yo tocar todas las puertas,
> y suplicar a no sé quién perdón,
> y hacerle pedacitos de pan fresco
> aquí, en el horno de mi corazón.

And in this cold hour, when the earth
Exhales human dust and is so sad,
I would like to knock at all the doors,
And beg pardon, I know not from whom,
And make him little pieces of bread
Here, in my heart's oven.

Imperial nostalgias

'Nostalgias imperiales' are the only poems which are written in the tradition of poems of provincial or rustic life which were much in vogue at the turn of the century. But even these poems which are strongly marked by the influence of the Uruguayan Modernist, Julio Herrera y Reissig centre on the spiritual loss of the indigenous peoples. By choosing to evoke the 'imperial nostalgias' of the Peruvian Indians, Vallejo relates the universal loss of faith to the specific peoples whose degradation he had witnessed both in the northern areas of Peru and during his brief stay in the Sierra de Pasco, where the sad plight of the modern Indian was even more evident.[43] Thus the first four sonnets of 'Nostalgias imperiales' are structured around images of desacralization and emptiness. There is a closed chapel, a desecrated altar with the bell tolling in the distance, the snow-white eyes of an old woman coloured by a 'blind sun without light', a lake (of stillness or stagnation) in which the Inca Emperor and Sun-God Manco-Capac weeps as he drowns. Cut off from any possibility of future, the figures and landscapes are bathed in the fading light of what has gone.

> ya en las viudas pupilas de los bueyes
> se pudren sueños que no tienen cuándo.

> Now in the widowed pupils of the oxen
> Timeless dreams are stagnating.

Emptied of spiritual life, the people and landscapes become signs of loss and in 'Oración del camino', the parallel between the defeat of the Incas and the loss of Christian faith is explicitly made:

> Ni sé para quién es esta amargura!
> Oh, Sol, llévala tú que estás muriendo,
> y cuelga, como un Cristo ensangrentado,
> mi bohemio dolor sobre su pecho.

I know not for whom is this bitterness!
Take it, oh dying Sun,
And wear my outcast's pain
Like a bleeding heart of Jesus on your breast.

Yet when the poet declares 'I know not for whom is this bitterness', he betrays the impossibility of returning to racial origins by
writing Indianist poetry. For what is impossible is no longer this
or that religious belief but the notion of any original truth what-
soever and it is the consequences of this which are to be worked
out in *Trilce*.

The poetics of contingency

There is a parallel between Vallejo's rejection of God the Father,
unique creator of the universe, and his own questioning of the
poet-creator. During the writing of the poems of *Los heraldos
negros,* he had already glimpsed the relativity of language and
begun the process of laying bare the man-made origins of those
seemingly given structures of values. Trying vainly to make sense
of the world, he finds himself with a language whose rules he did
not invent and which again and again proves an instrument for
mystification. The poet cannot control his creation. So at some
point another analogy suggests itself – that of a female principle
who works with primary materials whose nature is already given.
This 'she' makes her appearance in 'Babel':

> Dulce hogar sin estilo, fabricado
> de un solo golpe y de una sola pieza
> de cera tornasol. Y en el hogar
> ella daña y arregla; a veces dice:
> 'El hospicio es bonito; aquí no más!'
> ¡Y otras veces se pone a llorar!⁴⁴

> Sweet home produced without style
> Abruptly from one single piece
> Of rainbow-coloured wax. And in that home
> She undoes and does, and sometimes says:
> 'My shelter is nice; come over here!'
> But other times, she weeps!

The home is a place of shelter and rest, of origin and birth.[45] And
it is precisely the polyvalency of this constituting metaphor which
suggests the contingency which is also the motive of the poem.
The building of the tower of Babel was undertaken by men who

spoke the same tongue and strove to reach Heaven, an impious ambition for which Jehovah punished them by multiplying tongues. The abrupt creation of this 'sweet home' (like the poem itself) out of a single though varied substance is no miracle. The God who had declared his creation to be good is replaced by a female who can only manipulate what is already given and occasionally admire, occasionally sorrow at, her own handiwork. The poem suggests something very different from the Romantic view of creation and one which eventually affects the very condition of Vallejo's poetics, driving him away from traditional analogies and 'imagery' in the direction of conceptual and grammatical figures and especially those like the pun and paronomasia which underscore the treachery of language. Romantic alienation – the notion that individuation is the original sin, a superfluous gesture on the part of nature and the source of the deepest suffering – will however never entirely disappear from his poetry even when it becomes overlaid with another kind of alienation, that of one-dimensional man.

3

THE BODY AS TEXT
NATURE AND CULTURE IN
VALLEJO'S POETICS

Throughout Vallejo's poetry, the human body is presented as a text in which the history of the species has been documented. Arms signal the fact that they have refused to become wings, the legs are columns on which *homo erectus* first raised himself over nature; eyes are fatal pilots, nails vestigial claws. From 'Enereida' (*Los heraldos negros*) in which the child is one of the human words produced by a human creator, to the 'Lomo de las sagradas escrituras' (The back of the Holy Scriptures) in which the body is a grammar of evolution;[1] from *Trilce* in which the individual is a single edition of the book of nature (poem 69) to the book produced by the dead Republican hero of *España, aparta de mí este cáliz*, Vallejo's poetry consistently seeks to inscribe this silent history which is the work of the species. And this physical order (often present in the poems as an animal, as microbe or bacteria or as a silent witness) inserts itself within the very clamour of conscious life.

For what the document of the species tells is the story of evolution; what culture nurtures in us, however, is the conviction of our unique fate. This conflict is forever re-enacted within human consciousness itself in which the moment when man stood on his feet and appeared to dominate nature is the source of a hubris which language itself supports. It is this association of writing with false consciousness that has such important consequences for Vallejo's poetics and goes right to the heart of certain traditional analogies between microcosm and macrocosm. In the process of demystification, which began with *Los heraldos negros,* pun and paronomasia are the battering rams which break down the logocentrism implicit both in Christian faith and in the poetics Vallejo had inherited from Modernism and Symbolism; for, by playing on fortuitous acoustic similarities, puns introduce all kinds of contradition and ambiguity.[2] In *Los heraldos negros,* Vallejo was still at the beginning of his discovery of the instability of language. It is, perhaps, at this stage, little more than a recognition that words such as 'love' and 'passion' no longer serve to designate both cosmic and individual design since these are at odds. Metonymy and synecdoche, on the other hand, become privileged figures precisely because they lend themselves less easily to inflationary claims. To say 'foot' may reduce the individual to a role as traveller through life but it does not imply anything about 'head' or 'heart' nor does it open the door to holistic assumptions. Further certain metonymys and synecdoches – the body and the house, for instance, form 'sets' which are flexible enough to allow the poet to explore the relation of physical life to the cultural superstructure. And by establishing a homology between the body and the house, Vallejo is then able to show how nature is codified and given a human imprint through the family itself.

In 'Canciones del hogar' which constitute the final group of poems in *Los heraldos negros,* the house in Santiago de Chuco with its pictures of saints, its altars and candles, the corridor and the 'poyo' (the stone bench) which marked the limits between the outside and the inside, his father's leather armchair, become the spatial configuration of consciousness.

The first of the 'Canciones del hogar' to be published was 'Encaje de fiebre' (Feverlace) which appeared in the Trujillo newspaper, *La Industria* in September 1916.[3] It describes the poet's return to his family home where the pictures of saints on the wall evoke a sense of nostalgia for the order and meaning of Christian faith. Instead of real faith, the poet feels only an 'illusion of Orients'; yet the random objects around him acquire significance precisely because of their association with the central figures in the tableau – the father and mother:

> En un sillón antiguo sentado está mi padre.
> Como una Dolorosa, entra y sale mi madre.
> Y al verlos siento un algo que no quiere partir.

> In an ancient chair my father is sitting.
> And like a Dolorosa, my mother comes and goes.
> I watch and feel a something which would not break away.

The 'something which would not break away' is a kind of rebellion against the very individuation which the parents themselves originated when they brought him into existence. The father on his 'ancient chair' is the bearer of a seed which has been transmitted by successive generations from the beginning of time. The mother as 'Dolorosa 'represents the synchronic pattern of human relationships with her 'coming and going'. The meaning that the poet reads into this text allows a moral conclusion:

> Porque antes de la oblea que es hostia hecha de Ciencia,
> está la hostia, oblea hecha de Providencia,
> Y la visita nace, me ayuda a bien vivir . . .
>
> Because before the wafer of that host made by Science
> Is the host in the wafer made by Providence,
> The visit is born and helps me to live well.

The poet gives priority to a 'providence' incarnated in his own family over science (perhaps more accurately translated here as knowledge) for he still sees the family as superior as a moral force to science (or the laws of nature). Evolution cannot provide a moral paradigm but the father and mother can.[4]

But though father and mother may provide an ethic that transcends the animal's struggle for existence, they do not promise eternal life. Because his parents were well into middle age when he was born, Vallejo was particularly conscious of the sadness of ageing and the loss vitality which is an indication that men and women have no more function in life. It is precisely because in old age senses become dimmed with the passing away of the biological function that he saw his parents as 'pure' and 'abstracted' in poems like 'Los pasos lejanos' (Distant steps). The home which the poet evokes here is not a plenitude but the loneliness of a place 'without noise, /Without news, without green, without childhood'.[5]

Even more than his mother's old age, it was his father's ageing that touched Vallejo because of its sad futility. In 'Enereida' (January poem) he makes the father into a paradigm of the human creator, but he is a creator who is part of succession and time and not somewhere beyond time in the dimensions of eternity. The title is one of Vallejo's lexical inventions, for 'Enereida' conflates 'enero' (January) and La Eneida (The Aeneid). January is the New Year in Peru, but also the beginning of the summer so that the title refers both to nature's cyclical renewal and to the linear succession of human life transmitted from father to son:

> Mi padre, apenas,
> en la mañana pajarina, pone

sus setentiocho años, sus setentiocho
ramos de invierno a solear.
El cementerio de Santiago, untado
en alegre año nuevo, está a la vista.
Cuántas veces sus pasos cortaron hacia él,
v tornaron de algún entierro humilde.

Hoy hace mucho tiempo que mi padre no sale!
Una broma de niños se desbanda.

Otras veces le hablaba a mi madre
de impresiones urbanas, de política;
y hoy, apoyado en su bastón ilustre
que sonara mejor en los años de la Gobernación,
mi padre está desconocido, frágil,
mi padre es una víspera.
Lleva, trae, abstraído, reliquias, cosas,
recuerdos, sugerencias.
La mañana apacible le acompaña
con sus alas blancas de hermana de caridad.

Día eterno es éste, día ingenuo, infante,
coral, oracional;
se corona el tiempo de palomas,
y el futuro se puebla
de caravanas de inmortales rosas.
Padre, aún sigue todo despertando;
es enero que canta, es tu amor
que resonando va en la Eternidad.
Aún reirás de tus pequeñuelos,
y habrá bulla triunfal en los Vacíos.

Aún será año nuevo. Habrá empanadas;
y yo tendré hambre, cuando toque a misa
en el beato campanario
el buen ciego mélico con quien
departieron mis sílabas escolares y frescas,
mi inocencia rotunda.
Y cuando la mañana llena de gracia,
desde sus senos de tiempo
que son dos renuncias, dos avances de amor
que se tienden y ruegan infinito, eterna vida,
cante, y eche a volar Verbos plurales,
jirones de tu ser,
a la borda de sus alas blancas
de hermana de caridad. ¡Oh, padre mío!

My father,
In the bird-morning, just puts
His seventy-eight years, his seventy-eight

Winter branches in the sun.
The Santiago cemetery, anointed
With the joyful new year, is in sight.
How many times his footsteps cut toward it,
And returned from some humble burial.

Today it's been a long time since my father went out!
The children's giggling disperses.

Other times, he spoke to my mother
About city life, about politics;
And today, supported by his illustrious cane
Which might have sounded stouter in his Government years,
My father is unknown, fragile,
My father is the eve of something.
Distracted, he takes away and brings back relics, things,
Memories, suggestions.
The gentle morning accompanies him
With its white wings of a sister of mercy.

This is an eternal day, an ingenuous day, a choral
Prayerful day;
Time is halo'd with doves
And the future is peopled
With caravans of immortal roses.
Father, everything is still awakening;
It is January that sings, it is your love
That resounds down Eternity.
You'll still be laughing at your little ones,
And there will be a triumphal hubbub in the Voids.

It will still be a New Year. There will be *empanadas;*
And I'll be hungry, when the Mass is rung
From the blessed bell-tower
By the good, lyrical blind man with whom
My school-fresh syllables conversed,
And my rotund innocence.
And when the morning, full of grace,
From its breasts of time
Which are two renunciations, two advances of love
Which extend and plead infinitely, an eternal life,
Sings, and lets fly plural Verbs,
The tatters of your being,
At the white edge of the wings
Of a sister of mercy – oh my father!

The poet's father unlike the authoritarian 'Our father' is fragile
and aged. His temporal journey takes him to the cemetery into

which, one by one, his friends disappear for ever and where nature's joyful resurrection suggests the primacy of the natural order. Nature and time thus speak of a 'joyful new year' and rebirth, though this does not signify the rebirth of the individual. With old age, the father becomes abstracted from life and 'takes away and brings back, relics, things, / Memories, suggestions'. And the sister of mercy who accompanies him in old age is not a human being but personified time.

Vallejo's father is, then, a creator whose function is over. Yet, unexpectedly, at this point in the poem, the mood shifts from peaceful resignation to an affirmation of life and of the future. That 'bird-morning' is now 'eternal day', the 'ingenuous day', the 'choral, prayerful day' of naive belief. This future time which had appeared to be synonymous with death and non-being is crowned with doves and peopled 'with caravans of immortal roses'. And it is not simply nature but time itself which transmits a message of joy. Instead of the terror of the Romantic poet, poised on the brink of an empty no-time, the poet discovers a New Year that 'resounds down Eternity', obliterating the silence of the grave with laughter, bustle and 'bulla triunfal'. It is a joy reminiscent of Blake, unusual in Vallejo, although characteristically, this populated, human future is represented not as a beatific, wordless vision but as 'hubbub', that hubbub which throughout his poems marks conscious life. But it is also an ironic vision for, by addressing the prayer to 'my father', by reading the oracle of nature's resurrection, the poet violates our notion of time and eternity. If fathers and sons are once again to be united, the sons must remain eternally sons, the poet must remain eternally a child learning to spell out his first words. The poet's pious hope is contrary to the nature of existence and the reader knows, even as the poet strains in the opposite direction, that there is no way of overcoming succession and having a simultaneously existent human trinity. The joker in the pack is time itself, that 'morning, full of grace' which suckles the generations and gives birth not to Logos, but to 'plural verbs'. The ending of the poem as a prayer to 'my father' is a reminder of the humanity of this creator.

The poem is more than a profane prayer, being a conscious exploration of the consequence of replacing 'Logos' by 'plural verbs'. 'In the beginning was the Word and the Word was made flesh' says John the Evangelist. That Biblical pronouncement unites Father, Son and Holy Ghost in the one person of the Trinity, from which all meaning, all significance and all Christian symbols take their substance. Once the creator is situated in time, he must be divided from his sons; there must be plurality. That this has profound consequences for language is demonstrated by the text itself, for not only are the children seen as plural words but the very learning of the syllables no longer ensures Christian salvation. The 'good, lyrical blind man' with whom the poet shared his first syllables refers to Santiago, the blind bell-ringer of Santiago de Chuco, but also to that vital moment when the child separates himself from the 'pulsational' symbiosis with the mother and becomes conscious of the self, the moment when he learns to speak. The joyful vision which this child has of his father's immortality in the continuous chain of the species is properly associated with childhood when the individual is conscious of his separate identity but not of his mortal state.

Yet 'Enereida' is the only poem in which Vallejo was able to view the succession of generations and the parental role in this with anything approaching joy. And when in *Poemas humanos,* he returned to this theme in 'Un hombre está mirando a una mujer' (A man is looking at a woman), he wrote a bitter parody of the Song of Songs.

Considering Vallejo's isolation at this point from the discoveries of Freud and his circle, the family poems are remarkably prescient. In many of them, he mimes children's games as playful re-enactments of the drives of Eros and Thanatos. For instance, a poem addressed to his brother Miguel who died in adolescence, recalls a game of hide-and-seek which, rather like the game *fort-und-da* described by Freud represents a playful stage of cognition.[6] In Vallejo's poem, however, hide-and-seek is a prefiguration of death:

> Ahora yo me escondo,
> como antes, todas estas oraciones
> vespertinas, y espero que tú no des conmigo.

> Now I hide myself,
> As I used to do, during all those evening
> Prayers, hoping that you will not find me.

Playing hide-and-seek provides the child with an excuse for skipping prayers which are intended to ward off evil, so that there is an element of guilty omission, associated with the game which makes Miguel's 'disappearance' seem like punishment for the poet's lack of faith:

> Oye, hermano, no tardes
> en salir. Bueno? Puede inquietarse mamá.

> Listen, brother, come out quickly,
> Right? Mother might get worried.

Adult perception charges every word with irony for the child's worried mother stands in opposition to the 'mother nature' for whom the death of one individual is a matter of indifference or necessity. In this context, the innocent words used in everyday discourse – words like 'bueno', 'oye' take on ironic connotations since what is 'good' or 'right' on the cosmic level may be tragedy to the human individual.

The presence of the trinity of father, mother and child in Vallejo's poetry has been the source of some misunderstanding. While it is true that the conflict between the needs of the species and the pains of individuation recurs in *Los heraldos negros*, *Trilce* and *Poemas humanos* and while it is also true that he carried his distaste for reproduction into his personal life by refusing to bring children into the world,[7] the poems resist the anecdotal. In *Trilce,* in particular, the reliving of childhood is not so much nostalgic as a method for exploring that significant break at which consciousness begins, a moment which is transferred from the natural to the cultural level by the body/house homology. For instance, in the third poem of *Trilce,* the voice of a child left behind in the family home asks the innocent question:

> Las personas mayores
> ¿a qué hora volverán?

> When will the grown-ups
> Come back?

The Spanish phrase for grown-ups, 'personas mayores' introduces a note of irony. By putting it at the beginning of the poem, the poet asks another subliminal question, in what way are these people 'mayor'?, what is there about adulthood which is qualitatively 'greater' than childhood? This is the question to which the poem now responds:

> Da las seis el ciego Santiago,
> y ya está muy oscuro.

The blind Santiago calls out six o'clock,
And it's already dark.

The hour that Santiago calls marks the transition between the
daylight hours and night-time. We would expect the conscious
adult stage to be likened to daytime, as against the child's pre-
conscious night but everything in the poem suggests the reverse
for it is a blind man who presides like a minor deity over the transition from day to night. For the child, the future is dark because
of his ignorance though he unconsciously senses that adult life is
closer to death and silence.

As in 'A mi hermano Miguel', the child's fears of darkness
anticipate adult reality; the poet / child warns his brothers and
sisters not to go out 'por donde / acaban de pasar gangueando
sus memorias / dobladoras penas' (where stooping pains have
just passed stuttering out their memories). So the adult world is
associated in the child's mind with age, pain and memory as well
as with the discontinuity illustrated by the verb, 'stuttering'.
Quite logically he has no wish to tear himself out of his protected
though confined state. But there is no way he can remain in the
paradise of pre-consciousness and as the poem progresses so does
his anxiety to leave and follow the others into adult life. Again,
his games foreshadow adult life:

> Ya no tengamos pena. Vamos viendo
> los barcos. ¡el mío es más bonito de todos!
> con los cuales jugamos todo el santo día,
> sin pelearnos, como debe de ser:
> han quedado en el pozo de agua, listos,
> fletados de dulces para mañana.

> Let's not be sad. We can look at
> Our boats. Mine's the best of the lot!
> With which we play the livelong day –
> Without fighting, just as we ought to do;
> They've stayed in the water tank, already
> Laden with sweets for tomorrow.

This very language with which the child tries to persuade his
brothers and sisters to stay is charged with time and with comparison. The individual always sees himself as the most important
figure in the world and when the child boasts that his boat is the
best, he unwittingly prefigures the dissension of adult life. The
Spanish for livelong day, 'todo el *santo* día', though a mere cliché,
recovers some of its original force as the reader separates this

holy childhood day from adult consciousness. The child's notion
of what 'ought to be' – the plenitude of the family, is hardly possible even as he demands it: by the final lines of the poem, he is
himself clamouring to get out into the adult world.

> Llamo, busco al tanteo en la oscuridad.
> No me vayan a haber dejado solo,
> y el único recluso sea yo.

> I call out and grope in darkness.
> Don't let me have been left alone,
> Don't let me be the only one left behind.

The poem's dynamic depends on the opposing tensions of the
child's wish to stay within childhood and the gradual formation
of his desire to follow others into the 'outside' of the adult world.
The use of certain grammatical forms, such as the continuous
present – 'se están acostando todavía' (they are still going to
bed) – reveals the undertow of time itself which imposes its inevitable pattern over the childish will. And the formation of that
will and the beginning of individuation is what makes the innocence of childhood so ironically ambiguous.

The journey of life and the house/body homology

It was natural enough, given the remoteness of Santiago de
Chuco that Vallejo should have depicted the life process as a
journey and one of his early poems, 'Los arrieros' (The mule-
drivers) turns the muletrain which took him to the railhead at
Menocucho into a symbol of the purposeful thrust of the life
force in contrast to the aimlessness of the conscious individual. It
is significant too that one of his short stories, 'Más allá de la
vida y la muerte' (Beyond life and death) should be structured
around a journey home.[8] But in *Trilce*, the house will become a
place of birth which is metamorphosized into the mother's body.
   We can observe this very process in poem 61:

> Esta noche desciendo del caballo,
> ante la puerta de la casa, donde
> me despedí con el cantar del gallo.
> Está cerrada y nadie responde.

> El poyo en que mamá alumbró
> al hermano mayor, para que ensille
> lomos que había yo montado en pelo,

por rúas y por cercas, niño aldeano;
el poyo en que dejé que se amarille al sol
mi adolorida infancia . . . ¿Y este duelo
que enmarca la portada?

Dios en la paz foránea,
estornuda, cual llamando también, el bruto;
husmea, golpeando el empedrado. Luego duda
relincha,
orejea a viva oreja.

Ha de velar papá rezando, y quizás
pensará se me hizo tarde.
Las hermanas, canturreando sus ilusiones
sencillas, bullosas,
en la labor para la fiesta que se acerca,
y ya no falta casi nada.
Espero, espero, el corazón
un huevo en su momento, que se obstruye.

Numerosa familia que dejamos
no ha mucho, hoy nadie en vela, y ni una cera
puso en el ara para que volviéramos.

Llamo de nuevo, y nada.
Callamos y nos ponemos a sollozar, y el animal
relincha, relincha más todavía.

Todos están durmiendo para siempre,
y tan de lo más bien, que por fin
mi caballo acaba fatigado por cabecear
a su vez, y entre sueños, a cada venia, dice
que está bien, que todo está muy bien.

I dismount my horse, this night,
At the door of the house, where
I said farewell at the cock's crowing.
It is shut and no one answers.

The stone bench from which Mamá lighted the way
For my older brother, to saddle
The backs that I had ridden bare,
Through streets and neighbourhoods, a rural boy;
The bench on which I left my painful childhood
To grow yellow in the sun . . . And this bereavement
That frames the portal?

God's in a foreign peace,
And the animal, as if also calling, snorts;
Sniffs about, striking the pavement. Then he doubts,
Whinnies,
Pricks up his ears.

Papa should still be up, praying, and perhaps
He'll think I'm late.
My sisters, humming their simple
Clamorous illusions,
Preparing for the coming party,
And there's hardly anything missing.
I wait, I wait – my heart's
An egg about to be laid, but forestalled.

The numerous family we left
Not long ago, and today no one waits, and not even a candle
Was put on the altar for our return.

I call again, and nothing.
We grow quiet, and begin to sob, and the animal
Neighs and neighs again.

They are all asleep forever,
And it's so much for the best, that at last
My horse grows tired of tossing its head
And, half asleep, with each nod of its head, says
That it's all right, that everything is all right.

Night and morning become, in the opening lines, a telescoped
life-span, between the cockcrow of dawn (which reminds us of
Peter's denial of Christ) and the prodigal's return. Day's journey
and the life-span each generate different clusters of images which
throw each other into relief and sometimes overlap. The prodigal
returns to find an empty house. The crowing of the cock at day-
break which had signalled his departure suggests the larger
framework in which the journey is life itself and the cock announces the dawn of consciousness. The poem can, indeed, be
read as allegory in which both God and animal nature represented by the horse are outside the human universe. The poet's
descent from the horse (and the journey of life) represents a
momentary hiatus and the space in which the poem itself becomes possible. The 'poyo' or stone bench of the house in Santiago de Chuco thus becomes the marker which separates the
plenitude of childhood from the emptiness of adult life. The
poem shifts between an allegorical and an anecdotal level because of a range of ambiguities and puns whose very nature
seems to underline the absence of Logos. Thus the stone bench
on which his mother 'lighted the way' for the elder brother is
also the place where the mother had given birth to him. This play
on the word 'alumbrar' in its dual significance of 'to light up' and

'to give birth' reveals the ambiguous nature of the mother who is the source of individual consciousness but also of the life which subjects every individual to the drive of the species. For instance, the elder brother saddling 'backs that I had ridden bareback' sets up an opposition between the cultural act of *saddling* (and dominating) nature and the younger child's more primitive bareback riding. Adult life on which the elder brother is already embarked involves the separation from nature and the younger child though closer to nature must inevitably follow the same course.

Unlike the animal, however, the human individual is endowed with memory, reason and hope which are the source of his illusory desire for the plenitude of family life and the feast which should celebrate the prodigal's return. In reality, no return to childhood is possible and the traveller feels his frustration as an unhatchable egg which obstructs his throat i.e. the very organ associated both with speech and the act of communion. Since there is no way to be outside time like God, he can only respond to the emptiness of the house of identity by imitating the animal's resignation.

'Esta noche desciendo del caballo' is unusual in suggesting an allegorical reading of this kind. Possibly the Quevedan sonnet which seems to have inspired the opening lines encouraged the strategy of the poem.[9] Elsewhere in *Trilce*, the metamorphosis of house into body is much more complex. For instance, in poem 65, 'Madre, me voy mañana a Santiago' (Mother, I go tomorrow to Santiago), the house to which the prodigal son returns is the mother's body. Because the house is an artefact produced by human beings, its identification with the body suggests that the mother is not simply an instrument of nature but also the agent in a socialization process:

> Me esperará tu arco de asombro,
> las tonsuradas columnas de tus ansias
> que se acaban la vida. Me esperará el patio,
> el corredor de abajo con sus tondos y repulgos
> de fiesta. Me esperará mi sillón ayo,
> aquel buen quijarudo trasto de dinástico
> cuero, que pára no más rezongando a las nalgas
> tataranietas, de correa a correhuela.

> Your arch of astonishment will await me,
> The tonsured columns of your uneasiness
> That ends life. The patio will await me,

> The corridors with festive
> Mouldings and decorations. My grandfather chair
> That good big-jawed bulk of dynastic
> Leather that no longer growls at the great-grandchild
> Buttocks, from leather strap to thong.

The rhythm and the semantic weight of the lines fall on that repeated future tense – 'me esperará' – although the very importance that the poetic device bestows on them underscores the
irony for the certainty which is promised is the continuation of
material existence through the family. The mother is the temple
of the species whose womb is an 'arch of astonishment' and whose
legs are 'tonsured' columns as if to indicate her sacrificial role
and the fact that on her, rests the edifice of the species. Moreover, the 'corredor de abajo con sus tondos y repulgos / de fiesta'
has the very configuration of the womb decked out, as it were,
not only for the prodigal's return to nature's fold but for that first
coming at birth. Like González Prada, Vallejo dwells on procreation as an unselfish act, a non-supernatural moral paradigm.[10]
And this is reinforced later in the poem by lines which describe
the father's penetration of the mother's body as if he were a wor-
shipper humbly prostrating himself in order to enter the temple
as half a man, as essentially incomplete. 'Bajo los dobles arcos de
tu sangre, por donde / hay que pasar tan de puntillas, que hasta
mi padre / para ir por allí, / humildóse hasta menos de la mitad
del hombre, / hasta ser el primer pequeño que tuviste' (Under
the double arches of your blood through which / One can only
pass on tiptoe so that even my father / To go up there, / Bent
down until he was half a man, / Until he was the first child that
you had).

The fact that arches suggest civilization is important since this
indicates that human life is something more than animal reproduction without casting doubt on its material basis. Further, the
body is described as a grandfather chair, i.e. as 'furniture' passed
on from generation to generation, and as 'aquel buen quijarudo
trasto de dinástico cuero' ('That good big-jawed piece of dynastic
leather'). The adjective 'quijarudo' is formed by analogy with
linajudo or lineaged and this analogy again associates the descent
of species-man with the document of the body which is the sign
of his evolutionary inheritance and the chair is 'big-jawed' as if

to emphasize the devouring animal lurking under the human skin. Finally the grandfather chair is also described as chastizing the backsides of successive generations 'de correa a correhuela' thus once again emphasizing the continuity of life and the fact that it is a discipline to which each individual must submit in turn.

The message of the species is thus codified in the house and family structures although once the family is abandoned, the human imprint is effaced and there is mere submission to the needs of the species. Further, no amount of socialization can alter the fact that natural creation cannot supply the same moral force as Christianity had once done. Hence the poet's outcry:

> Oh si se dispusieran los tácitos volantes
> para todas las cintas más distantes
> para todas las citas más distintas.

> Oh if only the silent flyers were at hand
> For all the most distant connections
> For all the most distinct appointments.

On the literal plane, this is simply an expression of longing for a mother love which might have the totalizing force of divine grace. However, the use of paronomasia reveals the extent to which Vallejo's poetics were now freed from the myth of presence even while, on the surface level, he demands a Logos. For paronomasia occurs at the very climax of the poem to suggest the fortuitous character of all creation. The process of signification is here set in motion, so to speak, by the apparently accidental connection between 'cintas' and 'citas' and between 'distantes' and 'distintas'. Further, the very triviality of the difference (a single phoneme) between 'cintas' and 'citas' foregrounds the nature of language itself and the rules of differentiation and identity which govern speech.[11] Language here while ostensibly demanding something different reveals its own non-supernatural mechanisms and thus thrusts the poem to the final demystification in which the poet resigns himself to his natural origin:

> Así, muerta inmortal.
> Entre la columnata de tus huesos
> que no puede caer ni a lloros,
> y a cuyo lado ni el Destino pudo entrometer
> ni un solo dedo suyo.

Así muerta inmortal.
Así.

So, immortal dead.
Beneath the colonnade of your bones
Which cannot fall even with weeping,
And in whose side Destiny cannot place
A single finger.

So, immortal dead.
So.

The return of the prodigal in *Trilce* 65 has led back to the unalterable certainty of the journey of the species of which the mother is both the human agent and the victim.

In some poems, however, this process of humanizing the species is reversed. What appears to be human and individual history is shown, in reality, to be the species drive. Poem 47, for instance, begins:

Ciliado arrecife donde nací
según refieren cronicones y pliegos
de labios familiares historiados
en segunda gracia.

Ciliated reef where I was born
According to chronicles and documents
Of embellished, familiar lips
In second grace.

'Arrecife' and 'historiados' belong to the opposing extremes of nature and culture though it is plainly nature which has priority. 'Ciliated', a curiously technical term which Vallejo probably took from Haeckel links the ciliated cells of the spermatazoa which fertilize the human egg to the simplest forms of zoological life. 'Arrecife' is one of a number of geographical terms – archipelago and peninsula are others – which Vallejo used in order to spatialize the relationship of individual to species. For though individuals appear to be islands, they 'de-island' themselves whenever they act in function of the species by reproducing their kind.[12]

The same lines show that this natural history of the individual is *documented* in the body itself, in 'cronicones y pliegos / de labios familiares historiados / en segunda gracia'. Unlike the Holy Scriptures, this document speaks not of original unity with its source in a creator but of a *second* grace or a *re*creation. And the

lips which issue this message (like the 'pliegos' of the body) are
the sexual organs themselves. The fact that it is a second grace
and not a unique event underscores the repetitive nature of
human reproduction and explains why, in the same poem, the
guardian angels who preside over the child's birth are 'pericotes
viejos' (old parrots). Yet, ironically, the very character of the
human family ensures the development of a false pride, of consciousness of the self as unique so that the lofty and priestly pretensions of the individual stand in ludicrous contrast to his real
status:

> Se va el altar, el cirio para
> que no le pasase nada a mi madre,
> y por mí que sería con los años, si Dios
> quería, Obispo, Papa, Santo, o talvez
> sólo un columnario dolor de cabeza.

> The altar goes away, the candle lit
> So that nothing would happen to my mother,
> And lit for me so that with the years, I would be,
> God willing, Bishop, Pope, Saint, or perhaps
> Only a columnary headache.

The altar *goes,* displaced by the conviction of a natural creation
in which there is no room for popes, bishops or saints and in
which the individual is nothing but the cypher, the number 1
which the poem brings into being. Thus the poem shows both
the traces of religious belief left over in human consciousness
from the myth of supernatural creation and the geography of the
species which the birth and death of individuals cannot alter.

The human mother stands between the divine and natural
worlds. To the child, she offers both too much and too little for
she showers love on the child thus endowing him with an individual consciousness which is thereby overdetermined. In the
well-known poem, 'Tahona estuosa de aquellos mis bizcochos'
(Warm oven of those my biscuits) the mother not only *re*produces but produces the food of individual existence which sticks
like a crumb in the gullet of the grown man. In this poem (*Trilce*
33), the mother becomes an ambiguous figure for she is both the
vessel of the species and the source of individuation. The poem
recreates the moment when the child is still scarcely conscious of
himself as an individual, still wearing a 'tress for each letter of
the alphabet'. This 'tress' of hair is plainly an attribute of civilized

nan and in other poems is associated with 'combing', 'plaiting' and 'weaving' which are activities that refer to culture rather than nature.¹³ In poem 31, the association of the social activity of plaiting hair with the learning of the alphabet clearly identifies speech with the socialization process.

The dawn of consciousness is explored in greatest detail in *Trilce* 52 which describes the child's unwillingness to get out of bed (and be born) and the games which, in the guise of play, make him conscious of his separate identity.

> Y nos levantaremos cuando se nos dé
> la gana, aunque mamá toda claror
> nos despierte con cantora
> y linda cólera materna.
> Nosotros reiremos a hurtadillas de esto,
> mordiendo el canto de las tibias colchas
> de vicuña ¡y no me vaya a hacer cosas!
>
> Los humos de los bohíos ¡ah golfillos
> en rama! madrugarían a jugar
> a las cometas azulinas, azulantes,
> y, apañuscando alfarjes y piedras, nos darían
> su estímulo fragante de boñiga,
>   para sacarnos
> al aire nene que no conoce aún las letras
> a pelearles los hilos.

> And we'll get up whenever we
> Feel like it, though mummy all brightness
> Wakes us with melodious,
> Lovely motherly anger.
> We'll giggle over it,
> Biting the edges of the warm blankets,
> Of vicuna skin. 'No, don't tickle me!'
>
> The smoke of the huts, oh urchins
> In the branches! – they would get up early to play
> With the blue, blue-ing kites,
> And grabbing stones and pebbles, they would give us
> The fragrant stimulus of dung,
>   to bring us
> Into the infant air that has not yet learned the alphabet,
> To fight for their kite-strings.

The game, like many of those in *Trilce*, is an ironic foreshadowing of adult life. The mother feigns anger and teases the child out of the symbiotic animal warmth of the vicuna blankets. In this way she performs the tasks of nature and, indeed, her teasing the child out of bed is a prelude to the birth process itself.

With the expulsion of the child into the 'infant air', a series of connections is set up between the child, the smoke of huts and kites which can be seen as symbolic of individual destinies. The child stands between the purely natural process (like that which produces dung as excess from bodily consumption) and culture symbolized by the smoke from the hearth.

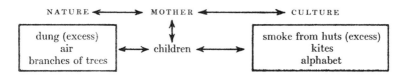

The 'urchins in the branches' stands in apposition to the 'smoke of the huts' – a grammatical device which suggests, not metaphoric transference so much as a common structuring principle in the two terms, based on production, consumption and excess. Thus:

functioning of body (survival)	functioning of species (survival through reproduction)	functioning of culture (fires in huts)
dung	child's consciousness of self as an individual	smoke
(excess over what is necessary for the body)	(excess over needs of species)	(excess from fire)

The fragrant smell of dung sends the children into the 'infant air' and this suggests that they are still at the pre-conscious stage though already engaged in the struggle for life since they fight over the kite-strings which may symbolize individual destinies. That this process of individuation begins before birth is suggested in the third stanza of the poem in which the 'we', the plural voice of the species, addresses an individualized 'tu' who 'will want to pasture / among omphaloid hollows, avid caverns, ninth months / My curtains'. The desire of this individual is, at this point, at one with the species, for he wishes to break the waters and so be born and partake of the feast of life. But the final lines of the poem bring into being a strangely divided individual – divided between a consciousness that is inseparable from culture and the unconscious silence of the species. The child arrives laughing at this feast of life:

le tomas el pelo al peón decúbito
que hoy otra vez olvida dar los buenos días,
esos sus días buenos con b de baldío,
que insisten en salirle al pobre
por la culata de la v
dentilabial que vela en él.

You tease the prostrate labourer
Who once again forgets to say Good morning.
Those his good mornings spelt with g for godforsaken,[14]
Which will come out of him
Through the butt of the v
Dentilabial that keeps watch within.

Mocking child and prostrate labourer are the two aspects of divided humanity, corresponding to the individual (culture) and the species (nature). The socialized child self-confidently uses the phatic expressions and courtesies of civilized life and already despises the submissive body which is enslaved to reproduction. Yet the joke is on the *conscious* individual for the dentilabial *v* (with its sexual connotations) keeps watch on the real purpose of life which is the continuation of the species. Because the *v* is a sexual sign and because this priority is imposed despite culture, no 'good morning' can promise anything but the passing of time and of the individual.

The ramifications of images and word play in poem 52 (even more complex than I have suggested here) is itself an indication of Vallejo's problematic. The exploration of the genesis of individual consciousness, the priority of reproduction over the cultural superstructure, the formation of a false consciousness which conceals the true purpose of existence could not but take Vallejo into forbidden territory. Peruvian society was as traditional as any in Latin America. If a D.H. Lawrence novel could be banned in England where there was at least a vocal liberal minority, then it is reasonable to conclude that Peruvian society imposed even stricter though unspoken limits on what could be said. Indeed shortly after the publication of *Trilce*, President Leguía would dedicate the country to the Sacred Heart. In this environment, obscurity, ellipsis and euphemism became Vallejo's weapons of self-defence.[15] Moreover it is interesting and significant that one of these devices – the substitution of food terms for sexual terminology (which we find in poem 52 and several other *Trilce* poems) – is common in popular culture and familiar from the North American blues singers.

The Holy Scriptures of the body

Though some of these constraints were removed when Vallejo arrived in Paris in 1923, his devastating attack on the individualized subject was too radical to permit him to dispense with parody, irony and word play. In this respect, he stands apart from the Marxist humanism epitomized by Neruda. Nevertheless, in one of the first poems he wrote during his stay in Paris, 'Lomo de las sagradas escrituras' (Back of the Holy Scriptures), he makes a far more explicit attempt than in *Trilce* to demystify the process of creation:

> La talla de mi madre moviéndome por índole de movimiento
> y poniéndome serio, me llega exactamente al corazón:
> pensando cuanto cayera de vuelo con mis tristes abuelos,
> mi madre me oye en diámetro callándose en altura.
>
> Mi metro está midiendo ya dos metros,
> mis huesos concuerdan en género y en número
> y el verbo encarnado habita entre nosotros
> y el verbo encarnado habita al hundirse en el baño,
> un alto grado de perfección.

> My mother's height moving me because of the nature of motion
> And to be serious, it reaches exactly to my heart:
> And thinking how many fell in flight with my sad grandparents,
> My mother listens to me in diameter, silent on high.
>
> My metre is already measuring two metres,
> My bones agree in gender and number
> And the incarnated Word is here among us
> And the incarnated Word reaches, as it sinks into the bath tub,
> A high degree of perfection.

In these lines, all the spatial metaphors which had once referred to a theocentric universe – 'on high', 'fall' – now refer to natural descent. The Scriptures which tell the story of individual creation are written in the organs of the body itself. The final comic synthesis, in which the incarnated Word sinks into the bath tub, reminds us of Archimedes's law and the dawn of scientific knowledge which eroded belief in supernatural causes. In 'Encaje de fiebre', the poet had still been able to believe that providence prevailed over science. In 'Lomo de las sagradas escrituras', science prevails but allows no dignity, no *hubris* in the human individual. More eloquent than the babble of consciousness is this dumb text of evolution. The mother as immediate cause of his existence is silent; the dead ancestors 'fallen'. There is no sound from these creators who are responsible for his existence and whose inheritance is incarnated in the poet's own body. This living body constitutes a grammar of organs which, as long as life lasts, can never fail to complete the sentence which is individual existence. 'So much life and I never forget the tune', Vallejo writes in one of the *Poemas humanos*.[16] Competence and performance may be separate phenomena in the speech acts of conscious life but in the silent tongue of the species, they are inseparable.

4

THE END OF THE SOVEREIGN
ILLUSION: *TRILCE*

The book was created in a complete vacuum. I am responsible for it.
I take the entire responsibility for its aesthetics. I give myself in the
freest possible way and this is my greatest artistic achievement. God
knows how sure and real this freedom is. God knows how much I have
suffered so that the rhythms will not transgress freedom and descend
into license. God knows to what dreadful limits I have gone in fear,
terrified that everything would come to an end there for my poor
living mind.[1]

Trilce is an extreme book, revolutionary in its exploration of an
authentic language, yet curiously at odds with the fact that
between 1918 and 1922 the poet still seemed to be living within
the structures of Romanticism, still paying homage to the
rhetoric of José Santos Chocano and practising the 'bohemianism'
that had come to seem the indispensable mode of existence for
the poet. It seems as if, while exploring the pains and delusions
of the individuation principle that was the heritage of Romanticism, Vallejo also glimpsed that terrifying vision of utter emptiness and chaos, described by Laforgue:

> Oh! qu'il n' y ait personne et que Tout continue!
> Alors géhenne à fous, sans raison, sans issue.[2]

The crisis that produced *Trilce* was probably precipitated, as
much as anything, by the profound contradictions Vallejo discovered between the Romantic exaltation of the self and the
displacement of man from the central role in creation which had
followed from evolutionist theory. It was very much a crisis of
the time, shared, for instance, by a writer who was just becoming
fashionable – Henri Barbusse – in whose early novels, *Les sup-
pliants* and *L'enfer*, the self had been questioned to the point of
destruction. Or so Gonzalo Zaldumbide suggested in his essay on
Barbusse:

We have nothing left but eyes that watch, a mind that enquires, a
heart that gives and asks the infinite; that is to say, a man who is like
all other men without any special characteristics. And since individuals

79

appear to be non-existent, ephemeral repetitions of the same indefinite unity, *what does this or that matter?* [my italics][3]

A similar indifference threatens the *Trilce* poems. In them the individual voice becomes fitful, indistinguishable from the banal monotony of life. A volcanic eruption has taken place, destroying the hierarchies of the past, leaving man to confront a universe in which he has no special purpose or importance. This 'geological' upheaval of the very grounds of self is dramatically represented in poem 57:

> Craterizados los puntos más altos, los puntos
> del amor de ser mayúsculo, bebo, ayuno, ab-
> sorbo heroína para la pena, para el latido
> lacio y contra toda corrección.
>
> ¿Puedo decir que nos han traicionado? No.
> ¿Que todos fueron buenos? Tampoco. Pero
> allí está una buena voluntad, sin duda,
> y sobre todo, el ser así.
>
> Y qué quien se ame mucho! Yo me busco
> en mi propio designio que debió ser obra
> mía, en vano: nada alcanzó a ser libre.
>
> Y sin embargo, quién me empuja.
> A que no me atrevo a cerrar la quinta ventana.
> Y el papel de amarse y persistir, junto a las
> horas y a lo indebido.
>
> Y el éste y el aquél.
>
> The highest points craterized, the points
> Of the love of upper-case being, I drink, go hungry, ab-
> Sorb heroin for the pain, for the weak
> Kick and in defiance of all correction.
>
> Can I say that they have betrayed us? No.
> That they were all good? Not that either. But
> There's good will there, no doubt,
> And above all, being's like that.
>
> So who is it loves himself so! I seek myself
> In my own intention which should have been my own
> Work, in vain: nothing attained freedom.
>
> And yet who drives me?
> I bet I won't dare shut the fifth window.
> And the role of loving one's self, and persisting, along with the
> Hours and what can hardly be owed.
>
> And the this and the that.

'El éste y el aquél' echoes Barbusse's 'this and that' as if the destruction of what Vallejo calls elsewhere the 'sovereign illusion' must reduce individuation to accidental differences. Beginning with the premise that 'the highest points' of being have been 'craterized', that these points represent 'love of upper-case being', the poet shows how the 'I' becomes reduced to a function, to a subject who drinks, fasts and absorbs heroin. The Spanish language helps here, since the subject–pronoun *yo* can be dispensed with: so that by saying 'bebo' instead of *yo bebo* the poem already illustrates the absorption of the subject category into verbs which denote activity. Because of this premise, the questions the poet asks in the second stanza – 'Can I say that they have betrayed us? . . . That they were all good?' – are meaningless since they depend on Christian and humanistic assumptions about man (if someone is to blame, then original sin is implied; if all were good, a Rousseauesque view of man follows). But neither of these can be applicable if the 'I' has been 'craterized', if there is no moral choice, if 'nothing attained freedom'. The poet has to conclude with a vague allusion to Kant – that there is 'doubtless a good will' and 'above all, being's like that' – in other words, the exploration of the self ends with the tautological statement, 'I am'.[4]

Having no transcendental design or purpose and no freedom to make moral choices, the poet is left with the puzzle of his own motivation. 'Who drives me?' he asks, couching the question in terms that demand 'God' or a humanized, transcendental demiurge as his answer. Yet this question produces two contradictory responses. On the one hand, he does not dare to 'close off the fifth window', the window being the Mallarméan symbol for escape into the ideal, 'fifth' because the number four connotes for him the prison-like confinement of the categories of time and space.[5] Yet in contradiction to this he also adduces self-love and persistence in his own being (in the Spinozan sense). So the self turns out to be both the need to escape from the human condition and persistence within it.

The names of Kant, Rousseau and Spinoza are not cited arbitrarily. Vallejo mentions philosophers in several poems. But in *Trilce* 57, he is also concerned to reduce their systems to the commonplace – 'goodness', 'good will' 'persistence in one's own being' – precisely because he wishes to parody the inadequacy of philosophic explanations of the self, which are also 'craterized'

by the death of God. What can finally be said of the self by the
end of the poem is that it is reduced to this inexplicable persistence in its own being: 'el papel de amarse y persistir, junto a
las / horas y a lo indebido. / Y el éste y el áquel.' The very
inarticulacy of the conclusion suggests the impossibility of defining the self in a coherent way. The role of the individual
cannot be conceived apart from 'las horas' (time as never-ending
succession) and 'lo indebido' (contingency). All else becomes
absorbed into the 'this and that' as if there is nothing but the
demonstrative pronouns left to denote the discrete but accidental
differences which are all that is left to the individual.

The illusion of the self's importance is shored up by individuation which, however, serves the species. Subjectively speaking,
the individual is motivated by pleasure, though pleasure itself is
essential only because it is a mechanism for survival:

> esta horrible sutura
> del placer que nos engendra sin querer,
> y el placer que nos DestieRRa! (poem 60)

> this horrible suture
> Of pleasure that begets us without our wanting
> And pleasure which ExiLes us!

The oddly capitalized 'DestieRRa' is emphasized in such a way
that we attend to its original meaning – to 'de-earth'. The lines
represent man as being born of pleasure which is also the source
of his alienation from nature. This paradox is not new, though
we find few writers who translate this more directly into syntax,
lexicon and orthography. Much of the strangeness of *Trilce* arises
from the almost superhuman attempt to create a language of
truth – 'verdadismo', Vallejo was to call it[6] – in order to decon-
struct all those categories which, as Nietzsche had shown, had
come to appear given and eternal though in fact they are 'anthro-
pomorphic through and through'. 'What we take to be stable
truths', Nietzsche had written, turn out to be 'a mobile army of
metaphors, metonym, anthropomorphisms, in short a sum of
human relations which became poetically and rhetorically intensified, metamorphosed, adorned and, after a long usage, seemed
to a nation, fixed, canonic and binding'.[7] Nietzsche's conclusion
is striking:

Only by forgetting this primitive world of metaphors, only by the
congelation and coagulation of an original mass of similes and pre-

cepts, pouring forth as a fiery liquid out of the primal faculty of human fancy, only by the invincible faith that this sun, this window, this table is a truth in itself; in short, only by the fact that he forgets himself as subject and what is more as an artificially creating subject; only by all this does he live with some repose, safety and consequence; if he were able to get out of the prison-walls of his faith for an instant only, his self-consciousness would be destroyed at once.[8]

This was like the terrifying void which Vallejo glimpsed in *Trilce*. Later on, Vallejo would relate language closely to the ideology of individualism, and in one of his articles he talks of the 'blind and unchecked supremacy of Archimedes's law and the crudely positivist enthusiasm which has been responsible for bomber planes and war', relating this to the crisis in civilization from which the only salvation could be a new Logos: 'the supremacy of the Word which discovers, which unites and which takes us beyond transient self-interest and egoism'.[9] By this, he did not of course mean some avant-garde revolution of the word, nor did he believe that by spelling 'destierra' 'DestieRRa', he would change man or society. It is rather that consciousness and language are one, and there can no more be a new consciousness without a new language than there can be a new language without a new consciousness. But in *Trilce* he is faced with a de-mystifying task – that of showing the inoperability of traditional images and metaphors, the speciousness of 'harmony' in the Modernist sense. That is why the poems lurch forward in a series of shocks, discontinuities, verbal games, outrageous puns. That is why *Trilce* rejects homogeneity of mood, refuses comfort and solace. That is why the poems are anti-divine, anti-prophetic, anti-heroic, satiric.[10]

Tearing the blindfold from the eyes

In order to go on, we do not need to look up, but ahead. For too long we have populated the Firmament with the phantoms of our imagination and given substance to hallucinations forged by fear and hope; the time has come to throw off the blindfold from our eyes and see the Universe in all its beauty and also in all its implacable reality.[11]

Vallejo had not only read González Prada but also Max Müller and possibly even Feuerbach, so he was well aware of the way men had externalized their hopes, incarnating them in god-like figures; and how they had needed to express immaterial things in material ways. He is not content to reflect this in his poetry but must make language enact the process in such a way that human capacity for self-delusion is exposed. The opening lines of poem 19 are a striking example of this.

> A trastear, Hélpide dulce, escampas,
> cómo quedamos de tan quedarnos.

> To strum, sweet Helpide, you clear up
> How we are from so much staying.

A conventional analysis which selects one of the many possible connotations of 'trastear' (to shift around, to chatter, to put the bridge into the guitar or to strum) immediately runs into difficulties, first because none of them can possibly fit with 'escampas' but more seriously because the interest of the poem centres on the making of myth not on interpretation. By giving Hope a Greek name (Hélpide) and capitalizing the initial letter, Vallejo is creating his own deity; and it is a deity who can only be spoken of in language which derives from the material world – 'trastes' or 'escampar' (which derives from *campo*). The poet has elevated hope but can only refer to it in words which draw him back to the material world. Unlike the Christian God, Hélpide cannot reveal a beyond but only 'clear up' the given. The poem turns into a parody of the annunciation, with hope replacing both Saint Gabriel and the Holy Ghost and appearing in a stable which has all too evident signs of animal nature:

> Hoy vienes apenas me he levantado.
> El establo está divinamente meado
> y excrementido por la vaca inocente
> y el inocente asno y el gallo inocente.[12]

> Today you come to me just as I've risen.
> The stable is divinely pissed
> And defecated by the innocent cow
> The innocent ass and the innocent cock.

Hélpide comes to the poet at the moment when he has 'risen', an ambiguous term since it might refer to his getting out of bed in the morning or to man rising out of his animal status and standing on his feet. In *Trilce,* the feet and shoes become important synechdoches for man's journey through life which is different from the animal's existence only because of consciousness. When man first stood on his own two feet, he began the evolutionary process which awakened consciousness; but this in turn led to self-glorification. Man tends to ignore his own animal nature, making gods to suit his own ideal image. By identifying 'Hélpide' with Saint Gabriel and the Holy Ghost, and by addressing his prayer to this personified emotion, the poet lays bare the human origin of religious myth. Indeed the very words of the prayer devirtualize the message by showing how incompatible 'hope' is with the evidence of our senses which confirm our animal nature:

> Penetra en la maría ecuménica.
> Oh sangabriel, haz que conciba el alma,
> el sin luz amor, el sin cielo,
> lo más piedra, lo más nada
> > hasta la ilusión monarca.

> Penetrate the ecumenical mary.
> Oh saintgabriel, let the soul conceive,
> The without light love, the without-heaven,
> The most stone, the most nothing,
> > Even to the sovereign illusion.

We have already seen how in *Los heraldos negros* Vallejo destroys Christian myth by transforming Christ into Christs. In poem 19, the 'ecumenical mary' is no longer Mary the Mother of God, but a common world-soul which is without consciousness (light), without heaven – in other words, blind, material and undifferentiated. Though the syntax of the verse is ambiguous, it is clear that it is no longer God who is to bring forth salvation but hope which is not transcendent and which, when united with the ecumenical mary, can give birth only to self-delusion. So Vallejo is showing us the 'god-making' process at work and at the same time revealing the truth 'in all its implacable reality' (to use González Prada's phrase[13]). For as soon as we recognize that myth is nothing but a construction that men put upon reality in order to understand it, then it ceases to be effective.

> Mas si se ha de sufrir de mito a mito,
> y a hablarme llegas masticando hielo,
> mastiquemos brasas,
> ya no hay dónde bajar,
> ya no hay dónde subir.

> Se ha puesto el gallo incierto, hombre.

> But if we have to suffer from myth to myth,
> And if when you speak to me you come chewing ice,
> Let us chew coals, then.

> There is no place to descend,
> There is no place to rise.
>
> The cock has begun to doubt, man.

The instability of language is underscored by the purely natural opposition of 'chewing ice' and 'chewing coals' for neither substance belongs to the supernatural order. Man's suffering clearly is of this earth. The poet's response to the coldness of hope can only be physical and this in turn removes him far from any Christian notion of salvation and resurrection. The poem ends on a comic note. The cock which had, with its crowing, signalled Peter's denial of Christ is now unsure of itself; the animal world no longer confirms the supernatural order but speaks only of uncertainty.

Poem 19 shows us that the whole ground on which human existence had rested for centuries has crumbled away. With it, there has been a vast upheaval in language and in symbol. Mary, Saint Gabriel, the cock can no longer fill their functions as signs in a sacred text since there is no longer a supernatural message to transmit. The projection of human hopes and emotions, their personification in gods and myths has turned into an uncomfortable paradox, for man both makes and destroys his own gods. That is the price of consciousness.[14]

The demystification of poetry

'The poet', said Coleridge, 'brings the whole soul of man into activity, with the subordination of its faculties to each other according to their relative worth and dignity. He diffuses a tone and spirit of unity that blends, and (as it were) *fuses,* each into each, by that synthetic and magical power to which I would exclusively appropriate the name of Imagination.'[15] The cognitive and psychological functions which Coleridge ascribes to poetry have become deeply-ingrained assumptions among modern critics. Poetry puts, according to Elizabeth Sewell, 'language to full use as a means of thought, exploration and discovery'.[16] I. A. Richards, speaking of one special kind of poetic language, metaphor, describes it as 'the supreme agent by which disparate and hitherto unconnected things are brought together . . . for the sake of the effect upon attitude and impulse which springs from their collocation and from the combinations which the mind establishes between them'.[17] The difficulty arises when we pass from description to prescription, as Octavio Paz seems to do when he writes of the image which 'does not explain; it asks to be recreated and literally, to be relived. The discourse of the poet is incarnated in poetic communion. The image transmutes man and converts him in turn into image, that is, into a space in which the contraries are resolved.'[18] The alchemical term 'transmute' suggests the liberation of man from phenomenal contradictions and this power of poetry to achieve something beyond words, to achieve once again the identity of word and being, has prevailed in a great deal of modern poetry from the Romantics to Heidegger.[19] The alternative is either a poetics of the free play of the sign or a poetry which opens up contradiction and is akin to satire, parody, insult. To the seventeenth-century poet all these possibilities were open because they had their place in the totality of divine providence. When, in the nineteenth century, poetry came to occupy the empty space left by the death of God and religion, it also lost some of its playfulness as well as its critical function which was displaced into other kinds of discourse. At the same time, the word 'image' comes to replace the 'figure' of older rhetoric precisely because it must fill the place of vision in religious experience. Vallejo's poetry, on the other hand, now turns against the image itself and whilst he uses traditional analogies – the road of life, the house of identity – he resists recognizing these as signposts of another reality. This explains why he turns his attention not only to the symbol-making and myth-making processes themselves but also reveals how grotesque and inadequate a consolation they are. This is the significance of poem 36, which takes the Venus de Milo as a symbol of perfection and of art's power to create harmony, only to discover the impossibility of deriving harmony and perfection from limited, finite experience. For harmony implies simultaneity and life is lived as linear succession.

> Pugnamos ensartarnos por un ojo de aguja,
> enfrentados, a las ganadas.
> Amoniácase casi el cuarto ángulo del círculo.
> ¡Hembra se continúa el macho, a raíz
> de probables senos, y precisamente
> a raíz de cuanto no florece!

¿Por ahí estás, Venus de Milo?
Tú manqueas apenas pululando
entrañada en los brazos plenarios
de la existencia,
de esta existencia que todaviiza
perenne imperfección.
Venus de Milo, cuyo cercenado, increado
brazo revuélvese y trata de encodarse
a través de verdeantes guijarros gagos,
ortivos nautilos, aunes que gatean
recién, vísperas inmortales.
Laceadora de inminencias, laceadora
del paréntesis.

Rehusad, y vosotros, a posar las plantas
en la seguridad dupla de la Armonía.
Rehusad la simetría a buen seguro.
Intervenid en el conflicto
de puntas que se disputan
en la más torionda de las justas
el salto por el ojo de la aguja!

Tal siento ahora al meñique
demás en la siniestra. Lo veo y creo
no debe serme, o por lo menos que está
en sitio donde no debe.
Y me inspira rabia y me azarea
y no hay cómo salir de él, sino haciendo
la cuenta de que hoy es jueves.

¡Ceded al nuevo impar
                    potente de orfandad!

We struggle to thread ourselves through the eye of a needle,
Face to face with the conquered.
The fourth angle of the circle is almost ammonia-ized.
The female complements the male, on the basis
Of probable breasts, and precisely
On the basis of that which does not bloom!

Are you there, Venus de Milo?
You act crippled, hardly budding,
Encircled by the plenary arms
Of existence,
Of this existence which neverthelesses
A perennial imperfection.
Venus de Milo, whose lopped-off, uncreated
Arm swivels and tries to elbow itself
Through greeny stuttering stones,

The end of the sovereign illusion {89}

East-rising nautili, yets scrabbling
Recently, immortal vespers,
Lassoer of immanences, lassoer
Of the parenthesis.

Refuse – and all of the rest of you – to plant your feet
In the double security of Harmony.
Refuse symmetry, indubitably.
Intervene in the conflict
Of points that are disputed
In the most ruttish of joustings,
The leap through the eye of the needle!

Thus I sense my little finger
And on my left hand, besides. I see it and believe that
It cannot be mine, or at least that it is
Not where it should be.
And it angers and irritates me
And there is no way to get out of it, except taking
Into account that today is Thursday.

Yield to the new and potent odd numbers
                    of orphanhood!

What is immediately apparent in Trilce 36 is the 'material' nature
of the language. *Pugnar* comes from *pugno* (fist) so that the
poetic 'we' which struggle to thread themselves through the eye
of the needle are firmly related to bodily action. The 'eye' of the
needle is the empty space in which individual consciousness
manifests itself in its striving to 'thread' i.e. to perform an action
which is the very reverse of being or of presence. The human
being is in perpetual confrontation with his own efforts to be the
continuity in a linear process which, however, he perceives only
as an individual, as discontinuity.[20] Reversing the old arguments
for the existence of God which induced the existence of a perfect
being from the imperfections of the world, Vallejo reveals human
imperfection through the striving for continuity and perfection.
The key word is *almost*. The fourth angle of the circle is '*almost*
ammonia-ized' but the circle of perfection will never be realized,
a failure that is emphasized by a characteristic device of which
I shall have more to say later. In Spanish *armonizar* sounds very
similar, though not quite identical, to *amoniácase* 'to ammonia-
ize'. The fourth angle of the circle is not harmonized but ammo-
niacized and this outrageous device illustrates exactly the point
Vallejo is trying to make, that there is no Platonic ascent from

imperfect phenomena to perfection. *Almost* cannot be made into totality, ammonia will never be harmony and incompleteness will never terminate in completion. In fact 'amoniácase' instead of 'armonizase' is like a Freudian slip; it substitutes what is really in our minds for what we intended to say.

There is another characteristic of the human condition that makes transcendence impossible, namely the separation of human beings into two sexes, a primal division which derives from the different functions of the male as the source of the seed and the female as the source of life and nourishment. Because we are either male or female, we can never be 'whole', and because of the linear nature of life we are separated from our origins. What Vallejo proposes is the creation of a new harmony by image and symbol. He will square the circle, continue the male in the female – both of which operations suggest conditions that are impossible in the real world. Yet, instead of creating a new reality, Vallejo's poem shows the absurdity of such a pretension, and shows it by turning the Venus de Milo, the armless goddess who symbolizes perfection, into a grotesque figure. Venus's armlessness is part of the real world; she is within the 'plenary arms of existence' and if existence is a *plenum,* everything that is, is *here.* What is absent cannot signify anything but *what is not there in reality.* Yet, traditionally, art has been supposed capable of 'bodying forth' the intangible, a process which Vallejo's poem now begins to enact with comic results. Venus's arm, which is either cut off or uncreated (since it is not there, it does not matter which), tries to elbow its way into existence; but because existence implies discontinuity, succession, potential, the arm's material incarnation can only be imagined as incongruous. It will elbow itself 'through green-stuttering stones', 'east-rising nautili', 'yets scrabbling recently', 'immortal vespers'. The uncreated arm is related to the cosmos which is all process and unrealized potential;[21] but potential can only be imagined in temporal terms. Even when we say 'not yet', we imply a *yet* and hence imply succession rather than the simultaneity which harmony demands.

The Venus de Milo belongs, however, to art or culture rather than nature. Even so, Vallejo cannot liberate her from the cosmic process, cannot make a sculpture the symbol of immortality or totality. She is described, at the end of the third verse, as a 'lassoer of immanences', a 'lassoer of the parenthesis' – as if art were, in Husserl's terminology a 'bracketing' which did not alter the conditions of existence.[22] To contemplate this Venus, therefore, is not to be reminded of the eternal but rather to be reminded of those very limits which condition existence in the material world.

Plainly this poem challenges any Platonic notion of aesthetics. When the poet turns once again to his listeners ('y vosotros'), demanding that they refuse harmony and intervene in the process, his imperative tone is otiose. Man *is* within the process and cannot escape even through art; for Venus fails to mediate between this world and the beyond. Man's only possible creativity is bound to the life-process itself and the 'most ruttish of joustings' (the sexual act) which will allow him to thread himself through the eye of the needle and continue the linear thread of succession of the species. The Venus de Milo has, in fact, reminded the poet not of a perfection not of this world but of the individual's function in terms of the species, in which all that does not serve it is redundant, like the useless little finger which he feels as 'surplus' on his left hand ('I *see it and believe* that it cannot be mine'). Having failed to envisage an eternal, perfect beauty in the Venus de Milo's absent arms, he now sees and believes the message of his own body which tells him that he has more body than he really needs. The only use of the little finger is to enable him to count and hence to understand the temporal succession – the fact that Thursday is the fifth day of the week (if we begin with Sunday). The finger, though it may make the poet angry, nevertheless signals the truth. Moreover, the word he uses to express his irritation, 'me azarea', contains suggestions of *azar* or chance, in other words suggestions of contingency. At the end of the poem, he is forced to recognize himself and others as cyphers in a dialectic progression:

> ¡Ceded al nuevo impar
> potente de orfandad!
> Yield to the new and potent odd numbers
> of orphanhood!

I shall return later to the fact that the language of the poem is that 'roughened, impeded language' of which the Formalists speak.[23] What is important is that this dense text itself forces us to recognize the impossibility of the analogy-making process. Vallejo's aesthetic thus stands in striking contrast to that of the

Modernists, epitomized in Rubén Darío's poem 'Yo persigo una forma' (I seek a form) which makes Venus the visible proof of a perfection not of this world.

> se anuncia con un beso que en mis labios se posa
> al abrazo imposible de la Venus de Milo.

> [The vision] is heralded with a kiss impressed on my lips
> With the impossible embrace of the Venus de Milo.

But between *Prosas profanas* and *Trilce,* there has occurred a change in the very conditions in which the image is produced. Analogies between the visible and the invisible world no longer come so easily; the material world has lost its power of suggesting the infinite. Even the universe does not appear to have any coherence or plan, or it appears to defy man's sense-making abilities. Hence the prevalence of catachresis – for instance the treble-sound of poem 25 which is 'nasalized' into an icicle:

> Y la más aguda tiplisonancia
> se tonsura y apeálase, y largamente
> se ennazala hacia carámbanos
> de lástima infinita.

> And the most acute treblesounding
> Is tonsured and lassoed and slowly
> Becomes nasalized towards icicles
> Of infinite pity.

In poem 26, we have another example:

> Nudo alvino deshecho, una pierna por allí,
> más allá todavía la otra,
> > desgajadas,
> > péndulas.

> Whitish knot undone, one leg over here,
> The other further over there,
> > Split off
> > Penduluming.

A third example may be found in poem 73:

> Y quien tal actúa ¿no va a saber
> amaestrar excelentes digitígrados
> para el ratón. ¿Sí . . . No . . .?

> And he who acts like this, must he know
> How to train excellent digitigrades
> For the mice? Yes? No?

In all these the initial image is made to perform in a way which negates its primary characteristics and it quickly becomes metamorphosed into something different, the knot into hanging, straddling legs, the treble sound nasalizes, grades are tamed. The effect is comic because of that animation of the inanimate which Bergson described as the source of laughter. And this in turn means that we perceive it as disparity, not fusion or harmony. What we have to attend to is not connection but disconnection, the patent inability of either nature or culture to add up to a totality.

Perverse symbols

This lack of connection can best be illustrated with reference to a number of poems whose subject is not the 'I' but some symbolic thing. If we take, for example, by way of contrast, a poem like Mallarmé's 'Les fenêtres', we may assume that we must attend to certain window-like analogies and associations. Windows frame the outside world yet protect us from it; they allow us to 'see through' rather than simply to see. As soon as we turn to Vallejo's poems, the difference is striking. He has, for instance a piano which journeys through the body, a piece of glass which is to be consumed like a communion wafer, a room which speaks dialects and is cone-shaped. None of these objects behave as we would expect them to behave. It is as if, instead of using 'window' to stand metaphorically for all the things it usually stands for – transparency, a view on the outside world, etc. he made it stand for something quite uncharacteristic such as heaviness or opaqueness. By defamiliarizing 'piano', 'room', 'glass', Vallejo suggests the intractability of the objective world when we try to convert it into metaphor and symbol. A good example is poem 44, whose subject is an oddly-behaved piano:

> Este piano viaja para adentro,
> viaja a saltos alegres.
> Luego medita en ferrado reposo,
> clavado con diez horizontes.
>
> Adelanta. Arrástrase bajo túneles,
> más allá, bajo túneles de dolor,
> bajo vértebras que fugan naturalmente.
>
> Otras veces van sus trompas,
> lentas asias amarillas de vivir,

van de eclipse,
y se espulgan pesadillas insectiles,
ya muertas para el trueno, heraldo de los génesis.

Piano oscuro ¿a quién atisbas
con tu sordera que me oye,
con tu mudez que me asorda?

Oh pulso misterioso.

This piano journeys inward,
Journeys by joyful leaps.
Then it meditates in iron-bound repose,
Nailed together with ten horizons.

It goes on. It crawls through tunnels,
And beyond, through tunnels of pain,
Under vertebrae elusively fugue-ing, naturally.

At other times, its trumpet tubes go,
Slow yellow asias of living,
Go into eclipse,
And insectile nightmares inspect and pick themselves,
Dead already to the thunderclap, herald of genesis.

Dark piano, at whom do you peer
With your deafness that hears me,
With your muteness that deafens me?

Oh mysterious pulse!

As soon as we try to make a symbol of the piano, we find ourselves in difficulties. To be sure, it is a mysterious pulse which is
'inside', and so we might take it to refer to Valdelomar's principle
of rhythm which will lift us back to our source in God.[24] But
Vallejo's piano neither emits sound nor is played by anyone.
Instead, it is 'nailed together with ten horizons' and meditates in
'iron-bound repose'. Furthermore, it is a piano that journeys
through the body. Instead of a series of analogies and associations:

man – piano – harmony – God

we have

piano – journey – meditation – rest – journey

In other words, where we would expect sound and silence, we
get movement and rest. But in making this substitution, Vallejo
suggests an association between sound and succession which is
just as valid as the one we normally make between the instrument and the simultaneous emission of sounds in harmony. More-

over he draws a joking parallel between the piano and the body
which 'fugues naturally'. Thus a new analogy is established
between body and instrument as *function,* not between body and
cosmic harmony. This silent piano which travels through the
body is an anticipation of those dumb animals and insects which,
in *Poemas humanos,* incarnate a life force which stands in opposition to consciousness.

At this point in the third verse, the piano undergoes a new
metamorphosis, acquiring tubes in eclipse and insectile nightmares which 'pick themselves'. The problem with this verse is
that it goes in several directions at once, two of which derive
from the pun on 'trompa' (tube) which might be either a musical
instrument or a Fallopian tube. These diverse meanings suggest
simultaneously music and birth, that pulsation of the musical
rhythm and of life itself which is again brought together in the
'Oh pulso misterioso' of the final line. Yet it is precisely the characteristic of this poetry that it impedes and frustrates sense-
making so that the 'trompas' now in turn develop a proliferation
of associations of their own – they are 'slow yellow asias of living',
which move 'into eclipse' and 'insectile nightmares inspect and pick
themselves', 'dead already to the thunderclap, herald of genesis'.
Each new image is so concrete as to become superimposed on its
antecedents so that the original is lost to view. Yet all these associations suggest cosmic events so that they are not unconnected.
Living is linked not to the individual but to the pullulating masses
of the East (the yellow asias), time is not individual time but the
cosmic time of the eclipse; and what is removed by the delousing
process are the dead nightmares of religious belief. Each image
has in it something which belongs to the greater life of the
planetary system and which is non-human. Conflated, they suggest a cosmic scheme of things in which the individual is lost.
Not until the end of the poem is there any human subject and
even then this subject appears only as a voice interrogating an
incomprehensible and mysterious object. The 'piano', the internalized rhythm, is deaf because it cannot receive the communications
of the individual and its silence (since it cannot communicate
with the subject) is deafening. So the disjunction between life
process and individual desires is complete; and the image of a
species fixing the individual with a mute and wondering gaze as
if totally separate will come to obsess Vallejo more and more in

his later poems. That 'mysterious pulse' which occasioned lofty
Modernist rhetoric is now turned into an alien force.

One could cite many other examples of poems in which the
language offers resistance not only to our sense-making efforts
but even to the very act of utterance. Often the opening lines of
a poem form a tongue-twister. For instance, poem 25 begins,
'Alfan alfiles a adherirse . . .', poem 23 starts with 'Tahona
estuosa de aquellos mis bizcochos . . .'. Alliteration as in 'Vusco
volvvver de golpe el golpe' (poem 9), awkward combinations of
consonants increase the intractability of the poem so that they
transmit neither recognizable messages nor agreeable sounds.
This deliberate impeding of comprehension is further increased
by Vallejo's orthographic, syntactic and typographical inventions
which are perhaps the more obvious features of *Trilce* and on
which critics have frequently commented. For instance, he may
place capital letters at the middle or the end of a word as in
'nombrE' or he may break verse lines in awkward places. In poem
58, he arranges the final words vertically instead of horizontally
across the page. In poem 13, 'estruendo mudo' is spelled backwards as 'odumodneurtse', etc. And far from these devices being
exercises in virtuosity, they point to the reverse, to the powerless-
ness of invention in the face of the iron laws of necessity. For instance, to capitalize the final letter of nombrE instead of the first
letter of someone's name shifts importance to the end and also
causes us to reflect critically on the use of the initial capital letter.
This is an aspect of *Trilce* to which I shall return later for it not
only increases the resistance and density of the text but plainly
has a cognitive function as well.

In this prisonhouse of language, the subject seems to be defined only by what *cannot* be known and said.[25] In poem 54,
'El forajido tormento', it is a 'foreign storm', something from outside the subject which is the active agent. The poetic 'I' is something which is acted on, defined by limits beyond which the
subject cannot go.

> A veces doyme contra todas las contras,
> y por ratos soy el alto más negro de las ápices
> en la fatalidad de la Armonía.
> Entonces las ojeras se irritan divinamente,
> y solloza la sierra del alma,

se violentan oxígenos de buena voluntad,
arde cuanto no arde y hasta
el dolor dobla el pico en risa.

Sometimes I come up against all the againsts
And at times I'm the blackest of peaks
In Harmony's inevitability.
Then my eye-sockets become divinely irritated,
And the mountain of my soul weeps,
Oxygens of good will are violated,
All that does not burn is burned and even
Suffering doubles back its beak in laughter.

Both 'a veces' (sometimes) and 'por ratos' (at times) suggest
the discontinuity of experience. The self is, by definition, the
locus of contradiction and limitation. The willing subject is replaced by 'I' which appears motivated by forces outside the
limits of individualism. 'Harmony' thus becomes a 'fatality' because the subject cannot help being in tune with the cosmic
forces though he is conscious of the self only as he attempts to
transcend his condition as part of nature. Scaling heights and
going beyond his physical possibilities thus produces undesirable
effects – the 'mountain of my soul weeps', 'oxygens of good will
are violated'. The higher man aspires, the more he must suffer by
straining against his true nature and the less oxygen (of Kantian
good will?) does he have. Yet straining against the limits can
only increase suffering.

arde cuanto no arde y hasta
el dolor dobla el pico en risa.

All that does not burn is burned and even
Suffering doubles back its beak in laughter
(or: dies laughing).

These lines are reminiscent of the paradox found in 'cancionero'
and seventeenth-century poetry. But Vallejo is not interested in
the analogy between the sensation of love (whether divine or
profane) and physical sensation, nor the paradox that we take
pleasure in what makes us suffer. He is much more concerned
with showing the contortions of language itself as soon as words
try to reach beyond empirical knowledge. What burns is 'all that
does not burn', all that lies outside the possibility of physical
law. The verse ends in a grotesque image, a parody of Prome-

theus. 'Doblar el pico en risa' not only means 'to die laughing'
as if suffering is overcome by the absurdity of the individual
situation but 'pico' also suggests the Promethean vulture. It is as
if having seized fire, having attempted to dominate and imitate
God, the subject finds himself defined by the very impossibility
of being anything more than a finite individual.

It is now obvious why catachresis, oxymoron (or condensed
paradox) and paradox itself are central to *Trilce*. Metaphor based
on analogy gives the illusory sense of coherence and makes the
world into the poet's mirror or the poet into the mirror of the
world. Now the mirror is broken. Left with fragments of the old
analogies, with dead metaphors and with a syntax which makes
the 'I' the subject of willing and of acting, the poet's task turns
into an examination of the fragments or glimpses into the void.

The prisonhouse of self

In *Trilce*, the world defies human control. 'El forajido tormento'
and 'Este piano' are objects which resist humanization even as
the poet attempts to internalize them. Conversely, 'time' and
'death' come alive and are transmogrified, participating as active
subjects in contrast to the human individual who is often represented as the sick man or the patient. The sun as centre of the
cosmos and source of energy takes on a particular importance,
though the poet often speaks of the planet in comic or familiar
terms:

> ¿Los soles andan sin yantar? ¿O hay quien
> les da granos como a pajarillos?   (poem 70)

> The suns go without eating – or is there someone
> Who gives them seed as if to little birds?

or again:

> Ni ese bueno del Sol que, al morirse de gusto,
> la desposta todo para distribuirlo
> entre las sombras.   (poem 39)

> Nor that good fellow Sun who, on dying from choice,
> quarters everything for distribution
> among the shadows.

Plainly Vallejo is laying bare the familiar and even childish
manner in which we try to bring within the realm of understand-

ing the universal but totally non-human source of energy. Death
too is given summary treatment, being personified as a 'great
baker' who makes man pay 'in curious coins' for the 'warm, ir-
refutable, baked, transcendent value' of life. In one poem, Death
is down on its knees bleeding and apparently vanquished:

> La Muerte de rodillas mana
> su sangre blanca que no es sangre.
> Se huele a garantía.
> Pero ya me quiero reír.   (poem 41)

> Death on its knees lets flow
> Its white blood that is not blood.
> It smells of a guarantee.
> But already I feel like laughing.

The poet's laughter can only be bravado. Yet it is the poet's
hyperbolic enactment of man's cavalier attitude to death which
displays human pretension in all its absurdity. Time, too, is
treated with disrespect. In poem 21, he refers to 'diciembre con
sus 31 pieles rotas / el pobre diablo' (December with its broken
31 skins / Poor devil). In poem 60, daytime becomes a hyper-
active newborn child:

> Día que has sido puro, niño, inútil,
> que naciste desnudo, las leguas
> de tu marcha, van corriendo sobre
> tus doce extremidades, ese doblez ceñudo
> que después deshiláchase
> en no se sabe qué últimos pañales.

> Day which has been pure, childish, useless,
> Born naked, the leagues
> Of your journey go running upon
> Your twelve extremities, that frowning doubling
> Which then unthreads itself
> In I know not what ultimate diapers.

Day is a grotesque little monster running on twelve limbs which
are duplicated like the hours of day and night. But more important is the way this active time is made to contrast with the
poet who in the same poem speaks of his 'patience' as 'made of
wood', 'vegetable'. The examples of this humanization of time
could be multiplied. June acquires shoulders on which the poet
stands and laughs. Morning softens up its fine hair (poem 63).
The afternoon is a cook serving inedible food (poem 46). Wed-

nesday has its nails dethroned. Time marches, drives a motorcar,
runs on rails, conjugates in the past tense. The week has its
throat cut. But plainly all these attempts to humanize only
heighten the arrogance of man's appropriation of the world.
Coleridge described art as that which humanized nature and
infuses 'the thoughts and passions of man into everything which
is the object of contemplation'. Now Vallejo appears to show us
the futility of this.

The most striking example of this is poem 50 'El cancerbero',
where the very limitations of human existence turn into a prison
guard who has all kinds of contradictory and grotesque attributes:

> El cancerbero cuatro veces
> al día maneja su candado, abriéndonos
> cerrándonos los esternones, en guiños
> que entendemos perfectamente.
>
> Cerberus handles his padlock
> Four times a day, opening
> And closing our breastbones, with a wink
> We perfectly understand.

'Four' is the number of limitation – there are *four* elements, *four*
seasons. Cerberus, the deity that presides over the frontier between life and death, is here personified as the limit between
being and non-being, but also as the master in a master / prisoner
relationship in which the prison is also the human body. Between
warder and prisoner there is perfect understanding, for in effect
they are indistinguishable. Man's existence depends on Cerberus
who thus comes to personify not simply limitation but the condition of existence, and hence consciousness. There is more than a
hint here of the Platonic separation of master (soul) from slave
(body) or of master (ego) from slave (nature), not to mention
the Hegelian master / slave relationship. All these personifications
represented attempts to explore the nature of consciousness which
is, above all, man's reflection upon his own nature and hence
implies a sense of separation from nature. In this poem, the self
is imprisoned by a warder whom like time, sun, death, the poet
treats with condescension or disrespect.

> Con los fundillos lelos melancólicos,
> amuchachado de trascendental desaliño,
> parado, es adorable el pobre viejo.
> Chancea con los presos, hasta el tope

los puños en las ingles. Y hasta mojarilla
les roe algún mendrugo; pero siempre
cumpliendo su deber.

Por entre los barrotes pone el punto
fiscal, inadvertido, izándose en la falangita
del meñique,
a la pista de lo que hablo,
lo que como,
lo que sueño.
Quiere el corvino ya no hayan adentros,
y cómo nos duele esto que quiere el cancerbero.

With his dull, melancholy basis,
Boyish and transcendentally dishevelled,
On his own two feet, the poor old man is adorable.
He jokes with the prisoners, to the brim
Fists in crotches. And the gay fellow
Even gnaws on a crumb or two; but always
Doing his duty.

Between the bars, he thrusts the fiscal, unnoticed
Point, hoisting himself up on the little phalanx
Of his little finger
On the track of what I speak,
What I eat,
What I dream
The crow wants no privacy
And how the wishes of this Cerberus pain us.

Like all the conditions under which life is lived, this Cerberus
presents contradictory characteristics which defy understanding.
He is described as 'boyish', 'dishevelled', 'adorable' yet funda-
mentally 'melancholy'. He jokes with the prisoners, placing his
fist in their crotch (the closed hand being symbolic of defiant
masculinity) as if he were challenging their manhood. He 'gnaws
on a crumb' for them and yet is just 'doing his duty'. To the
prisoner, he is familiar and yet an object of contempt; certainly
there is nothing fearful or very oppressive about him. Yet he is
'corvino' (crow-like) and the crow is a bird of prey who feeds
on dead carcasses: he stands 'on his own two feet', a sign in
Vallejo's poetry of human as against animal consciousness. What
the poet tells us, then, is that the prisoner feels separate from the
Cerberus who keeps him imprisoned, yet he cannot discover any
part of the self which is not accessible to Cerberus. In other
words he has no essence, for the warder 'pokes his fiscal, un-

noticed point' through the bars of the prison and raises himself to the level of the 'little phalanx of his little finger' – a significant vantage-point, for the little finger is a characteristically human member yet also useless, the redundant reminder that hands were once feet and claws. The little finger allows Cerberus to be on the track of what the prisoner eats, speaks and dreams – in other words, to become internalized, so that the prisoner is virtually indistinguishable from his warder. The only thing that distinguishes him is consciousness of his imprisonment which implies that the subject is defined by individuation.

> Por un sistema de relojería, juega
> el viejo inminente, pitagórico!
> a lo ancho de las aortas. Y sólo
> de tarde en noche, con noche
> soslaya alguna su excepción de metal.
> Pero, naturalmente,
> siempre cumpliendo su deber.

> The immanent old man, Pythagorean, plays
> Within a clockwork system,
> Along the wide channels of the aortas. And only
> From dusk to night, by night
> Is anyone able to evade his metal exception.
> But, naturally,
> Always doing his duty.

The little word, 'naturally' is not merely a filler. It reminds us of 'nature' and of the fact that Cerberus is 'doing his duty' according to nature and so is identifiable with the life force which is also immanent in man, part of an internal time-mechanism. He is described as Pythagorean because he represents the universal rhythm beating in man's very blood (but mortal blood). Cerberus, being a 'metal exception' which prevents him sharing the fate of the transient individual, is only to be escaped by night, presumably when the individual dies and is released from his human condition.

The personification of the imprisoning conditions of life enables Vallejo to explore consciousness in a new way, showing the irony of man's sense of superiority over the conditions which imprison him. And more than irony, it is the grotesque personification of the inexplicable which takes us to the very source of man's attempt to make his world understandable.

All too often critics have read the 'prison poems' as anecdotes based on Vallejo's own prison experience when, in fact, they are explorations of the imprisoned and divided self. If any doubt were possible of Vallejo's deep involvement in the problems that arose from this Romantic alienation, poem 22 should be sufficient evidence that one of his main concerns was the inadequacy of individualism. The poem begins:

> Es posible me persigan hasta cuatro
> magistrados vuelto. Es posible me juzguen pedro.
> ¡Cuatro humanidades justas juntas!
> Don Juan Jacobo está en hacerío,
> y las burlas le tiran de su soledad,
> como a un tonto. Bien hecho.

> It's possible that as many as four
> Magistrates might chase me back. It's possible, they might
>   judge me as pedro.
> Four just humanities joined!
> Don Juan Jacobo is in the act,
> And the joke pulls him out of his solitude,
> Like an idiot. Well done!

Clearly the subject feels himself in conflict with the species. He is a pedro denying his saviour – in other words the species in general. There are four humanities because four is the number of limitation and since there are four races of man, the four magistrates represent the totality of humanity. Yet in Schopenhaurian terms, the species tricks the individual by making him feel that he is different from all others, that he has some purpose other than that of the continuation of life. That is why even Don Juan Jacobo (Rousseau) is drawn out of his solitude since he represents an untenable position based on abstract individualism and not on the prior claims of the species. In this poem, the individual has no space left to occupy and becomes a mere fugitive from his destiny as instrument of nature. At the poem's end, the subject can only state tautologically, 'Heme' (Here I am), having no other attribute but existence itself.

But the prisonhouse from which the subject attempts to escape is also time and there is no way in which the poet can return to original time, to that symbiosis of mother and child. With early childhood, the direction of adult life, the rectilinear progression towards death is already set:

> Severas madres guías al colegio,
> asedian las reflexiones, y nosotros enflechamos
> la cara apenas.   (Poem 74)

> Severe mother-guides at school,
> Hem in our bendings, and we hardly
> Aim our faces.

Once set on the road, the child merely follows it to the prison-house of adult life. And in this bleak and lonely individualism, there is perhaps no more than the comradeship of sharing a common fate. Vallejo explores this in one of his finest poems, poem 58 which is a subtle projection of the formation of moral attitudes which are plainly in conflict with the species' struggle for life:

> En la celda, en lo sólido, también
> se acurrucan los rincones.
>
> Arreglo los desnudos que se ajan,
> se doblan, se harapan.
>
> Apéome del caballo jadeante, bufando
> líneas de bofetadas y de horizontes;
> espumoso pie contra tres cascos.
> Y le ayudo: ¡Anda, animal!
>
> Se tomaría menos, siempre menos, de lo
> que me tocase erogar,
> en la celda, en lo líquido.
>
> El compañero de prisión comía el trigo
> de las lomas, con mi propia cuchara,
> cuando, a la mesa de mis padres, niño,
> me quedaba dormido masticando.
>
> Le soplo al otro:
> Vuelve, sal por la otra esquina;
> apura . . . aprisa . . . apronta!
>
> E inadvertido aduzco, planeo,
> cabe camastro desvencijado, piadoso:
> No creas. Aquel médico era un hombre sano.
>
> Ya no reiré cuando mi madre rece
> en infancia y en domingo, a las cuatro
> de la madrugada, por los caminantes,
> encarcelados,
> enfermos
> y pobres.
>
> En el redil de niños, ya no le asestaré
> puñetazos a ninguno de ellos, quien, después,
> todavía sangrando, lloraría: El otro sábado
> te daré de mi fiambre, pero
> no me pegues!
> Ya no le diré que bueno.

En la celda, en el gas ilimitado
hasta redondearse en la condensación,
¿quién tropieza por afuera?

In the cell, in what's solid, even
The corners squat down and hug themselves.

I apportion the naked who wither,
Double over, go to rags.

I dismount the panting horse, snorting
Strings of slaps and horizons;
A foamy foot against three hooves.
And I help him: Get up, beast!

Less would be required, much less, of what
It is up to me to set in order
In the cell, in what's liquid.

The cell-mate used to eat the wheat
From the hills, with my spoon,
When at my parents' table, as a child
I used to fall asleep chewing.

I encourage the other one:
Come back, go that way round that corner;
Hurry . . . quick . . . Come on!

Unnoticed I adduce, I plan,
By the pious, rickety bed:
Don't believe. For that doctor was a healthy man.

I won't be laughing when my mother prays
In childhood and on Sunday, at four
In the morning, for travellers,
Prisoners,
The sick
And the poor.

In the childrens' little pen, I won't aim
My fists at any of them, who, afterwards,
Still bleeding, might cry: Next Saturday
I'll give you my lunch, but
Don't hit me!
I won't even say Good, do it.

In the cell, in the gas that is boundless
Until growing round in condensation,
Who stumbles outside?

There is a counterpoint in this poem between 'solid', 'liquid' and 'gas' which has more than a hint of Haeckel's account of the creation of the universe. Vallejo's counterpoint however reminds us of the physical underpinning of consciousness, imagination and memory. The 'I' of the poem is snugly ensconced in a cell of identity whose corners 'squat down', as if moving nearer to the ground. This confined state does not prevent the prisoner from acting or planning to act on others, upon the 'naked' who, despite their nakedness behave like suits of clothes for they 'wither, double over, go to rags' as if they were not creatures of flesh and blood. The moral aspirations of the 'I' are out of kilter; his consciousness consists of 'arreglando', of putting the world into a coherent pattern which will make sense, though as one image follows another it becomes clear that the world defies his understanding.

Separate from 'others', he is equally apart from the animal world, having descended from his horse which bears all the signs of having journeyed from the beginning of animal creation. Using a numerical symbolism on which I shall comment later, Vallejo suggests both the linear principle of life (the foaming foot) and its motor force – the triad of father, mother and child involved in the continuation of the species. The individual is not only 'arreglando' but 'helping' the animal on its journey, an absurd pretension since the animal needs no help nor any encouragement. Yet what is important here is the subject's sense of being privileged and apart from nature.

The voice that comes to us is the centre of activity, 'arranging', 'planning', 'whispering', 'remembering', but it is a voice which expresses solitude and separation, in contrast to a past when he was the peaceful centre of a world in which connections had not broken down, in which his 'cell-mate used to eat the wheat / From the hills, with my spoon, / When at my parents' table, as a child / I used to fall asleep chewing'. But in the present, the voice of consciousness is that of plotter or the futile comforter near the sick-bed of life, beside which he is so redundant as to be 'unnoticed'. The adult consciousness is connected by memory to a past which enables him to relive his careless childhood. The child's mockery of prayers for sufferers, his natural aggressiveness, his quarrels, reflect the truth of his preparation for a struggle for life. Thus the poem becomes a conflict between human nature which is well-prepared for adult strife and the 'unselfishness' which family and religious training make him see as morally right but which results in a divided and alienated adult.

The poem ends on a highly suggestive and ambiguous note:

In the cell, in the gas that is boundless
Until growing round in condensation,
Who stumbles outside?

Who indeed? For inside, there are only the laws of matter creating form out of condensation. And these physical laws exist, as the poem demonstrates, irrespective of the individual and with no regard for an ethic of 'doing good' or 'giving'. So the voice of the poet unable to find any response in the present, nor anything but guilt in his memory of the past turns to the 'outside' whose message is equally ambiguous – for a stumbling, hesitant step in the beyond is not the message of an all-powerful Creator.

The geography of the given

If the prison is a projection of the restricted space which consciousness inhabits, landscape turns into a geography of the given. Years later, writing from Paris, Vallejo would identify the given with city streets and he would breathe with relief in the Spanish countryside away 'from streets, tracks, corners, telegraphs, towers, theatres, newspapers, writers, hotels, combs, soap – from everything that, in one way or another, is a pathway. Behold me free of thought'.[26] In *Trilce*, there are many traces of these well-marked paths – roads, arrows, pointing fingers – which signal the programming of the species. In place of a Romantic landscape which mirrors the poetic self, the plains, mountains, oceans and valleys of these poems speak to us of a world that is already created, which can offer no surprise and promise no fulfillment.

Oh valle sin altura madre, donde todo duerme
horrible mediatinta, sin ríos frescos, sin entradas de amor.   (Poem 64)

Oh valley without mother-heights, where all sleeps
In a horrible half-tone, with no fresh rivers, with no entrances of love.

This landscape has two time-frames – that of the individual and that of the cosmos. The individual journeys in and through time and is limited to a rectilinear path down which he follows the previous generation. 'Cómo arzonamos, cara a monótonas ancas' (How we saddle, facing monotonous rumps), he exclaims in poem 10. And there is also the cosmic time of creation, of the mountains and the seas against which the individual is a mere speck.

> Pacífico inmóvil, vidrio, preñado
> de todos los posibles.
> Andes frío, inhumanable, puro.
> Acaso. Acaso.   (poem 59)

> Pacific, immobile, glass, impregnated
> With all the possibles.
> Cold Andes, pure, not humanizable.
> Perhaps. Perhaps.

This is Haeckel's creation rather than a Biblical one. Out of this motionless, seemingly timeless Pacific emerge all possible forms of earthly life and the mountains themselves. It is a creation which accords no particular importance to man. The 'perhaps' which appears to open up a crack within the given in the final line of the verse is the slenderest thread on which all desire for transcendence has been hung: yet Nature is not an oracle which transmits a sense of humanity's importance. Rather the reverse. In poem 69, the ocean's book can be read only for an 'inconsolable' message and the sky can no longer suggest a heaven in poem 63.

> Cielos de puna descorazonada
> por gran amor, los cielos de platino, torvos
> de imposible.   (poem 63)

> Skies of the puna disheartened
> From a great love, silvery skies, frowning
> With the impossible.

The heart has literally been taken out of the universe with the death of God and only consciousness and memory now plague the poet who recognizes that the plenitude he seeks is death.

Me acuerdo de mí mismo. Pero bastan
las astas del viento, los timones quietos hasta
hacerse uno,
y el grillo del tedio y el jiboso codo inquebrantable.

I remember myself. But the sails of the wind
Suffice, the rudders quiet until
They become one,
And the grasshopper of boredom and the humped unbreakable elbow.

Human identity is inseparable from memory; yet it is set against the fact that there is only one monotonous fate. The 'asta' suggests the sails of a windmill so that despite the fact that there are winds coming from different directions, the basic motion of life is the same; the rudder can only guide in one direction, the grass-hopper has only one note and the 'humped unbreakable elbow', a synecdoche for the human body in its function of eating and therefore survival, is our only destiny. And the irony is further enhanced by the juxtaposition of the reflexive (and solipsistic) 'me acuerdo de mí mismo' with 'Pero bastan / las astas del viento', a phrase which rhythmically underscores the monotony and repetitiousness of life.

Intertextuality

Vallejo does not meet the opposition nature/culture head on but tends to work against existing texts, whether those of González Prada and Valdelomar or other poems. Thus he appears not only to be correcting the false consciousness of his predecessors but also revealing their values to be relative and not eternal. There is no more graphic illustration of this than his 'parody' of a poem by Samain, 'L'automne' (included in the Diez-Canedo and Fortún anthology), which is a nostalgic evocation of human alienation healed by the essential harmony of nature:

Comme dans un préau d'hospice ou de prison,
L'air est calme et d'une tristesse contenue;
Et chaque feuille d'or tombe, l'heure venue,
Ainsi qu'un souvenir, lente, sur le gazon.

Le Silence entre nous marche . . . Coeurs de mensonges.
Chacun, las du voyage, et mûr pour d'autres songes,
Rêve égoïstement de retourner au port.

Mais les bois ont, ce soir, tant de mélancolie,
Que notre Coeur s'émeut à son tour et s'oublie
À parler du passé, sous le ciel qui s'endort,

Doucement, a mi-voix, comme d'un enfant mort.

The separate selves (the 'nous' of the poem) are isolated, wrapped up in a mood which nature also reflects; but as the poem progresses, the introspection turns into a mood of acceptance as the individual forgets his own past and is absorbed into the cosmic process. In Samain's poem, nature is humanized – autumn 'bleeds', the air is 'sad' – and for this very reason, a silent discourse can be established between man and landscape. It was this, no doubt, which struck Vallejo, suggesting as it did an underlying harmony between man and nature. But if it impressed him, it was precisely because of its soothing and complacent falseness, which induced him, in poem 55, to write a poetic refutation.

Samain diría el aire es quieto y de una contenida tristeza.
Vallejo dice hoy la Muerte está soldando
cada lindero a cada hebra de cabello perdido,
desde la cubeta de un frontal, donde hay algas,
toronjiles que cantan divinos almácigos en guardia,
y versos antisépticos sin dueño.

El miércoles, con uñas destronadas se abre las propias uñas
de alcanfor, e instila por polvorientos
harneros, ecos, páginas vueltas, sarros,
zumbidos de moscas
cuando hay muerto, y pena clara esponjosa y cierta esperanza.

Samain would say that the air is calm and of a contained sadness.
Vallejo says today Death is welding every limit
to every thread of lost hair, from the little tub
of a frontal, where there are algae, herbal balms
which sing divine guardian seed-beds and
antiseptic lordless verses.

Wednesday, with dethroned fingernails opens
its own nails with camphor and through dusty
sieves instils echoes, turned pages, sediments
the buzzing of flies
when there are dead, and clear spongy grief and a certain hope.

In Samain's poem, the reader can only envisage death as a return to the greater totality of nature. In Vallejo's poem, death begins where the living body ends; there is no possible humanization of nature outside the individual, which is represented not by roses or trees but by algae and herbal balm. We can accept falling leaves as a sign of the ephemeral, or singing birds as images of harmony and beauty, but it is hard to make 'algae' or 'toronjil' into reflections of human moods. To be sure, 'toronjil' is a medicinal plant, but here it sings a message of *divine seed-beds,* suggesting a biological world which flourishes irrespective of the individual; and its verses are 'antiseptic' – that is, proof against the infections that assail mortal man. The message of 'Wednesday' is equally uncomfortable, for this slot of time performs a

storage process with its 'dethroned fingernails', suggesting that
having lost its grip on life and actuality, it has left only detritus.
Death (experienced with the loss of every hair) tells man of his
finitude, of a creation not made for his exclusive benefit. Each
dehumanized image reinforces the fact that man is no longer a
sense-producing animal, that it is not he who determines the
conditions of his existence.

In his preface to the second edition of *Trilce*, José Bergamín
rightly pointed out the assault made by the poet on grammatical
structures in the interest of poetic logic, seeing this as a child's
eye view of the world at the very moment of dawning consciousness. But we should add that this does not make the poetry ingenuous. The estrangement produced by the destruction of the
hierarchies, the replacement of an acting subject by time and
death, the reduction of the individual to the condition of a sick
man, reading the newspaper and waiting for death, is a device
which lays bare the skeleton beneath the flesh of humanism. Far
from reflecting human moods, nature and time are utterly alien,
the soldiers of a foreign army. It is time, not the poet, who makes
the Orphic descent into the underworld, leaving the individual
facing the emptiness of his own destiny:

> Ya la tarde pasó diez y seis veces por el subsuelo
> empatrullado,
> y se está casi ausente
> en el número de madera amarilla
> de la cama que está desocupada tanto tiempo
> allá . . . .
> enfrente.

> Already afternoon has gone sixteen times through the
> patrolled underground,
> And is almost absent
> In the number of yellow wood
> Of the bed so long unoccupied
> there . . . .
> in front.

The regular disappearance of the afternoon into an underground
no longer peopled by gods but 'patrolled' by more menacing un-
named forces cannot provide any basis for the pathetic fallacy
and indeed, only conjures up images of absence – the eventual
absence of time itself, and the unoccupied waiting bed which is

like the waiting tomb. Man's goal in his linear journey is 'ahead'
and there will be no Orphic return to life.[27]

The absence of design

The elevation of time and death to the subject category is, as we
have already remarked, not unusual in Vallejo's poetry. Following
the Romantic tradition, he still perceives the alienation of the individual as inherent in existence. So, in poem 56 'Todos los días
amanezco a ciegas' (Everyday I wake up blind), he represents
the individual as 'thread', 'teeth', 'pillar', i.e. as mere parts in a
whole whose totality it is not given to him to grasp.

> Flecos de invisible trama,
> dientes que huronean desde la neutra emoción,
> 　　　　　　　　pilares
> libres de base y coronación,
> en la gran boca que ha perdido el habla.　(poem 56)

> Fringes of an invisible weave,
> Teeth which ferret from neutral emotion,
> 　　　　　　　　pillars
> Free of base and crown,
> In the great mouth which has lost its speech.

Similarly in poem 26, 'El verano echa nudo a tres años', man becomes:

> Deshecho nudo de lácteas glándulas
> de la sinamayera,
> buena para alpacas brillantes,
> para abrigo de pluma inservible
> ¡más piernas los brazos que brazos!

> Unfastened knot of lacteal glands
> Of the sinamayera,
> Good for brilliant alpaca
> Useless as a coat of feathers,
> Arms more like legs than arms!

The two disparate metaphoric systems in this poem suggest both
nature (man as an unfastened knot of lacteal glands) and culture
(the 'sinamayera', or clothseller and the coat). Man is separated
from the source and alienated to the point where his arms (which
should be used for embracing his fellows) are more legs than
arms. In other words, they too are in function of the linear journey

of species-man. Viewed as a cultural being man should be the woof and warp in a series of relationships. Yet his culture serves only as animal skin – the alpaca coat which helps him survive; as a coat of feathers (which would permit him to soar to the ideal), it is useless. The poem suggests, then, that however complex culturally, however separate he considers himself from nature, man is simply a beast of burden whose function is the continuation of the species. And what strikes us about all this is the dense concentration of figures, all of which signal the monotonous existential pattern.

Though we have spoken of systems of metaphor in these poems, we should also speak of metonymy and synecdoche. Plainly when Vallejo refers to 'lacteal glands', for example, he is making these stand for motherhood and the nourishment of one generation by another. And when he refers to 'pluma', he is obviously making a connection between feather–wing–soaring in order to suggest the ideal. Kenneth Burke believes that the basic strategy of metonymy is 'to convey some incorporeal state in terms of the corporeal and tangible'.[28] And much recent criticism has been exercised by these figures of contiguity which are seen as a form of verbal condensation and the characteristic figure of narrative.[29] In Vallejo's poetry, the part is not simply used for the whole ('feet' or 'legs') for the sake of verbal economy but in order to stress certain functions:

> Y las manitas que se abarquillan
> asiéndose de algo flotante,
> a no querer quedarse. (poem 47)

> And the tiny hands that curl up
> Seizing something that would float,
> When they would not stay behind.

This is a device which is particularly appropriate to the sexual organs since by designating their function in zoological or botanical terms – the 'dicotyledon group' of poem 5 or the reference to 'ovary' in poem 4 – he emphasizes function rather than the emotions we attach to sex. In the following example, the figures of contiguity turn the lovers into reproductive organs:

> se arrequintan pelo por pelo
> soberanos belfos, los dos tomos de la Obra,
> y no vivo entonces ausencia,
>   ni al tacto. (poem 9)

> Hair by hair, the sovereign jaws
> Are laced together, the two volumes of the Work,
> And then I do not live absence,
>   not even to the touch.

The bodies of the lovers become 'hair' and 'jaw' which, in turn, refer euphemistically to the sexual organs. They link man to the animal since semantically they can refer to both humans and animals. By further identifying the sexual 'jaws' with the two volumes of the Work, the poet makes an analogy between the primal act and the sacred text of creation. Further, it is only when performing the sexual act that the subject is truly 'present'. However, in the process of showing this, Vallejo reverses all that we usually associate with human love as transcendence of the animal state. In this poem, the idealization disappears and sex becomes simply coupling for the purpose of reproduction.

Though sexual activity brings us into harmony with the species, it is an activity which cannot be regarded as peculiarly human, and this adds significance to the anatomical naming of parts according to their exact scientific terminology; for science looks at man in terms of species and not as an individual. But Vallejo carries the process of humiliation even further by transforming the human being into pure animal, by ignoring man's historical progress and making him into a mere episode in animal evolution. This transformation is often comic or grotesque:

> El encuentro con la amada
> tánto alguna vez, es un simple detalle,
> casi un programa hípico en violado,
> que de tan largo no se puede doblar bien.   (poem 35)

> The meeting with the beloved
> So much sometimes amounts to a simple detail
> Almost a race programme in-violate
> Which is so long that it can't be folded well.

The 'race programme' in which his own meeting with the beloved is simply an episode has been going on since the beginning of time and cannot be 'folded' since evolution cannot be put into reverse. In another poem, the pair turn into 'travelling saucepans' whose contents 'spill over into the unanimous shade'. In poem 71, the Schopenhaurian conflict between natural design and the *hubris* of the individual is momentarily resolved as the subject becomes, in the act of copulation, species-man.

Calla también, crepúsculo futuro,
y recógete a reír en lo íntimo, de este celo
de gallos ajisecos[30] soberbiamente,
soberbiamente ennavajados
de cúpulas, de viudas mitades cerúleas.
Regocíjate, huérfano; bebe tu copa de agua
desde la pulpería de una esquina cualquiera.   (poem 71)

Hush too, future twilight,
And go away to laugh privately, at this rutting
Of russet fighting-cocks haughtily,
Haughtily armed with blades
Of domes, and cerulean widowed halves.
Rejoice, orphan; drink your glass of water
At any corner bar.

From the vantagepoint of that future twilight, the human being
has only the status of a rutting cock; the inflated 'macho' (pride)
reiterated in the 'soberbiamente,/soberbiamente' amounts to no
more than being able to match up with his widowed half as if
human beings were no more than those maimed androgynes
whom Aristophanes describes in Plato's *Symposium*. The poetic
voice appears to stave off, as it were, both the ultimate mockery
of death and the *hubris* of the universal 'orphan' he addresses
and whose greatest joy can only be in that common act which
can be shared by anybody. Pride usually associated with our
difference from one another and our individualism is an attribute
of the species; the human being is least alienated when he is least
specifically human. Thus in poem 30, he speaks of sex as the
'aromatic truth touched on the raw', for 'The antenna of sex is
connected / To what we are without knowing it.' This reminds
us of Freud, of course, and Vallejo's poetry as I shall show in
the next chapter often allows intuitions of these unconscious
drives by means of puns or slips of the tongue. Thus in *Trilce* 71,
'cúpola' which we usually associate with a cathedral dome and
hence with man's proudest spiritual achievements is uncomfort-
ably close to 'cópula' which is the motive of the poem.

What *Trilce* presents us with, then, on the level of the signifier
is a language which impedes harmony; on the level of the signi-
fied there is the frustration of closure. Thus contradiction and
disharmony are forced upon the attention of the reader. However,
this is far from being the kind of freeplay of the sign or the
degree zero writing envisaged by some contemporary critics.

Vallejo's poetic language is marked by intention and it is finally the whole field of semantics that comes into question. Nor can the reader be expected to create meaning as Octavio Paz would have him do.[31] For the area of conflict which Vallejo's poem reveals is no less than that unhealable breach between nature and culture. To be whole, the individual has only to reverse the evolution process and become once again that 'free brute / Who enjoys where he wants, where he can' (poem 13). Yet as Vallejo shows in this same poem, the very act of thinking, consciousness itself prevents plenitude.

Species/individual, nature/culture are then the irreconcilable interests which thrust themselves into poetry itself, since poetry traditionally strives after harmony, yet uses language which, because of the fact that one word must suffice for disparate functions, is constantly in danger of acting against the poet's wishes and intentions. Such disparity is, of course, another name for irony and irony is, as Octavio Paz has shown, 'the wound through which analogy bleeds to death'.[32]

5

THE DISCOURSE OF THE
GIVEN: *TRILCE*

A group of children have thrown a ball on to the roof and one of them exclaims at once, 'I'll put away my book and see if I can make the ball come down.' I adduce these childish examples, because it is among children that such heroic methods of creative adventure or discovery are most frequent. Men are too cunning and practical to trust such intuitive adventures.[1]

In *Trilce*, the poet's stance is essentially ironic. That is to say, the truth bubbles to the surface despite the strong support language gives to self-delusion. Puns, unguarded language, automatized words whose original significance is suddenly laid bare – all these open doorways to the reality principle. What Vallejo finds beneath the comforting structures of language is not the 'marvellous' of the Surrealists[2] but the iron laws of necessity, the dialectical patterns of nature, and the disharmony between the laws of nature and man's desires.[3]

We find, as in *Los heraldos negros,* that the first and last poems of *Trilce* put poetic creation within a parenthesis beyond which there is silence and non-being. Unlike the earlier collection, which had made the poet into the incarnation of Romantic alienation, these poems of *Trilce* deal with creation in a larger sense, showing a process of geographical formation, an ecology of animal life and nature which allows little place for the individual and still less for the poet-creator. The poems present us with a creation which has already come into being; the waters have been separated from the land; the species have been created. There are elements, climate, day and night. Nowhere is Vallejo's monistic viewpoint clearer than in these poems in which the poetic voice emerges from the 'given' as a superfluous and gratuitous act outside the economy of nature yet dependent on it. In poem 1, the entire natural cycle is presented as an 'other', alien to the poet who pleads for 'more consideration'.

> Quién hace tánta bulla, y ni deja
> testar las islas que van quedando.

117

Un poco más de consideración
en cuanto será tarde, temprano,
y se aquilatará mejor
el guano, la simple calabrina tesórea
que brinda sin querer,
en el insular corazón,
salobre alcatraz, a cada hialóidea
grupada.

Un poco más de consideración,
y el mantillo líquido, seis de la tarde
DE LOS MAS SOBERBIOS BEMOLES

Y la península párase
por la espalda, abozaleada, impertérrita
en la línea mortal del equilibrio.

Who is so noisy that he keeps
The islands that remain from testifying?

A bit more consideration
Since it will soon be late
The better to assay
The guano, the simple treasurey stench
That the briny pelican unwittingly proffers
In the island heart
At each hyaloid
squall.

A little more consideration,
And liquid humus, six in the afternoon
OF THE PROUDEST B FLATS

And the peninsula stands on its two feet
Backward, muzzled, unperturbed
On the mortal line of equilibrium.

The poem immediately strikes a reader as strange, for though its
structure seems to make sense, its vocabulary defies our expectations. Words like 'testar', 'guano', 'tesórea', 'grupada', 'hialóidea'
are not only 'unliterary': they have not accumulated the kind of
cultural or historical allusions which make them readily assimil-
able. We might think of 'motorcars' or 'ice-cream cones' as unliterary but they are at least familiar. The language of Vallejo's
poem resists even these non-literary associations. Not surprisingly,
as a result, the poem has given rise to the most diverse interpretations.[4]
In general terms, the poem gives us a demystified demonstra-

tion of 'creation', not as a *fiat lux* but rather by analogy with the formation of the guano islands from the excrement of marine birds (pelicans). The islands are the by-products of the bird and have nothing to do with its life-cycle nor with the prior geological formation of the world. The poet's voice asking, 'Who is so noisy', emerges as a solitary appeal against a life-force which produces islands (individuals) as by-product but does not allow those islands to leave any legacy. There is no substantial continuity between one generation and the next. The economy of man and civilization is one in which individual creation is the accidental surplus of the life force which, like Freud, Vallejo expresses as 'clamour'.[5] The individual's desires, however, are different. He needs 'more consideration' because though caught within the continuous succession of the species, he values the by-product, the 'calabrina tesórea' (treasure stench). The contradiction in the poem is between the march of the species and the individual's attempt to read significance into his mortal life, the 'guano' which is the involuntary product of a 'briny pelican', 'at each hyaloid squall'. In mythology, the pelican is a bird which feeds her young from her own breast: so this bird (who also helps to produce the guano which is used as a fertilizer) refers both to a system of natural reproduction and to the excremental. The word 'grupada' (storm) is linked to a series of natural events and substances which are produced without regard to the desires of the subject. But 'grupada' has also the suggestion of 'group' and the hidden pun is a reminder that natural creation is not the work of the individual, nor does it simply produce islands but arises out of a coupling which, in reality, serves the species.[6]

The irony of the poem lies in the disparity between the noisy demand of the individual and the implacable natural process which reaches its crescendo in the third part of the poem:

> and liquid humus, six in the afternoon
> OF THE PROUDEST B FLATS

The word 'proud' connotes the human and the cultural as opposed to nature. Yet this crescendo is played on a single, monotonous note – the B flat – so that the secret monotony of life thrusts itself to the surface. The process is brought to a halt not in order to give 'more consideration' to the subject but because it has reached a limit beyond which there is only the silence of non-being. 'Muzzled' and 'unperturbed', species-man stands on the mortal line of equilibrium, trapped in the linear labyrinth of nature. Unable to prolong his individuality beyond death, he is defined not by his use value to the species but by surplus (excrement). Thus the opposition of nature and culture is, at another level, seen as the opposition between reproduction and excrement, between use and surplus.[7] And it is this economy system which generates the fundamental and insoluble tensions of the poems.

I have spoken of the 'individual' but in *Trilce* 1, there is only a voice which we assume to be that of someone rebelling against the iron laws of existence only to be lost within the process. The plea for 'A little more consideration' reminds us of a reproachful neighbour upbraiding a noisy and inconsiderate tenant; the fact that the complaint is levelled against nature itself only makes it the more ironic. For it is nature which must triumph. At the climax of the poem, at six in the afternoon – which marks the threshold between day and night – the voice disappears, the process is suspended, a transformation which is indicated on the level of the signifier by a change in the phonemic pattern from k and t to a predominance of plosives p and b.

The structuring principle of the *Trilce* poems nearly always turns on this primary opposition between the cosmic view and the individual's perception of his life as discontinuous, fragmented, essentially separate from others. And this basic opposition generates others – between the essential and the contingent, between nature and culture, species and individual and between the cyclical time of the cosmos and the unrepeatable time of the human life-span. Yet this opposition is not between equally forceful elements since the natural and the cosmic are primary, a fact that is only concealed because language being a product of culture masks reality.

Thus though the poet creates havoc with the language, as if affirming his freedom to do as he likes with the material of his craft, the deeper structures often reveal the laws of necessity and represent the immovable frontiers beyond which he cannot go. On the surface level, Vallejo uses the syntax to mime the repetitive, confused and fragmented surface of experience. He abandons formal structures in most poems, building the poems on repetition, anaphora (the repetition of a word at the beginning of a line), on enumerations. And he uses the conjunction 'and' to link disparate elements.[8] Yet we have already seen how in the first poem of *Trilce*, movement continues despite the objections of the individual voice. 'La creada voz rebélase y no quiere / ser malla, ni amor', he wrote in poem 5; but again and again, the manipulation of the language by the poet results in secret connections which are made to appear the involuntary revelations offered by language itself which is never completely controlled by the speaker.

False consciousness and the Freudian slip

There are two contrary thrusts in the first poem of *Trilce* which correspond to the distinction that Fernand de Saussure makes between *langue* and *parole*.[9] *Langue* is language as given, the corpus of words and grammatical structures built up by a social group; *parole* is the language spoken by any particular individual – in other words, language in use. In many of the poems of *Trilce*, Vallejo seems to be rebelling against the given and attempting to transform it into an instrument adequate to human experience. When he writes in *Trilce* 6 for instance, 'El traje que vestí mañana' (The suit I wore tomorrow), he uses correct syntax but the sentence shocks because the adverb refers to future time, yet modifies a verb in the past. 'Aquella mi lavandera' (That my washerwoman) sounds odd because we do not normally use the distancing demonstrative 'that' with the possessive pronoun. These examples could be multiplied and have often been noted by critics[10] yet they have a paradoxical effect since they both indicate a rebellion against the prisonhouse of language yet somehow suggest its intractability. For instance, in poem 1, the poet writes 'en cuanto será tarde, temprano' (since it will soon be late), and though this is not incorrect, in everyday speech the speaker would avoid both the pedantic 'en cuanto' and the ambiguous juxtaposition of 'tarde' and 'temprano'. Hence Vallejo foregrounds the unusual cluster of words though not in the interest of poetic rhythm or construction but rather to force together the two contradictory adverbs of time so that the dual nature of 'tarde' springs to life. For 'tarde' means not only late (which has subjective overtones since it must be late for someone) but also refers to the last part of the day before nightfall and thus anticipates the 'six in the afternoon' and the 'mortal line of equilibrium' on which the poem inevitably ends. It is as if even in consciously selecting words, the poet cannot entirely free them from other kinds of associations which betray his intention.

Invention, then, turns out to be a double-edged weapon. When, for instance, in poem 36, the poet writes of his little finger: 'Lo veo y lo creo y no debe ser*me*' (thus giving the verb *ser* an unusual pronoun complement), he relates *being* to a noun that indicates the most contingent part of his body, a part moreover which he observes as if it were not himself. Yet in trying to protest that it should not be so, he also is forced to conflate the verb and the complement as if reinforcing what he would like to deny. In this way even the most conscious selections and distortions of language appear to emphasize the immutability of the laws of life. And the poem which often appears in its opening lines to be an act of rebellion against language and against the biologically given often ends by affirming what cannot be altered. So in poem 53, the poetic voice comes up against that immutable frontier which is temporal rather than spatial to end on a note of exasperation:

> Veis lo que es sin poder ser negado,
> veis lo que tenemos que aguantar,
> mal que nos pese.
> ¡Cuánto se aceita en codos
> que llegan hasta la boca!

> You see what is without possibility of denial,
> You see what we have to put up with,
> Whatever the cost.
> How many elbows are greased
> To reach our mouths!

The irony of this last verse is that language *can* deny, can conceal the truth, which is, nevertheless, obvious, readily available. This is why the instability of language itself becomes such an important aspect of these poems.

Colloquial discourse lends itself most readily to ambiguity precisely because it depends on a limited number of words which are made to serve a great many different functions ranging from the phatic to the sententious. Spanish, for instance, is particularly rich in ambiguous temporal expressions. *Tarde* used as an adverb means late but as noun means afternoon. *Mañana* can mean

either tomorrow or morning as in the phrase 'Una mañana sin
mañana' (poem 8). The most flexible elements often turn out to
be the most common verbs – *dar, ver, echar, ser, estar* which are
used in a vast range of idiomatic expressions. *Ser* and *estar* which
distinguish rather more finely than the English verb between
being as attribute and being as a state are also commonly used as
auxiliaries. They serve alike for metaphysical and existential statements and for the most commonplace, phatic utterances. This
flexibility is of great importance in *Trilce* since the same expression can be used to suggest a meaningless chatter which tries to
drown the silence of non-being and at the same time can suggest
the obvious truth which the subject refuses to see.

This instability is never clearer than in certain 'dialogue' poems
in which the subject appears to be speaking to another person or
persons whose response the reader never apprehends. Vallejo
achieves the maximum of instability by wresting the conversation
from any context so that we do not know what the 'appropriateness conditions' are. In *Trilce* 51, for instance, a speaker accuses
his partner of lying but there is no standard by which we can
judge what is truth and what is a lie.

> Mentira. Si lo hacía de engaños,
> y nada más. Ya está. De otro modo,
> también tú vas a ver
> cuánto va a dolerme el haber sido así.
>
> Mentira. Calla.
> Ya está bien.
> Como otras veces tú me haces esto mismo,
> por eso yo también he sido así.
>
> A lie. I was only kidding,
> That's all. It's all over. Otherwise,
> You too are going to see
> How much I'll suffer from doing it.
>
> A lie. Hush.
> It's all right.
> Since you did this to me before,
> Now I'm treating you the same way.

The language of the poem never departs from the conversational
but it sets up a web of accusation and counter-accusation in
which the reader is left with no criteria of truth. Divorced from
a system that can guide our view of the truth and falsehood of

the statements, divorced from empirical facts, the poem can only indicate the emptiness of the sign. Yet it is this very emptiness which also makes it possible for words to be charged with contradictory intentions. When, for instance, at the end of poem 35, the poet concludes his meeting with the beloved with the banal, 'Otro vaso y me voy. Y nos marchamos, / ahora sí, a trabajar' (Another glass and I'll be off. And now we really / Will go to work), in isolation the words suggest nothing more than phatic speech. In ordinary conversation, we would understand them to mean that the speaker was going back to his job after taking a break. However the context of the poem has reversed the values we might ordinarily attach to 'vaso' or 'trabajar'. The 'glass' is a euphemism for the sexual act which, for the species, is the real business of life whilst human work is a surplus activity. And this reversal of values is achieved by making sex into a food, into something which is immediately necessary for survival.

To speak of the sexual act in terms of food corresponds, as has already been observed, to a whole series of equivalencies between eating and entering, expelling and leaving, consumption and reproduction which displace the subject from the centre of the production process. But because the poet's utterance is an individual utterance, the only way this subliminal system can make its appearance is through puns, slips of the tongue and errors of pronunciation. We have already come across several examples of these. For instance, the v is constantly substituted for b or vice versa as in 'Vusco volvvver de golpe el golpe' (poem 9). At first sight, this seems simply to be an estrangement device. In Spanish b and v are pronounced in almost identical fashion so that 'Vusco' looks like a spelling error for 'busco'. But then come those three vvvs in 'volver' which remind us that the v-sign is a common obscene gesture, the sign of the vulva. The individual's conscious statement unwittingly betrays the instinctual act. In Trilce 52, 'Y nos levantaremos cuando se nos de / la gana . . .', the prostrate labourer who forgets to say 'buenos días' cannot pronounce the b for 'baldío' (waste) because the 'buenos días' 'insisten en salirle al pobre / por la culata de la v / dentilabial que vela en él'. The reverse mis-spelling which replaces the b for v has the effect of an over-insistent euphemism. In poem 4, for instance, during the sexual encounter, there is a playful interjection, 'Qué la bamos a hhazer' in which the mis-spelling of vamos and the exaggerated aspiration of the (usually silent) *h* draws comic attention to the tautological question.[11]

Many of the neologisms and lexical conflations in *Trilce* are related to punning. In poem 5, for instance 'oberturan' (to overture) is a conflation which suggests not only *obertura* but *overa* (a bird's egg-sac) thus linking music, which for Vallejo suggested sequence as much as harmony, to reproduction.[12] In poem 8, there is a new adjective which either combines *falto* and *hiato* or is a conflation of *Allí falto:*

> alguna
> vez hallaría para el hifalto poder,
> entrada eternal.

> some
> Time, I might find for the I-am-missing power,
> Eternal entry.

Not only is 'hifalto' a pun but it piles into one word different kinds of emptiness and absence. Whereas in *Los heraldos negros,* Vallejo might have used *nada* (nothingness), in this poem he makes the negative into a power, an energy whose attribute is the very absence of the subject.

Another example of the carpet-bag word is to be found in *Trilce* 5, a poem dedicated to the 'dicotyledon group':

> Grupo dicotiledón. Oberturan
> desde él petreles, propensiones de trinidad,
> finales que comienzan, ohs de ayes
> creyérase avaloriados de heterogeneidad.

> Dicotyledon group. Petrels
> Overture from it, propensities to trinity,
> Finales which begin, ohs of ouches
> You might believe gegawed with heterogeneity.

In the final line ('you might believe gegawed with heterogeneity'), the lexical invention is 'avaloriados'. This suggests, *valor* (both value and courage) and *abolorio* (a cheap ornament). Thus heterogeneity (the difference between sexes which is a function of the reproductive process) determines other attributes like the individual's sense of his own worth. The verse scrupulously avoids mentioning the human pair, however. Instead there is the 'dicotyledon group', 'finales' and 'overtures' (that is a pair which mark different moments of time) and also the 'ohs' (a cry of joy) and 'ouches' (a cry of suffering) which indicate conflicting emotions. There are then three types of heterogeneity which can account for most of the surface variety of life. The substitution of the *v* for *b* in 'avaloriados' not only allows him to suggest the individual's pride in this variety and the tawdriness of that pride but also the sexual origins of all difference.

Vallejo often employs another device, rather similar to the Freudian slip in which an automatic phrase or a cliché does not quite come out correctly. In poem 49, he has 'hasta el hueso' (till the bone) when we might expect *hasta luego* and in poem 50, he writes 'punto fiscal' where we would expect *punto final*. Instead of *qué hora son* in poem 18, he applies time to space; 'si vieras hasta qué hora son cuatro estas paredes'. In all these cases there is a subliminal cliché behind the estranged phrase so that we are led, as it were, to apprehend both the automatic usage and a quite different order of significance. The fact, for instance, that the walls add up to four o'clock in poem 18 illuminates the fact that time is our prison. There are vast numbers of these estranged though commonplace phrases in *Trilce* whose function is to indicate the repetitive, automatic nature of what people take to be consciousness while also revealing the reality principle from which they have been generated. This is particularly striking in the case of sententious and idiomatic phrases which Vallejo often twists out of all recognition. Poem 53, for instance, ends:

> ¡Cuánto se aceita en codos
> que llegan hasta la boca!

(How many elbows are greased / To reach out mouths). This phrase suggests a whole series of idiomatic expressions from *alzar uno el codo* (to eat and drink to excess) to *comerse uno los codos de hambre* (to be starving). These contradictory meanings are brought together subliminally in Vallejo's new phrase for it suggests the tireless activity of the human economy, the bending of the elbow to bring food to the mouth and, at the same time, the essential poverty of life; the further refinement of 'greasing elbows' in order to accelerate the whole repetitive process emphasizes the fact that even voluntary effort serves involuntary ends.

Frequently, however, the poet resorts to simpler tactics and merely positions a commonplace phrase so that some original significance now lost because of the devaluation of the word comes to the fore. There is an example of this in poem 28 when the subject sits at the friend's supper table listening to the empty chatter of some aunts:

> bisbiseando por todos sus viudos alvéolos;
> y con cubiertos francos de alegres tiroriros,
> porque estánse en su casa. Así, qué gracia.

> Encoring with all their widowed alveolus;
> And with frank tablesettings of joyful mouth-organs,
> Because they are home. So, what's new?

The subject's baleful, 'Así, qué gracia', is a jarring note in this cheerful scene in which open cavities, noise, repetition, signal the carefree clamour of life. The subject disassociates himself from this with a colloquial phrase in which the word 'gracia' is used in its devalued sense of 'charm' (So, what's the charm!), thus marking the extent of the degeneration of what had once been the gift of God.

Estrangement techniques and especially the pun and the Freudian slip help to disclose the reality beneath the surface even when the poem apparently enacts a state of false consciousness. We are here reminded that Freud, Marx and Nietzsche all postulated the notion of a false consciousness[13] and that all of them were concerned with 'demystification'. The irony of the *Trilce* poems is based precisely on this kind of disparity between the subject's avowed intention and the 'accidental' associations which a play on words brings to the fore. Vallejo, however, uses both the accidental slip – the 'hasta el hueso' instead of *hasta luego* – and the deliberate pun as ways of creating new kinds of associations. In pun and paronomasia, the arbitrary nature of the acoustic sign is exploited to the full and indeed, punning often causes laughter or a sense of outrage precisely because the same sequence of sounds has such a variety of semantic possibilities. Punning foregrounds the arbitrary nature of the acoustic sign but, as Freud has shown, may be a mechanism by which an unpleasant reality is displaced and covered over. Thus in one of his case-histories, a murderous impulse of one of his patients against an English boy called Dick becomes an obsession against being fat (*dick* in German).[14] In Vallejo's poems, an apparent 'slip' like

'Pienso en tu sexo' suddenly reveals the taboo. We would normally talk of thinking with *el seso* (the brain) but the slip makes brain a mere cover-up for the sexual dynamics of life. On the other hand when the poet writes in *Trilce* 11:

> 'Me he casado',
> me dice. Cuando lo que hicimos de niños
> en casa de la tía difunta.
> Se ha casado.
> Se ha casado.

> 'I'm married',
> She tells me. After what we did as children
> In her dead aunt's house.
> She's married.
> She's married.

the word 'casa' which echoes *casarse* is also associated with the dead aunt and therefore with the tomb. A hidden association is disclosed between sex and death. Of course the poet is only feigning the slip for the shock of discovery must be the reader's. But in doing so, he uses a device that is commonly found in the popular poetry of Latin America. The gauchesque poetry of the River Plate area in the nineteenth century and popular poetry in many other parts of Latin America abound in this kind of word play.[15] Vallejo, however, uses word play in order to set in motion a whole dynamic in which the poem reveals both the attempt of the ego to control reality and the underlying state of affairs. In poem 65, for instance, the poet cries out for a mother love that will guide him throughout life:

> Oh si se dispusieran los tácitos volantes
> para todas las cintas más distantes,
> para todas las citas más distintas.

> Oh if only the tacit guide wheels could be set
> For all the most distant cables,
> For all different occasions.

The paronomasia, 'cintas . . . distantes', 'citas . . . distintas', first claims our attention as a simple play on acoustically similar expressions. Yet there are all kinds of semantic connections beneath the apparently fortuitious equivalences. The many meanings of 'volante', for instance, which may refer to driving wheel, a frill or a flyer generate connections with *cinta* meaning ribbon (associated with frill), with cable (for 'volante' also means pulley-wheel) and with *cita* meaning rendez-vous (since 'volante' means a 'flyer' which announces meetings). The subject's desire for Logos, for a binding principle which would give significance to his life, produces the accidental surface tension of similarities and differences which point to the real nature of language as a mechanism which stands metaphorically for the given. The Logos which the subject demands is somehow mocked by the very 'given' which imprisons him.

In this way, punning and word play can suggest both the subject's attempt to manipulate the given and the secret limitations which he is powerless to affect. And even within the relative freedom of poetry, the very equivalences are always likely to demonstrate that the subject is not completely in control.[16] *Trilce* 7 which has frequently been 'interpreted' by critics is constructed precisely on this kind of tension:

> Rumbé sin novedad por la veteada calle
> que yo me sé. Todo sin novedad,
> de veras. Y fondée hacia cosas así,
> y fui pasado.
>
> Doblé la calle por la que raras
> veces se pasa con bien, salida
> heroica por la herida de aquella
> esquina viva, nada a medias.
>
> Son los grandores,
> el grito aquel, la claridad de careo,
> la barreta sumersa en su función de
>   ¡ya!
> Cuando la calle está ojerosa de puertas,
> y pregona desde descalzos atriles
> trasmañanar las salvas en los dobles.
>
> Ahora hormigas minuteras
> se adentran dulzoradas, dormitadas, apenas
> dispuestas, y se baldan,
> quemadas pólvoras, altos de a   1921
>
> I head without problem down the veined street
> I know so well. No problem,
> Really. And I plunged down to those kinds of things,
> And was passed.
>
> I crossed the street where rarely
> You get safely by, a heroic
> Sortie through the wound
> Of that raw corner, nothing by halves.

These are the highs,
That cry, brilliance of confrontation
The plunger submerged in its function of
                                   now!

When the street is heavy-edged with doorways,
And shouts its wares from discalced lecterns
Transtomorrow the salvos into tolling.

Now the minute-hand ants
Go in, sweetened, drowsy, re-
Luctantly to be emptied,
Burnt-out gunpowder, highs at   1921

The poem has all those devices – typographical, lexical, punning, which serve as estrangement techniques. Yet, because, unusually, the subject seems to be in control, and has direction (rumbo), there is an illusion of process in space and time. Yet the actions of the individual – 'rumbé', 'doblé', 'fondée' are all actions in the past which also define him – 'fui pasado'. This past is now part of a given, the geological formation of the self which, however, the subject vainly tries to 'plumb'. But perhaps the most remarkable aspect of the poem is the way that new areas are opened up *within the space of the given,* merely by word play. Thus 'sin novedad' in the first stanza is the phrase used in war-despatches for 'all quiet at the front' and so generates a number of war or warlike images – the 'salida heroica' (heroic sortie), 'herida' (wound). The geological and mining metaphor has generated 'esquina viva' (for *piedra viva* (bare rock)), 'fondear' (to plumb) and perhaps 'pólvora' (gunpowder) of the last line. A whole new set of associations opens up with 'doblar la calle' which literally means to cross the street. However *doblar* is also 'to duplicate' and *doblar la campana* is 'to toll a bell' so 'doblé la calle' generates 'a medias' (by halves) and 'doblar' (to toll) in line 15, which finally, because of its association with the church may have suggested the 'discalced' lecterns of line 14. 'Doblar' and 'nada a medias' suggest that it is in the sexual act that the subject feels himself truly present yet it is paradoxically here that he is also most trapped within the given, on the well-known street where there is no novelty. And it is at this point in the poem too that the subject disappears leaving the street insomniac with open doors, i.e. both empty and preaching the example of its own poverty. In other words time itself does its work, emptying experience like the busy ants of the last verse and converting the salvoes of victory into the tolling of funeral bells.

The thrust of the poem is summed up by the infinitive verb, 'trasmañanar', a lexical invention which conflates the notion of *trasponer* and that of *mañana* thus making time itself the energy behind a process which is common to all time whether past, present or future. Thus as the subject becomes emptied of significance after the climax of the poem (which may indicate the sex act), it is time itself which feeds on experience leaving only the empty date, 'altos de a 1921'.

Poem 8 not only shows us the passing of time at the expense of the identity of the subject but also lays bare the mechanism behind its own composition. Words and phrases suggest new images as if creation itself obeyed half-voluntary processes and as if the poet's apparent sense of direction were constantly being undermined by the ambiguity of words. Thus language does not so much denote experiences or objects as show that a limited number of words and expressions must cover a wide and even contradictory range of experience.

The perils of precision

There are certain kinds of language in *Trilce* which certainly do not lend themselves to ambiguous interpretation. Scientific language and numbers are univocal and precise unlike 'poetic' language. Onomatopoeia, though frequently used in poetry, is not only univocal but appears to be the only kind of language in which the acoustic sign is not arbitrary.[17]

Onomatopoeia and scientific language were, however, used by the Futurists in order to revolutionize poetry and ostensibly to bring it into step with modern life. Some of the less attractive results of this 'revolution' were published in *Cervantes* during the period when Vallejo was writing the poems of *Trilce* and Vallejo must have found Xavier Bóveda's poem on a street-car irresistibly comic for he parodied it in poem 32. Bóveda's street-car inspires the monotonous onomatopoeic rendering:

> tan, tan, tan, tan
> tan,
> Llega al final, el fin, y cambia el trole,
> chaf.

Clang, Clang, Clang, Clang,
Clang
The end of the line, the trolley's changed,
Crunch.

Vallejo's mentor, Valdelomar, had not been above this kind of
nonsense, though admittedly he uses it for comic effect when,
after describing an interview with the aviator, Santos Dumont,
he sends him off in his high-powered car with a "Rumb . . .
Rumb . . . Rumb . . . Sissss'.[18] Vallejo's poem begins:

999 calorías
Rumbb . . . Trrraprrr   rrach . . chaz
Serpentínica *u* del bizcochero
engrirafada al tímpano.

999 calories
Rumbb . . . trraprrr   rrach . . chaz
Serpentine *u* of the biscuit-vendor
Giraffed to the tympanum.

The poem was inspired, Haya de la Torre tells us, by the distorted cry of the Trujillo biscuit-vendor.[19] The cry is 'giraffed'
onto tympanum, because it is prolonged to the point of exaggeration and incomprehensibility yet immediately communicates
to the listener. Yet the poet's attempt to communicate physical
sensation through sound and through exact language eventually
breaks down. What Vallejo goes on to show is that scientific language and numbers can designate quantities that are far beyond
the existential comprehension of the subject. As the 'calories' in
the poem increase, the subject begins to gasp for air:

¡Aire, aire! ¡Hielo!
Si al menos el calor (– Mejor
                no digo nada.

Y hasta la misma pluma
con que escribo por último se troncha.

Treinta y tres trillones trescientos treinta
y tres calorías.

Air! Air! Ice!
If only the heat (– Better
                if I say nothing.

And even the same pen
With which I write is broken off at last.

Thirty-three trillion three hundred and thirty
Three calories.

The abstract language of science can designate 'unthinkable'
quantities, can treble energy without limit whereas the physical
limits of the individual are strictly circumscribed. When the pen
breaks, this signals the moment when language outstrips the
imaginative power of the poet.

Vallejo was fascinated and repelled by numbers which, in this
and other poems, seem to take on a life of their own, like the
coin in poem 48:

> Ella, siendo 69, dase contra 70;
> luego escala 71, rebota en 72.
>
> Being 69, it hits 70
> Then reaches 71, and bounces on 72

Many poets at this time were looking into the Cabbala or into
Pythagoreanism in order to find occult mysteries, evidence of a
divine world which could be read from numbers. For Vallejo
what significance they have derives from the fundamental patterns of nature. Indeed the numbers one to nine are known as the
natural numbers and the first four of them correspond to most
elementary patterns – the one, the pair, the triad and the four
points of the compass. We have *five* senses, there are *six* working
days of the week and a day of rest, making *seven,* there are *nine*
months of gestation, *twelve* months of the year. Yet it is the very
abstractness of numbers which makes the precision they suggest
more apparent than real. In poem 68, the exactness of numbers
is in tension with the theme of absence.

> Estamos a *catorce* de julio.
> Son las *cinco* de la tarde. Llueve en toda
> una *tercera* esquina de papel secante.
> Y lleuve más de abajo ay para arriba.
>
> *Dos* lagunas las manos avanzan
> de *diez* en fondo,
> desde un martes cenagoso que ha *seis* días
> está en los lagrimales helado. [The italics are mine.]
>
> It's the fourteenth of July.
> It's five in the afternoon. It is raining on all
> A third corner of blotting paper.
> And it rains alas more from below than from above.

>Two lakes my hands advance
>From ten deep,
>From a muddy Tuesday which six days long
>Is frozen in my tear-ducts.

Time and space can be designated with precision yet, for all this, the poet's world is upside down. Rain comes from below as if seeping up from the past instead of coming from the sky. The hands which grasp and embrace are lakes; thus though physically the poet is living on the fourteenth of July his emotional life seems to belong to that 'muddy Tuesday' of the past.

What numbers designate most of all is the empty repetitiveness of existence, and the pattern of succession against which the individual protests in vain. Thus in poem 5, the 'created voice rebels', striving to stay the monotonous generation of number by number:

>Pues no deis 1, que resonará al infinito
>Y no deis 0, que callará tánto,
>hasta despertar y poner de pie al 1.
>
>Ah grupo bicardiaco.
>
>So don't give 1, which will resound to infinity
>And don't give 0, which will be so silent
>Until it wakes up and erects the 1.
>
>Ah, bicardiac group.

The essence of human life is here reduced to a numerical pattern – the repetitive One, the zero whose egg-like shape provides the visual pun which generates the erection of the 1 and the reproduction of the whole monotonous and involuntary process, over and over again.

Numbers reduce the importance of the human in the poems of *Trilce*, yet this is because the whole life of the cosmos can be reduced to certain simple patterns. The dominant structures in *Trilce* are the binary opposites and contradiction, particularly that basic contradiction between the drive of the species and the perceptions of the individual which gives an ironic dimension to all the poems. But in addition to this, there is a triadic pattern which Vallejo in retrospect was to describe as a dialectic movement, even declaring that in this collection he had criticized and opposed 'dialectic determinism'.[20] Clearly at this stage, however, the triadic patterns have no relation to dialectical materialism or to any dialectics of historical progress but rather refer to the biological programming of the species. Hegel himself had related dialectics to reproduction when he described the process in terms of biological life:

The seed breaks free from its original unity, turns ever more and more to opposition, and begins to develop. Each stage of its development is a separation and its aim in each is to regain for itself the full riches of life. Thus the process is: unity, separated opposites, reunion. After their union, the lovers separate again but in their child their union has become unseparated.[21]

But in *Trilce*, it is the emptiness of this process which is emphasized: so in poem 10, the variety of life is annihilated by this reduction to a numerical pattern:

> Cómo detrás desahucian juntas
> de contrarios. Cómo siempre asoma el guarismo
> bajo la línea de todo avatar.
>
> Cómo escotan las ballenas a palomas.
> Cómo a su vez éstas dejan el pico
> cubicado en tercera ala.
> Cómo arzonamos, cara a monótonas ancas.
>
> How the yoked opposites are emptied out
> Behind. How the figure always shows
> Beneath the line of every change.
>
> How whales fit over doves.
> And how these in turn leave their beaks
> Cubed in a third wing.
> How we saddle, facing monotonous rumps.

Here the process is the reverse of the Hegelian dialectic in which the synthesis produces a higher stage. In Vallejo's dialectic, progress empties the original contraries so that the bare pattern becomes visible, so to speak. This in turn results in a pattern of abstraction into which whales and doves can both fit. Thus while everything is subsumed under this fundamental triad, nothing has any real life of its own; beaks can be metamorphosed into wings by the same 'cubing' process. This law of repetition and succession is particularly grotesque when those involved are human beings who pride themselves on their own individual and unique natures. The relation of biological succession both to the triadic pattern and to the alphabet are clearly suggested in poem 20. Here the subject is described successively as the 1, the sun and

the letter A. Yet he is also a self divided between the demands
of the species and his own pride in his individualism:

> Y he aquí se me cae la baba, soy
> *una* bella persona, cuando
> el hombre *guillermosecundario*
> puja y suda felicidad
> a chorros, a dar lustre al calzado
> de su pequeña de *tres* años.

> Engállase el barbado y frota un lado.
> La niña en tanto pónese el índice
> en la lengua que empieza a deletrear
> los enredos de enredos de los enredos,
> y unta el otro zapato, a escondidas
> con un poquito de saliva y tierra,
>   pero con un poquito
>   no má
>   s.

>   [The italics are mine.]

> And here I am dribbling with pleasure, I am
> One great person, when
> Williamthesecondary man
> Pushes and sweats felicity
> In streams, as he polishes the shoe
> Of his little three-year old girl.

> Beardy stands up straight and rubs one side.
> Whilst the girl puts her index finger
> On her tongue which is beginning to spell out
> The tangle of the tangles of the tangles.
> And she waxes the other shoe secretly
> With a little saliva and dirt
>   but with just a little
>   bi
>   t.

The first person has become the grossest of creatures, a kind of
inglorious voyeur observing the pleasure of Williamthesecondary.
Thus the 'I' feels detached from the body which is bearded as a
sign of the maturity of the race and stands up to re-enact that
moment of separation from nature. The bearded man rubs only
one side of the shoe for the species has developed a one-sided
sense of individualism; but the other side is secretly waxed by
the little girl with dirt (which indicates earthly origins) and
saliva (which appears to be a reference to sex). Yet saliva also
comes from a tongue which is beginning to spell out 'enredos' so

that even as the child does what is necessary to complete the journey of life she is also participating in that 'tangling' process which is none other than culture itself. The 's' slides off the end of the poem forestalling the closure that 'no más' would normally suggest. The process that the poem has enacted will continue *ad infinitum*.

Poem 20 represents one of the many attempts in *Trilce* to explore what we are 'without knowing it'. Because language appears to be an instrument of consciousness and consciousness is the superstructure erected from the very moment when the first anthropoid stood instead of walking on all fours, the involuntary and instinctive can only be revealed by performing 'accidental' slips and shocks. That is why Vallejo draws so extensively on devices like punning (whether audial or visual) and the 'Freudian' slip. Recognition of the silent work of the species thus becomes an essential element of his poetry. More important, *Trilce* already points to the disjunction which he makes in *Poemas humanos* between biological evolution and the attainment of a fully human status. Unlike the nineteenth-century thinkers (for instance Haeckel) who equated progress with evolution, Vallejo projects individualism as the surplus product of the human species. The aspirations of Christianity, now only present as meaningless traces in the language, had represented something different from deluded individualism but the attempt to derive a new Logos from the family Trinity only leads to the ironic recognition that the human body is a document which speaks of its own natural history but not of salvation. It is only gradually that the model of the text which predominates in the Spain poems comes tentatively into view as a form of inscription which points to more than the evolution of a species.

6

ART AND REVOLUTION

The word is stifled by individualism.[1]

Vallejo reached Paris on 11 July 1923, having travelled from Peru with Julio Gálvez, by all accounts a wild young man, who many years later was executed by a Falangist firing-squad in Spain.[2] Once his passage had been paid Vallejo had very little money left, and was soon to find himself in the financial difficulties from which he was rarely to be free. Never a bohemian, poverty did not appeal to him, and he would gladly have worked at any kind of job, even factory labour. He considered going home to Peru and he also tried to get a scholarship to study in Spain but nothing came his way.[3] Friends tell of him sleeping in the métro or bedding down in other people's studios and in the winter of 1924 he fell seriously ill.[4] In 1925, however, he found work as a secretary in the newly-opened press agency, the *Bureaux des Grands Journaux Ibéroamericains*, and he also began to contribute regular articles to *Mundial* and *Variedades*, two Lima periodicals.[5] In 1929 he went to live with Georgette Phillipart whom he later married, and with her he enjoyed a short period of relative stability. At the end of 1930, after two journeys to the Soviet Union, he was expelled from France and lived for some time in Spain before being allowed to return to Paris in 1932. From this period until his death he lived precariously enough on teaching and writing, and he was never to feel entirely free from financial worry.

To financial stress there was added, during his early years in Paris, that sense of estrangement that comes from adapting oneself to an alien culture. For, despite *Los heraldos negros,* despite *Trilce,* he was once again an unknown poet. Outside the immediate circle of his Paris acquaintances, many of whom were Latin Americans, few people had read his verse. A brief scoffing criticism of *Los heraldos negros* by the Spanish critic Astrana Marín appeared in a Madrid newspaper, but was worse than silence.[6] It was not until 1931 when the Spanish poet José Bergamín

138

brought out a second edition of *Trilce* in Madrid that Vallejo's poetry became accessible in Europe. Nor in the 1920s did he publish much new poetry. With the Spanish poet Juan Larrea he founded the magazine *Favorables-Paris-Poema* in which he published a few poems. A short story 'Sabiduría' appeared in José Carlos Mariátegui's periodical *Amauta,* and was later included in his novel *El tungsteno*. This, apart from a few poems published in Lima, constitutes the only work of his (apart from journalism) to appear in print between 1922 and 1931.[7]

All this could only have increased his sense of isolation and the growing feeling of personal crisis which came to a climax in 1927 and 1928. It was a crisis shared by many writers of the time, and amounted to what José Carlos Mariátegui had once described as an 'exasperation with the individual and with subjectivity' aggravated by the absence of any cohesive 'myth' which could give sense and purpose to the individual's life.[8] Both Mariátegui and Vallejo would eventually find that unifying myth in the Communist party.

Paris in the 1920s

Most of the friends and acquaintances of Vallejo's early years in Paris belonged to the literary and artistic avant-garde and many were Spanish or Latin American. There was the Cubist painter Juan Gris, the musician Eric Satie. Vallejo met Picasso and became a close friend of the Spanish poet Juan Larrea. The names of Morand, Pirandello, Valéry, Cocteau and Montherlant crop up in his articles. Yet despite a lasting friendship with the Chilean 'creationist' Vicente Huidobro (with whom he travelled to Spain in 1937),[9] Vallejo, even at this period, was far from sharing a view of poetry as some ultimate melting pot 'in which the extremes meet, where there is neither contradiction nor doubt'.[10] Vallejo was not given to making exaggerated claims for poetry even at his most enthusiastic; still less was he persuaded that the poet was necessarily in the vanguard of human progress. Amid the rich variety of possibilities offered by post-war Paris, Vallejo stands curiously aloof, spurning alike the Abbé Brémond's notion of 'pure poetry' and the élitist canons of taste set out by Cocteau in his essay 'Le secret professionel', to which Vallejo responded with his own refutation 'En contra el secreto profesional', in which he attacked the 'pseudo-new' in poetry and declared that poets became *avant-garde* 'out of cowardice or poverty'. But politics, in these early Paris years, pleased him even less. He was bored by the political rhetoric of Haya de la Torre who busily recruited for the *Apra* movement while passing through Paris. What Vallejo missed in society and art alike was that 'human note', the 'vital and sincere heartbeat'.

The notion that the artist should be politically committed was very much in the air at this time, nonetheless, and the principle spokesman for commitment, Henri Barbusse, was almost certainly a familiar name to Vallejo. Author of the novel *Clarté* and founder of the influential *Clarté* movement, one of the first intellectual movements in Europe to seek the active support of Latin American intellectuals,[11] Barbusse had become a most important advocate of an art committed to the people. His influence extended to Peru and José Carlos Mariátegui published several articles on the *Clarté* movement. Barbusse's *Manifeste aux intellectuels* of 1927 bluntly reiterated that the days of literature as an expression of the individual had gone, the luxury of private life had to be destroyed and a collective art must replace the art of the individual.[12] Vallejo who in 1931 translated *L'Élévation,* a rather mediocre novel by Barbusse, at first distrusted both him and Romain Rolland as 'professional apostles' and 'Christs in evening clothes'.[13] But by 1929 he was quoting Barbusse with apparent approval,[14] a significant change, for the French writer was to play a major role in the formation of the anti-fascist movement of the 1930s.

The Surrealists, who were also 'committed' in their diverse fashions, aroused contradictory responses in Vallejo, for though he always criticized them along with the rest of the avant-garde, he shared some of their attitudes.[15] The Surrealists regarded grammar, logic and establishment literature as ideological weapons for the maintenance of bourgeois order, and literary revolution as an indispensable ideological shock which would promote change both in man and society. Their vociferous soul-searching articulated one of the major questions for intellectuals at this time – the question, not whether the writer should be committed, but rather of the form commitment should take.

Vallejo's own response to the crisis of the times can be sensed both in his prose poems and in the articles he wrote for *Mundial* and *Variedades* between 1925 and 1931.[16] Many of the articles (which were sandwiched between society gossip) simply reported on the passing fads of the time. But he could not be blind to the aftermath of the First World War nor insensitive to the mood of post-war crisis. Indeed the war obsessed him. Did it mark the birth pangs of a new phase of society? He says as much when in an article on the Indian sage Krishnamurti, he suggests that the war had ushered in a new era and that each war-grave 'marked a new path' for humanity.[17]

The new sensibility

Despite his strictures on the avant-garde, it was to literature and art rather than to politics that Vallejo looked for evidence of the new sensibility. In those years in Paris, he made the most of concerts, ballet, motion pictures and art, of which he had been starved in Peru. He went to look at paintings by Juan Gris and Picasso, saw the Russian ballet and heard the music of Eric Satie, who unexpectedly became one of his idols. Satie has 'fratellini-ized music', he said (the Fratellini were a well-known family of clowns). 'In Satie', he wrote, 'one sees the way music has come to be a lofty, pure art, free and unconditioned, an art that ceases to be art. Perhaps this is the true path – to kill art by liberating it. Let nobody be an artist'.[18] Behind these words, lies the dream shared by so many at this time, of destroying the barriers be-tween art and life. After seeing Isadora Duncan, 'the barefoot dancer', the dream takes on bodily form for him, and he con-ceives of an art like dance 'that dances dance' and does not even need music.[19]

Even so, when he founded his own little magazine in collabo-ration with Juan Larrea, the views he expressed there are not easily classifiable under any of the usual 'ismos'. The journal, *Favorables-Paris-Poema* only survived to a second issue. It had brought together an eclectic group which included Vicente Huid-obro, Pierre Reverdy, Gerardo Diego, the Dadaist Tristan Tzara and the Cubist Juan Gris. Vallejo contributed poems, an article on Spanish literature (predictably critical), his own manifesto, 'Do not speak to the pilot', and an article on 'New poetry' in which he makes a scathing attack on those who believe that the mere use of words like 'cinema', 'motor' or 'radio' are signs of a new sensibility.[20] Unlike Mariátegui who had found some virtue in the avant-garde's mockery of the bourgeoisie,[21] Vallejo had no patience with the contemporary desire to shock at all costs, although his own manifesto, 'Se prohibe hablar al piloto' is not free of the faults he castigates in others. Yet despite its obscurity and the Artaud-like terrorism of the address to the establishment (in this case the Mexican writer Alfonso Reyes, a respected member of the Latin American intelligentsia), the manifesto has a serious underpinning, for it strives to draw the poet back to his vital roots:

Makers of images, give back words to men.
Makers of metaphors, do not forget that distances are proclaimed three by three.
Forgers of excellencies, see how the water comes by itself without need of lock-gates; water that is water to come, and not to beautify.
Forgers of perfections, I exhort you to present yourself hands first and once this has been done, you may then do the rest.[22]

By using the words 'maker' and 'forger' instead of 'creator', Vallejo emphasizes the demystification of poetry, which is *produced* as the workman produces things from his material, and not as a result of some divine inspiration. Poets should present themselves 'hands first' because poetry is produced by man as doer, not by man as thinker and prophet. The final disclaimer, 'Everything I say here is a lie', may simply have been a concession to the contemporary compulsion to mock at everything. But he added more seriously: 'I do not want to refer, to describe, to circulate nor to endure. I wish to catch birds by the second grade of their temperature and to catch men by the double-wide tongue of their names.'

The poems in prose

Once in Paris, Vallejo began to write prose poems: indeed, most of his poetic production between 1923 and 1931 took this form. In these poems, he came as near as he ever did to the 'dynamic chemistry of the *rapport*' which, he believed, made the new metaphor of the avant-garde a rather different project from the 'comparative alchemy of the metaphor of old'.[23]

The prose poem as conceived by the avant-garde and the Surrealists was the ideal vehicle for this new metaphor, the demonstration, so to speak, of the creative process; for in the prose poem, a framework of daily life could provide a point of entry into the other world of the imagination. André Breton's *Nadja* does precisely this; while mapping the topography of the Paris streets, the subject constantly defamiliarizes the scene by changes of perspective and grotesque juxtaposition. Vallejo's own experiments in prose-writing from his days in Lima already showed his interest in the unusual. The *Escalas melografiadas* (1923) were a series of brief sketches, many of them based on his prison experience but also imbued with a sense of estrangement. Yet there are also other concerns, as his most successful prose work of this period, 'Fabla salvaje', shows. In this story (clearly a story and not a prose poem), the peasant protagonist suffers paranoiac delusions after breaking a mirror, and in these delusions he constantly glimpses an unknown face. It is characteristic of Vallejo that this delusion should turn out to be occasioned by the wife's pregnancy and that the father should be driven to his death as the newcomer takes his place in the world.[24]

Once in Paris, however, Vallejo's writings began to change form. Obliquely, they translate the break with Santiago de Chuco, and the surfacing of Paris – and the urban experience – into consciousness. Each prose poem is an intense meditation, accentuated by repetition, on one of his obsessions, but most of all on the problem of identity.[25] Thus in 'Hay un mutilado' (There's a cripple), the mutilated man turns out to be not a cripple in his body but rather in his essence. Perhaps the most explicit of the prose poems on this theme is 'No vive ya nadie' (Nobody lives here any more) where all the elements that had once added up to individual identity – moral choice, meaningful relations with others – have disappeared, leaving only the body as the nucleus of different organs. The poem develops the familiar analogy between the body and a house:

What continues to function in the house is the organ, the gerundive and circular agent. Footsteps have departed, and kisses, banners and crimes. What is left is the foot, the lips, the eyes, the heart. Negations and affirmations, good and evil have disappeared. What goes on in the house is the subject of the act.[26]

The self is thus reduced to a 'gerundive' and 'circular' agent dedicated only to persistence in its own being. The use of the word 'gerundive' again illustrates the importance of the analogy with language and the breakdown of logocentrism which had already been performed in *Trilce*.

Nevertheless one of these poems stands out for its similarity with the mood of Surrealism. In 'Hallazgo de la vida' (Discovery of life) the poet appears to be inspired by 'spontaneous, fresh emotion'.

My delight comes from unprecedented emotion. My exultation comes from not having sensed the presence of life ever before. I have never felt this thing. He lies who says that I have. He lies and his lie wounds me to such an extent that it should make me unhappy. My delight comes from my faith in this personal discovery of life and no-one can reverse that faith. Should he do so, his tongue would fall out, his bones would fall out and he would have to risk borrowing someone else's in order to stand up before my eyes.[27]

It is not hard to read this as a parody of Surrealist proclamations, for the very repetition of the discovery of life becomes excessive and hence ironic. Once the subject finds himself in this 'unprecedented' region of pure discovery so dear to the Surrealists, he also finds that his own existence rests only on faith. In relation to others, he is mere *self*-assertion.

The crisis of conscience

Throughout the 1920s, Vallejo seems to have been vacillating between contradictory urges and convictions – between a longing to anchor himself in rational certainty and a sympathy for vitalism. He often expresses a belief that, out of the chaos of the post-war years, there will emerge some 'constructive motor force', able to 'function vitally'.[28] Unlike his European contemporaries, however, who found a vitality in the New World lacking in the 'over-cerebralized' culture of the West, Vallejo had nothing but contempt for most of his Latin American contemporaries who seemed incapable of creating a new spirit of 'truth to life and healthy genuine human inspiration'.[29] This vitalism helps to explain the attitude he took in an important controversy of the time.

In 1927, Diego Rivera, Mexican mural painter, member of the Communist party, anti-imperialist, issued a series of pronouncements on socialist art. One of these appeared in *Amauta* in January 1927. In forthright fashion, Diego Rivera proclaimed the end of bourgeois art and the dawn of an era of collective art. His declarations drew a response from Vallejo who saw his words as yet another misguided attempt to put programme before creativity. 'All political dogma', 'even the very best, is a repetition, a cliché, a dead thing compared with the creative sensibility of the artist', he writes, adding 'Theories, in general, embarrass and prevent creation.' The artist is not concerned with the immediate response to a particular issue but creates 'political concerns or nebulae' and these are 'vaster than any dogma and purer than any given set of concerns or ideals, whether national or universal'. The statement is important because Vallejo places, as he always does, creation at the point where consciousness awakens. The artist's task is 'to arouse, in a dark, subconscious, almost animal manner the political anatomy of man, awakening in him the ability to engender and internalise new concerns and civic emotions. The artist does not confine himself to the cultivation of new vegetation in the political terrain, and instead of modifying the geological composition of the earth, he must change it chemically and naturally.'[30] All this suggests that art functions at the level where pre-consciousness fades into consciousness, a level at which experience takes priority over conceptualization. Indeed, it is one of the constants in Vallejo's aesthetics, as far as we can judge from his scattered writing, that he gave priority to the raw material of experience which is always there, palpitating, so to speak, beneath the scaffolding of abstraction. This explains his diatribe against the new apostles, for instance, against those like Barbusse and Romain Rolland who set themselves up as international leaders, forgetting that the provincials at whom they preach 'are as intelligent as they are naive and know real tears, fresh laughter, warm bread, the water of affliction, the untutored furrow of profane love and anger – and they know nothing of literature'.[31]

But plainly these vacillations are not simply the result of abstract speculation. His articles make it plain that he is moved almost to desperation by social injustice, and in one of his letters to Pablo Abril he even suggests that a small group of angry people should get together and 'tear apart everything around us and within our reach'. Above all, he suggests, 'one must destroy oneself and then the rest. Without prior sacrifice, there can be no health.'[32] But though injustice inclined Vallejo towards socialism, he was far from accepting what he regarded as the dogmatic aspects of Marxism. 'Marxist philosophy as interpreted and applied by Lenin', he wrote in 1928, 'holds out a supporting hand to the writer whilst, with the other, it erases and corrects intellectual production in accordance with political expediency. Or at least that is the practical outcome in Russia.'[33] He has a real fear of escaping from one kind of sterility only to fall into another. 'As a man I can sympathise and work for the Revolution but as an artist, it does not lie in anybody's hands, least of all my own to control the political repercussions which might be concealed in my poems.'[34] But against the Scylla of socialist control, he sets the Charybdis of the bourgeois artist, 'this nauseous pen-pusher' (infecto . . . plumífero de gabinete) whom he described as inheriting the economic errors of the bourgeoisie.[35] Whereas the bourgeois artist is a self-serving individualist, the manual worker is possessed of 'natural health' and 'obvious wisdom'. The worker's intelligence 'does not flirt with many possible solutions of a conflict in order to function at last in accordance with mere dialectical expediency which is itself in conflict with the needs of the vital dialectic'. The difference goes back to work itself, to that contrast between the abstract manipulation of the intellectual and the productive labour of the worker.[36]

Vallejo's first visit to Russia was in October 1928, a time when he had just recovered from a serious illness. Significantly, he chose to go to the Soviet Union although there was some possibility of getting a return passage to Peru. It seems that he even thought of settling in Russia, but he returned to Paris after a few weeks, unable to stand the cold and the difficult living conditions.[37] On his return, he already saw Marxism in somewhat different terms, less as a dogma and more as praxis.[38] And he made an interesting comment on Marxism and determinism which shows how far he had moved in the direction of historical materialism:

The really new man is in the process of acquiring a rigorous consciousness of the free and creative possibility of his will, along with a sober sense of human responsibility towards history. Fatalism and determinism have no place in this supreme absorption of man in the creation of history – which he does not perceive as being outside the free motivations of his will . . .

The principle of good may be positive or negative . . . according to whether or not man manages to control his energies. In this case, tragedy is impossible and all solutions have their place in the vital process of man and society. The revolutionary feeling, created by Marx, proves precisely that history is always in a balance in which each side is controlled by the apathies or the activities of men and not by some secret or mysterious force, alien to human will.³⁹

This same article concludes with an attack on the 'impostors of revolution', 'the frauds', on those who 'play at being revolutionaries' – an allusion that seems to be directed both against the intellectual avant-garde and against the *Apristas*. His words mark the change from hesitation to committed praxis, a change in which his realisation that Marxist dialectic was not necessarily determinist must have been vital. It was not simply his first visit to Russia that produced the change but something closer to him – the internal struggles among the small group of Peruvians living in Paris, a struggle in which the two opponents were Haya de la Torre and José Carlos Mariátegui.

Long before his 'crisis of conscience', Vallejo had been interested in social justice, and had frequently spoken in his articles both of the brutality of modern society and of the tragic results that followed when technology outstripped human sensibility. There was nothing rigid, however, about his opinions and nothing which would make them incompatible with the 'Indo-americanism' of *Apra*, a movement with which he had strong ties because of his friendship with one of its ideologues, Antenor Orrego. This general concern for social justice did lead him, however, into more and more overt political positions including indignation at the execution of Sacco and Vanzetti and protest against the invasion of Nicaragua by American marines. Nor were his pronouncements on Latin America at all discordant with the *Apra* position. In 1927, he had attended a meeting organized by the League of Nations at which Gabriela Mistral spoke.⁴⁰ It provided him with the opportunity to complain of the emptiness of Latin American culture, its lack of interest for Europeans in contrast to the pre-Columbian Indian cultures. In other articles, he speaks of the devastating effect of the conquest on Latin America, and the emptiness of life which had resulted from this,⁴¹ and like many of his contemporaries, he was distressed by the imitative nature of Latin American culture and civilisation, finding that both bourgeois and Communist ideology were harmful to the continent since neither had sprung from the native soil. His 'Indianist' novel, *Hacia el reino de los Sciris*, on which he worked between 1924 and 1927, offers yet further evidence that he was greatly influenced by *Apra*'s emphasis on the originality of national cultures and the need for any form of government to be rooted in them.[42]

Yet ultimately Mariátegui proved the more powerful. Vallejo had been impressed by the first issue of *Amauta*[43] and clearly read it eagerly, whereas Haya's rhetoric appalled him. Yet to opt for Mariátegui was a serious ideological move, for instead of stressing the originality of American experience, Mariátegui believed socialism to be a universally applicable, international doctrine.

As long as *Apra* remained a loosely organized movement, uniting students, workers, peasants and intellectuals behind a broad anti-imperialist policy, there was no problem. Difficulties only arose when Haya, then in Mexico, tried to convert the movement into a political party, a move that brought a quick response from Mariátegui who declared in an editorial in the seventeenth issue of *Amauta* (September 1928) that, 'socialist materialism includes all the possibilities for the spiritual, ethical and philosophical development of man', and asserted that, though socialism (like capitalism) had originated in Europe, it was not specifically European.

The *Apra* cells abroad – in Buenos Aires, Mexico and Paris – were now obliged to decide between the new *Apra* party and Mariátegui's socialism. The Paris cell, which included Vallejo, Eudocio Ravines (who became a member of the Peruvian Communist party from which he later seceded), Juan Jacinto Paiva and Armando Bazán met on December 1928 and decided to support Mariátegui on the grounds that Haya de la Torre's new party was not a class party and therefore not socialist. 'Socialism is the direct and legitimate offspring and the dynamic and dialectical negation of capitalism. Socialism has emerged out of the factory, it has been nourished by the machine. The home of socialism is the city, which is the home of the worker, as the bourg was the home of liberalism. The countryside may be affected and imbued with socialism but it cannot generate or achieve it.'[44] Vallejo was among those who accepted this viewpoint, and with others formed the Peruvian Socialist party (29 December). He was also one of the signatories of a letter addressed to his Peruvian comrades which declared, 'The ideology we adopt in that of militant revolutionary Marxism and Leninism, a doctrine that we accept completely in all its aspects

– philosophical, political and socio-economic.' Their goals would be to train cadres and maintain contact with their comrades in Peru.[45]

The letter is an important indication of how rapidly Vallejo was moving in the direction of commitment, for the new party was the equivalent of a Communist party and linked to Comintern. Vallejo was also one of the signatories of a policy document, dated 29 December, which analysed the economic dependency of the Leguía régime and the penetration of Peru by foreign capital, and described the nature of the opposition forces. The document justified the inclusion of petty bourgeois elements in the party 'only when they renounce their personal points of view and accept the discipline, the programme, the points of view and the demands of the proletariat. Artisans, employees, students and writers may only enter the party if they agree to submit themselves at all times to the discipline imposed by workers and to *international* discipline.'[46] By a curious coincidence, an article by Vallejo on the 'Lessons of Marxism' was published in *Variedades* shortly after, though he had obviously written it several months before the meeting. It is an article that criticizes those who rigidly stick to a dogma and falsify reality in order to make it fit a theory, despite the fact that the *devenir vital* is so fluid and so charged with the unexpected. The 'scribes' of Marxism are traitors to its real spirit, 'eunuchs' who hold that Marx is the only philosopher of past, present and future history, a man who had legislated for the human spirit for all time. Vallejo excepts Lenin and Trotsky from these strictures, Lenin because he did not interpret Marxism too literally and brought about the Russian revolution despite the supposed immaturity of Russian capitalism. He praises Trotsky for his 'lessons in freedom' and for his opposition to Stalin, noting the significance of this new left within the left.[47]

The most interesting article published during this period of transition is one on 'The work of art and the life of the artist' (written in February 1929, published 6 May 1930) where he comes to grips with the problem of the relationship between art and life, declaring artistic production to be 'a true alchemic operation, a transmutation'. The artist is sensitive both to 'surrounding social concerns and his own individual concerns' though he does not merely reproduce these in the same form but changes them into 'pure revolutionary essences', different in form and identical in substance to the raw material. Art is like a tree in that we do not see the nourishment which is taken out of the earth:

> however, if the work is analysed deeply, in its innermost recesses there will necessarily be discovered not only the . . . social and economic currents but also the intellectual and even the religious currents of the time. The correspondence between the individual and the social life of the artist and his work is, then, inevitable and it operates consciously or unconsciously and whether or not the artist wants or intends it.[48]

Russia

> Bolshevism is humanism in action. The same can be said of Revolutionism or Communism that they are humanisms in action – that is, humanist idea and feeling together with the humanist and technical action which incarnates this ideal.[49]

In the deepest possible sense, Vallejo accepted Communism as *praxis* (the union of theory and practice) in the years between 1929 and 1931. Although he apparently did not join the Communist party before his arrival in Spain after being expelled from France at the end of 1930, the two years 1929 and 1930 saw a major revision of his opinions on art and politics. So much can be gleaned from his publications and from the rather meagre *carnet* of this time. He now began to see bourgeois artists and writers like Valéry, Gris and Benda in a different light. 'The Surrealists and Larrea seek the liberation of the spirit before the abolition of the bourgeois class conditions and even independently of it',[50] he wrote. He was now inclined to read socialism into his own past work and to regard committed writers and artists like Barbusse and Diego Rivera more favourably. He distinguished too between artistic revolution (in Proust, Giraudoux, Morand, Stravinsky, Picasso) and the 'thematic' revolution of such artists as Prokofiev, Rivera and Barbusse.[51] He was also very critical of the 'selective' sympathy of certain intellectuals who cannot really be stirred by the plight of the masses. Even so, lurking beneath his comments, there is still the concern that Marxism should not lose touch with the vital currents, a concern that remained with him throughout the rest of his life.

Two more visits to Russia confirmed these convictions. In October and November 1929 he was in Russia with Georgette; the fruit of the visit was his *Rusia en 1931*, published in Spain during the period when he was unable to go back to France. This was the only book of his that sold well. In October 1931 he briefly visited the Soviet Union to attend a congress. However a second book, *Rusia ante el plan quinquenal*, failed to find a publisher and did not appear in his lifetime.[52] Both books are of enormous interest since they reflect his thinking at a time when he was writing some of the finest of the *Poemas humanos*. Both, too, bear a family-resemblance to others on the same theme (Barbusse's *Russia*, for instance), for Vallejo was taken on the customary tour of collective farms, factories and schools. Yet underneath a mass of information which hardly trips lightly from his pen, there are some characteristic preoccupations. 'My aim is to give a picture of the Soviet process and interpret it rationally and objectively and from a technical point of view', he declares at the beginning of *Rusia en 1931*.[53] Many of the essays in the book are concerned with descriptions of the Soviet economy and the differences he sees between the American system of mechanization produced by the conveyor-belt and Soviet automation whose main object is to provide more leisure for the workers. He also comments on the traces of the *ancien régime* that he finds – the beggars and street people – though he is far more interested in seeking evidence of the emergence of the new man. Hence his interest in the family life of the Bolshevik militant and in the changes within the structure of the family. 'The Bolshevik knows that to be a revolutionary, one must first of all be a man in the truest sense of the word', he writes.[54] And in the militant, he recognizes a new man in whom sacrifice and courage were motivated not by individualism but by a collective ideal. One of the last articles he contributed to the Lima press was dedicated to Lenin whom, with Marx, he now considered to be one of the supreme examples of this new non-religious, wholly human ideal.[55]

Vallejo had arrived in Russia at a time when the struggle between the committed vanguard writers and the experimental avant-gardistes had reached a climax. A motley collection of Futurists, Formalists and experimenters who had regarded themselves as 'revolutionary writers' were to find themselves the targets of attack by the Union of Proletarian Writers. 'Socialist realism', though not yet regarded as the only possible art of the proletarian state, was clearly in the wind. Vallejo attempts to expound the ideas in a rather unconvincing chapter of *Rusia en 1931* in which he claims that artistic production is rational and realist.[56] Only when he turns to the cinema, however, does he show any real enthusiasm for Soviet art. During his visit, Mayakovsky had taken him to see *The Battleship Potemkin* and *The General Line,* and he was fascinated by what he regarded as 'cinedialéctico'. Here at last were new images – a line of tractors seen from a plane, pistons shot at close range below decks in a ship, the hand milking a cow and then the milking machine, 'the one emerging from the other in a Marxist historical leap'. 'Here the human forces of work find unexpected expression and images. This is the psychological gain unknown in subjective, capitalist cinema.'[57] A new form of psychology emerges which concentrates on collective emotions – the cry of rebellion, the pain of a wounded worker. It is the *verismo* of this cinema which most of all impresses Vallejo, its closeness to life.

Rusia ante el segundo plan quinquenal was written after a third visit to Russia to which he was invited as a delegate to the International Congress of Writers, along with other foreign intellectuals who sympathized with the Soviet Union. In this brief visit (he seems to have spent about ten days there in all), he visited Rostov, the Caucasus (where he was nearly killed when a stone fell from a crane just near where he had been standing) and spent two days in Moscow interviewing officials. The book he wrote after this visit was completed within two months of his return to Madrid.

In the four years between his first and third visits to Russia, Vallejo found important changes. His concerns were now less with monitoring the success of the Soviet system as expressed in production figures, much more with the profounder effects of the system on daily life, the class structures and on collective methods of work. A large part of this second book is devoted to conversations and visits he made with one of the hotel workers, a man who expresses himself in such clear political language that he must have had an important place in the party machine, though Vallejo evidently takes him to be an ordinary 'servant'. Whether this man did or did not represent the workers is less pertinent here than Vallejo's own concerns, above all his admiration for a system where the servant is no longer a slave and

where work is no longer classified according to a vertical series
of categories which makes intellectual work superior to manual
labour. Again he eagerly seizes on every scrap of evidence of the
new spirit, reproving his own kind for their individualism for
'we are so used to seeing nothing around us but those [base
material] interests that we find it difficult to conceive life from
the collective, generous and disinterested point of view of the
Bolshevik militant'.[58] And for a moment, at least, he sees the
machine as the liberator of man, freeing people from degrading
manual labour. 'Labour awaits this total and definitive redemption', he wrote. 'From the moment the first tool was invented,
redemption has been taking place . . .' . Technology will bring
about 'the definitive advent of joyful work'.[59]

   This vision of Utopia was not to remain steady or clear throughout the rest of his life, yet for all that, its power should not be
underestimated or held in low esteem. It is the slender possibility
of the practical realization of this dream that goes into the
making of the tragic vision of *Poemas humanos,* as if hope made
man's present fate all the more extreme.

Art and revolution

Both Vallejo's books on Russia included sections on art and
revolution and he also planned a book of essays with this title.[60]
His notes included twenty-seven sections covering theory, the
sociology of art, the relationship of art to technology, art and
dialectics, and the various 'isms' of the 1920s. Perhaps the most
interesting of these sections is the first in which he divides the
'arte de tendencia' – whether Fascist or Bolshevik – from propaganda art and 'free art', under which he classifies 'socialist, proletariat, imperialist-bourgeois, monarchic, conscious or subconscious
art'. He was clearly exercised by the problem of how to separate
a didactic art made necessary by the demands of the struggle,
and art in the truest sense of the word, whatever the society in
which it was produced.

   However, for some time after his 'crisis', he seems to have been
most concerned with attempting to understand the implications
of Marxism for his own work, for in Marxism he recognized a
tool which would allow 'a scientific interpretation of history' and

which might provide 'the constructive doctrine of future society'.[61]

In the late 1920s he had already begun a serious study of Marxism and even before living in Spain he was in contact with a number of Spanish intellectuals with similar sympathies. In May 1930, he visited Madrid in order to arrange for the printing of a second edition of *Trilce* with a preface written by José Bergamín, a Catholic poet with left-wing sympathies. And he had also established contact with Bergamín's friend and collaborator, Gerardo Diego. These contacts proved of the utmost importance when in December 1930, Vallejo was expelled from France for having engaged in militant activities and was therefore forced to live in Spain. The expulsion was his first brutal lesson in political commitment, for it was obvious that, since his visit to Russia, the police had taken an active interest in him, registering his visits to the Humanité bookstore, his attendance at meetings and his visits to the homes of other politically committed people.[62] His militancy also cost him part of his livelihood for his articles to *Variedades* and *Mundial* which had grown increasingly political in tone were no longer welcome. Although Vallejo was indifferent to the declaration of the Republic in Spain in July 1931, seeing it only as another form of bourgeois government,[63] his enforced residence in Spain was not without its compensations – not the least of which was that he was now among Spanish-speaking people. Soon after his arrival in Spain, he joined a Communist party cell where he apparently gave lessons in Marxist-Leninist theory.[64] Besides this, he made many friends, including García Lorca, whose experiments in reaching a new public through theatre greatly interested him, and Rafael Alberti, a member of the Communist party. For the only time in his years in Europe, he enjoyed a modest success. His articles on Russia, which had been published in the magazine 'Bolivar', came out in book form as *Rusia en 1931* (July 1931) which was recommended as a book of the month and went into three editions. His proletarian novel, *El tungsteno* came out in the same year. But after this initial success, he found himself increasingly frustrated. He earned money translating, but this could hardly make up for the rejection of his story *Paco Yunque* and his second book on Russia. Though he experimented in writing for the theatre, in an attempt to reach a wider public, none of his plays were staged. More frustrated than ever by this rejection in a country where, at least, they spoke his language, he returned to France, arriving in Paris in February 1932, to begin what turned out to be one of the saddest periods of his life, a period that was darkened by the outbreak of the Spanish Civil War in 1936.

Behind these frustrations there lay far deeper problems. Marxism had seemed to offer a new Logos, the hope of once again realising a whole man. But its practical realization was hard: hence Vallejo's problems in separating the tactical considerations of the era, his own position in bourgeois society and a valid new aesthetics. For it was the salvation of man that was at stake so that it was not simply a question for him of adopting a new style of writing but of discovering the artistic expression that corresponded to a new way of life.

This helps to explain why the lines he draws are not always the familiar Marxist ones. His strictures on Surrealism and the avant-garde, on Mayakovsky and Panai Istrati are thus not made on the grounds of their supposed decadence, but are directed towards their superficiality or their failure to wed new theory with new practice. He remained firmly convinced that poetry could never spring from ideas but must come from the 'dark nebulae of life expressed in a turn of phrase . . . in the imponderable of the word'.[65] In 1929, he expressed his admiration for Trotsky in words which reveal his anxiety to retain the dynamics of revolution within a post-revolutionary society.[66] More orthodox in his writings of 1930 and 1931, he retained his suspicion of abstract doctrine whether in art or politics and to the end was speaking of theoretical and practical 'cold' as if these words somehow spelled anti-life.[67]

Though these conflicts between the dynamics of life and the perils of abstraction were never entirely resolved, his notebooks show his determined effort to distinguish between revolutionary thought, proletarian art, Bolshevik art and socialist art. The need for such a distinction arose because of his conviction that art legitimately served an immediate 'party' purpose at the moment of revolutionary change but also because he also looked ahead to a time when once again there would be a genuinely social art, an art which he describes as 'socialist'. While Bolshevik art belongs to the transitional stage before the establishment of a truly socialist society, and while proletarian literature is a class literature, socialist art is the great art of the past and the present and the future, that which has transcended particular interests and psychologies and attained universality.[68]

Towards a materialist art

Immediately after his second visit to Russia, Vallejo began to explore new kinds of poetry and he also turned his hand to social narrative and to the theatre. The posthumously published *Poemas humanos* were to include several materialist poems – 'Gleba', 'Los mineros', 'Telúrica y magnética' – which belong to this period. However the impact of Russia was most direct on a number of plays that he wrote in the 1930s and on his 'proletarian' novel, *El tungsteno* which appeared in Spain in 1931.[69]

El tungsteno cannot simply be dismissed as a laborious attempt at socialist realism. Vallejo is here concerned not only with documenting and exposing injustice but also with the levels of consciousness of different characters and the relation of ideology to class. The 'sora' Indians who live in the *sierra* not far from the technologically advanced mines have no interest in private property. At the opposite extreme are the middle classes with their crude individualist philosophy. The highest stage of consciousness is reached by the militant mine-workers, especially the Marxist, Servando Huanca. The central problem of the novel was Vallejo's own – the problem of how the intellectual Benites (the surname of the poet's grandmother) can transcend the ideology of his class and become an ally of the workers. Before his vision of the Sacred Heart, an ideological turning-point in the novel, Benites is presented as an unsympathetic character who tacitly consents to brutal exploitation. He is obsessively concerned with his own health, hates shaking hands for fear of contamination and is devoted to the ideas of Samuel Smiles:

Everything in his room was always in its place and he himself was always in place, working, pondering, sleeping, eating and reading Smiles' Self-Help which he considered the best modern work. On church holidays, he leafed through the *Gospel according to St Matthew*, a little gold-tooled book which his mother had taught him to love and understand in all that it means to true Christians.[70]

Is this a caricature of the young Vallejo who had worked in the mines and the sugar plantations? It would not be surprising; nor that a vision of Christ had mediated the transition between the old Vallejo and the new. In the novel, Benites's vision of the Sacred Heart is based (with only minor modifications) on a similar incident in his short story 'Sabiduría' which he had published in *Amauta* in 1927.[71] Moreover, there was a long tradition, beginning with Renan and culminating in Barbusse's *Jesus,* of separating the person of Christ from the authoritarian figure of God the Father and making him a socially conscious reformer, even a revolutionary.[72] However, the modifications which Vallejo made to the episode before incorporating it in *El tungsteno* reflect a deep change in his own thinking – from a vague unease with materialism to a recognition of the conflict between Christian doctrine and capitalist society. In 'Sabiduría', the vision represents a brief transcendence of individualism during which Christ tells Benites that he must 'conform to the sense of the earth'. Christianity no longer promises an afterlife but does provide a moral ideal. Another of Vallejo's short stories, 'Vocación de la muerte', similarly suggests the moral influence of Christianity even on revolutionary thought.[73] Yet in *El tungsteno,* Christianity seems to be the ideology of the past rather than the present; the traces of religion which come back to Benites during his feverish delirium represent the best part of his consciousness, that which had resisted the crude individualism by which he normally lived. But the vision is immediately followed in the novel by a brutal incident in which the storekeeper and the 'authorities' of the mining community gamble for the storekeeper's mistress, Graciela; the men proceed to make her drunk and rape her so brutally that she dies. Benites, who has participated in the episode though not in the rape, feels a strong emotional revulsion, which is explicable given his Christian upbringing and his recent vision of the Sacred Heart, and this leads directly to his decision to join a protest led by Servando Huanca against forced labour in the mines. But the moral code of Christianity cannot provide a strategy for revolutionary *praxis*. Its significance in the novel is as a mediation between the old Benites and the new. Servando Huanca's protest is unsuccessful and twenty of the protestors are sent to the mines; however, the events unite the rebels against the system and encourage them to educate and organize. Benites, because of his class background, cannot take the lead, but is now prepared to become the ally of the socialist workers. Despite this impeccable conclusion which conforms rigorously to the tenets of socialist realism, there is a typically Vallejo touch in the final lines. The mine's timekeeper, who belongs to the revolutionary group, had been in love with the dead woman, Graciela. After a meeting of revolutionaries, he lies awake at night unable to sleep because words like 'industry', 'products', 'petty bourgeois', 'capital', 'Marx' keep floating into his consciousness while he is also grieving for his personal loss. In these final paragraphs, the language of class-consciousness appears abstract and meaningless. The timekeeper's suffering cannot be alleviated by his dedication to the cause, though socialism may eventually create a new society. Thus Vallejo never indicates that socialism will be the panacea for all suffering – only for the suffering that arises from exploitation.

El tungsteno is the most programmatic work that Vallejo wrote and its weaknesses are obvious. Perhaps its main interest is the insight it offers into the way Vallejo saw the ideological conflict between Christian sacrifice and selfish materialism which he had himself lived through. Another story he wrote at this time, *Paco Yunque,* is also rooted in his past – in his memories of the months he spent as a tutor to a landowner's son in the Sierra de Pasco. It is a somewhat sentimental tale of a servant's child who finds himself victimized by the master's son, who is in the same class in the village school. The master/slave relationship is here shown as penetrating the most innocent relationships.[74]

Vallejo's brief excursions into drama met with even less success than his narratives, though he felt that the theatre offered exceptional opportunities for the development of a new socialist art. The fragments of his extant plays, however, suggest that his real passion may have been for an art he could not practise – namely the cinema. While his articles and notebooks have comparatively little to say on the theatre, he wrote enthusiastically of Chaplin and Eisenstein.[75] The stage was the nearest he could get to this exciting and revolutionary medium, whose social possibilities seemed so much greater than those of poetry. Not surprisingly, given his lack of experience, he was unsuccessful in trying to get Charles Dullin and Gaston Baty to stage his farce, *Colacho hermanos.*[76] For better or for worse his genre was poetry, and during the period of his repeated failure as a dramatist, he was writing some of the great poems of the twentieth century.

The language of social struggle

One of the puzzling aspects of Vallejo's meditations on art and politics in the early 1930s is that despite his friendship with Lorca and Alberti, he appears to have made no attempt to follow their example and produce a poetry rooted in popular culture and written for oral performance. He came from an area in Peru rich in popular tradition, but his obsession was with the written word as an instrument of domination and a tool of liberation. Even after joining the Communist party, he did not see his task as one of closing the gap between the élite and the masses by drawing on oral tradition but rather as a more fundamental struggle with the social aspects of language itself. Logocentrism had given way to the poetics of free play of the sign as early as *Trilce*. Now, in 1930 and 1931, he became concerned with the emptiness of the sign, seeing a relation between the word which only has significance as a function in a particular situation and the rampant individualism of capitalism. His most important writing on this topic is to be found in an article he wrote called 'Duel between two literatures', in which he bases the differences between 'capitalist' and socialist literature on that between the language of individualism and a language rooted in new social relationships.[77] 'In capitalist society', he wrote, 'the word is empty . . . it suffers from an acute, incurable wasting disease . . . The relations that united human beings have broken down. The word of the individual with regard to collective experience has been truncated and suppressed in the mouth of the individual. We are dumb in the midst of our incomprehensible babble. It is the confusion of tongues arising from exaggerated individualism on which bourgeois economy and politics are based. Rampant self-interest has filled everything with its selfish intent, even words. The word is stifled by individualism. The most human form of social relationship – the word – has thus lost its collective essence and attributes.' So conflicting interests in bourgeois society are held directly responsible for the fact that people no longer communicate. 'Words such as faith, love, liberty, good, passion, truth, sorrow, effort, harmony, work, happiness, justice are empty or transmit ideas and sentiments which are different from those that they enunciate. Even the words life, God and history are hollow.' For the first time, Vallejo appears to relate that free play of language to class-conflict. A universal literature, he concludes, can only come into being once again with a society with a non-individualistic social infrastructure; then and then only can he look forward to the 'esperanto of co-operation and social justice', the 'tongue of tongues' which must come from proletarian consciousness.

This article helps us to understand why the *Poemas humanos* and the poems on Spain are complementary projects; why, on the one hand, he parodies the language of individualism, but on the other makes a Utopian attempt to inscribe a social text written by the Spanish people through sacrifice. For it is important to stress that there are not two Vallejos at this time – a Communist and an individual – but only a single project to forge a social and human future. Never completely at home in the novel and the theatre which, nevertheless, seemed to offer more immediate contact between writer and public, he soon turned back to his lifelong obsession – his confrontation with the act of writing itself.

7

THE DIALECTICS OF MAN
AND NATURE

Consciousness – that historical relationship between boat and water

Vallejo[1]

The poetry of the 1920s

To write about the *Poemas humanos* is an act of faith, since we shall perhaps never know whether the poems we now read under this title would have represented the final versions of the texts[2] nor whether Vallejo would have included all the poems (except the poems on Spain) that he wrote in the 1920s and 30s in a single collection.[3] In any event, *Poemas humanos* by no means represents a homogeneous body of work and there are two groups of poems which are plainly separable from the rest. The poems he wrote in the 1920s before the 'crisis of conscience' belong with in 'Poems in prose': a second group of poems – 'Gleba', 'Los mineros', 'Salutación angélica', 'Telúrica y magnética' – written after visiting Russia represent an experiment in social poetry of a type that anticipates *España, aparta de mí este cáliz*. Comparing these two groups of poems is a heuristic procedure which helps in the comprehension of what was plainly a crisis in his aesthetics as well as a crisis in his life.

The early Paris years, it must be confessed, did not produce much poetry. We find Vallejo, in the new environment of Paris, much concerned not only with his immediate problems (one of which was to learn to speak French) but also with the dazzling, contradictory and ebullient world of French art and letters.[4] Not until 1926 did two of his poems appear in the magazine which he himself had helped to edit, the *Favorables-Paris-Poema*. In August 1927, writing to Luis Alberto Sánchez to whom he sent some of his new work, he explained that he had been reluctant to publish his recent poems because of a 'vow of aesthetic conscience' not to let any of his poems appear in print except when he felt a deep need to do so, a need that must be 'as profound as it is extra-literary'. Luis Alberto Sánchez, who had initially

161

been dismayed by *Trilce,* now made up for this by publishing two poems in *Mundial* – 'Lomo de las sagradas escrituras' and 'Actitud de excelsa' (which Vallejo later called 'Altura y pelos'). Sánchez mentioned Vallejo's lack of recognition as a poet but forecast that "if any greatness is to survive among our poets, it will doubtless be this one from Trujillo', adding that he was 'above all things, the human poet'.[5] These poems and two others which he had published in his own review, *Favorables-Paris-Poema,* together with 'Nómina de huesos', 'Cuatro conciencias' (which would later be included in *Poemas humanos*) and 'En el momento en que el tenista' (which has only recently been published) seem to constitute his entire extant poetic production between leaving Trujillo and visiting Russia.

What characterizes these poems is that the concerns which engendered them are still very near the surface. At least one of them, 'En el momento en que el tenista', appears to violate his own principle that poetry should spring from emotions rather than from ideas for it is a recasting of a prose passage 'From Feuerbach to Marx'[6] which dispenses with most of the features of 'poetic language' and constitutes a brief gloss on other texts. Indeed the poem foreshadows that preoccupation with the act of writing itself which we shall find in *Poemas humanos* and which turns into a hypersensitive reaction to the written word. 'En el momento en que el tenista' is in fact a mock argument summed up in two lines which he excised:[7]

> Cuando un órgano ejerce su función en plenitud,
> no hay malicia posible en el cuerpo.

> When an organ functions perfectly
> There is no malice possible in the body.

The word 'malicia' which occurs in several of his articles suggests that consciousness is a surplus and demonic energy, which comes from the separation of the subject from the sense of his own body and from the world. Vallejo sees in a sport like tennis a perfect co-ordination of body and mind but then he mockingly goes on to argue that, were religious sentiment to be located in a bodily organ, then its perfect functioning would likewise exclude all possibility of self-consciousness and the believer would be 'casi un vegetal'. Thus the poem presents the antinomy of self-consciousness – self-forgetfulness so that if we accept the second term as perfection, then we must also accept the destruction of consciousness. '¡Oh alma! ¡Oh pensamiento! ¡Oh Marx! ¡Oh Feuerbach!' he concludes. The antinomy is, in fact, that of *Trilce* in which alienation was identified with existence. If Marx and Feuerbach are involved, it is precisely because they are philosophers who equate consciousness with the humanity of man: Feuerbach even goes so far as to hold that consciousness is joy in one's own perfection, is 'self-affirmation of the highest kind'.[8]

Poetry itself is the product of 'malicia' for by using the 'I' as the co-ordinating principle of the poem, the act of self-consciousness is consecrated. The grammatical category of the first person singular creates the illusion of an empirical 'I'; and literary history is muddied over by the confusion that arises from taking the 'I' of the poem as the personal statement of the poet. What begins to concern Vallejo in these poems of the 1920s is the very mechanism by which the poetic 'I' is produced and the illusion created. Thus in 'Altura y pelos', he poses a series of questions which separates the exceptional from the common denominator of social man:

> ¿Quién no tiene su vestido azul?
> ¡Quién no almuerza y no toma el tranvía,
> con su cigarrillo contratado y su dolor de bolsillo?
> ¡Yo que tan sólo he nacido!
> ¡Yo que tan sólo he nacido!

> Who does not have his blue suit?
> Who does not eat his lunch and take a bus,
> With the cigarette he has bargained for, with his aching pocket?
> I, who was born so alone!
> I, who was born so alone!

What is left when we take away man's automatized role in society is the category 'I' of which, however, only existence can be predicated. Naming also belongs to the social and the given:

> ¿Quién no *se llama* Carlos o cualquier otra cosa?
> ¿Quién al gato no *dice* gato gato?
> ¡Ay! yo que sólo he nacido solamente!
> ¡Ay! yo que sólo he nacido solamente! [The italics are mine.]

> Who is not called Carlos or whatever?
> Who does not say kitty kitty to the cat?
> Ay! I who was only born so alone!
> Ay! I who was only born so alone!

Script and writing constitute the means by which the subject separates the self from the common experience. And the exclamation 'ay, yo' re-enacts the very birth of this illusory creature. The poem thus reveals the process by which the 'I' comes into being through the differentiation of the subject category from the social.

In another poem of this period, 'He aquí que hoy saludo, me pongo el cuello y vivo', the opening lines represent a performative speech act and by their very utterance bring into being a subject who greets, who has a head connected to the body, and who lives.

He aquí que hoy saludo, me pongo el cuello y vivo,
superficial de pasos insondable de plantas.
Tal me recibo de hombre, tal más bien me despido
y de cada hora mía retoña una distanciA.

Here I am today giving greeting, fastening my neck and coming to life,
Superficial my footsteps, unfathomable my soles.
Thus I accept myself as a man, or rather thus I bid myself farewell
And from each of my hours there sprouts a distancE.

The subject is defined both as superficial and as unfathomable for on the one hand, the individual can be seen as a mere link in the chain of the species; on the other as the sum of the uncountable generations who have gone before. The 'I', therefore, has both a syntagmic and paradigmatic role. In this poem, the subject exists as an attempt to separate the self from the generic, as sheer differentiation from the mass.

Desde tttales códigos regulares saludo
al soldado desconocido
al verso perseguido por la tinta fatal
y al saurio que Equidista diariamente
de su vida y su muerte,
como quien no hace la cosa.

From sssuch normal statutes I greet
The unknown soldier,
The line of poetry pursued by fatal ink
And the saurian that daily Equidistances
Its life and its death,
Like someone who doesn't even care.

What the voice greets – the unknown soldier, the line of verse 'pursued by fatal ink', the motionless saurian life force – all represent what is illusorily immortal or permanent, all that is different from the transitory individual. And what finally defines the subject is little more than a grammatical category.

In the *Trilce* poems, Vallejo had presented both creativity and the individual as 'excess', something left over when the needs of the species have been fulfilled. These poems of the 1920s, however, begin to delineate a self who is not only biologically programmed but also lives and thinks within a socially given framework, and hence is in a prisonhouse that is ultimately humanity's own creation. A good many of the *Poemas humanos* represent the poet's insurrection against both biological enslavement and the reduction of individuals to a mere functional role within an environment they no longer appear able to control. Yet the poems are not homogeneous; and there are at least two groups of poems which present us with the twin alternatives of Utopia and Apocalypse. The first group lays bare the very process by which man structures and changes his reality; the second shows humanity at the end of its tether, doomed if it will not make the leap that will take them out of a destructive and individualistic course.

The production of man

'Salutación angélica', 'Los mineros', 'Gleba', and 'Telúrica y magnética' were all written soon after Vallejo visited Russia and are attempts to put into poetic practice, Marx's conviction that human beings produce themselves actively in a real sense and see themselves in a world they have made.[9] How well Vallejo knew the writings of Marx at this time is difficult to determine and perhaps the enquiry is otiose.[10] His journalistic writings reveal that he had a general grasp of Marxist theory and, more than this, that he believed that the Bolshevik incarnated a new possibility – that of reconciling the public and the private person and so healing the painful fragmentation of the self through social practice. Clearly, too, he did not consider Marxism simply as a faith replacing Christianity but rather as a *praxis* which could change both man and society. Thus, writing of the use of words like 'revolution', 'proletariat', 'international', 'capital', 'mass', 'social justice' etc. he describes them as *direct creations of the economic feeling and instinct of man* unlike the myths, 'God', 'Divine justice', 'soul', 'good', 'evil', 'eternity' etc. which are creations of religious feeling. In social doctrine, he writes, 'the dogmas proceed from the need or from a series of historical needs of production or, in other words, from the deterministic dialectic of technology'.[11] The articles on Russia reveal a Vallejo profoundly interested in labour, seeing work as the foundation of a new collective spirit which will flourish once the conflicts of the class-system have been overcome. The problem now is how this can be translated into poetry.

The three poems, 'Salutación angélica', 'Gleba' and 'Los mineros', not only deal with three new types of universal man – the Bolshevik militant, the miner and the peasant, but also with the way the world view of these men is structured. In 'Salutación angélica', for example, he contrasts a series of abstract national stereotypes with the Bolshevik's universal consciousness, but does so by laying bare the way such stereotypes are formed. For we tend to think of nations in relation to their place on the map; and this is how Vallejo presents them: the Slav in contrast to the palm-tree, the German between East and West is 'profiled against the sun', the Englishman on whose empire the sun never sets is described as 'endless'. Vallejo describes these national stereotypes as 'heaven threaded to earth by the winds' and as 'the kiss of limit on the shoulders' because they are ideal and abstract categories which have no real existence except to determine limits. In contrast, every part of the Bolshevik's body is a sign of relationship and communication:

> tu gesto marital,
> tu cara de padre,
> tus piernas de amado,
> tu cutis por teléfono,
> tu alma perpendicular
> a la mía,
> tus codos de justo
> y un pasaporte en blanco en tu sonrisa.

> Your marital gesture,
> Your fatherly face,
> Your legs of a beloved,
> Your skin by telephone,
> Your soul perpendicular
> To mine,
> Your elbows of a just man
> And a blank passport in your smile.

The 'elbow' and the 'legs' which in *Trilce* were synecdoches for man in his struggle for life and on his journey to death now acquire positive values; they are parts of a whole man whose function is to be universal and to bring about the communion of all men. By implication, Vallejo addresses this new man from a lesser, horizontal state, yearning for 'doctrinal heat in cold ingots' and the Bolshevik's 'added manner of looking'. The reference to ingots is significant; it anticipates the 'Spain' poems in which 'gold once again becomes gold', thanks to the sacrifice of the Spaniards, instead of representing the debased form of exchange and relationship in capitalist society. But within the context of 'Salutación angélica', the ingot represents the real value of a socialist society, backing, as it were, the 'doctrinal heat' which would otherwise be mere rhetoric. Meanwhile the poet admires the Bolshevik despite his own still fallen state:

Y digo, bolchevique, tomando esta flaqueza
en su feroz linaje de exhalación terrestre:
hijo natural del bien y del mal
y viviendo talvez por vanidad, para que digan,
me dan tus simultáneas estaturas mucha pena,
puesto que tú no ignoras en quién se me hace tarde diariamente,
en quién estoy callado y medio tuerto.

And I am speaking, Bolshevik, taking this weakness
In its fierce lineage of terrestrial exhalation:
Natural child of good and evil,
And living perhaps out of vanity, just so they will say so
Your simultaneous statures grieve me,
Given that you cannot fail to see into whom I daily get late,
Into whom I am silent and half one-eyed.

One of the key words is plainly 'simultaneous', for Communism proposed an unalienated state vastly different from that of individual man, imprisoned in linearity and divided both from his contemporaries and from the generations before and after him. The poet, however, is still the 'natural child of good and evil', a product of the struggle for life. His 'fierce lineage' is that of the species, his reason for living is vanity, his mode of being is something which the Bolshevik with his sense of human solidarity, his 'simultáneas estaturas' has overcome. The poet is 'callado' and 'medio tuerto' because he still has the alienated consciousness of individualistic man.

The importance of 'Salutación angélica' is that it proposes in an unequivocal fashion what will become a central issue in the 'Spain' poems – a poet-prophet who is not avant-garde or 'vanguard' but, as it were, bringing up the rear. It is not the poet who produces a new consciousness but the militant.[12]

'Los mineros' is a more complex poem, for it attempts to show the formation of consciousness through work. The voice, words, expression and ideas of the miners are formed directly out of the kind of labour they do:

Los mineros salieron de la mina
remontando sus ruinas venideras,
fajaron su salud con estampidos
y, elaborando su *función mental,*
cerraron *con sus voces*
el socavón, en forma de síntoma profundo.

¡Era de ver sus polvos corrosivos!
¡Era de oír sus óxidos de altura!
Cuñas de boca, yunques de boca, aparatos de boca
                    (¡Es formidable!)

El orden de sus túmulos,
sus inducciones plásticas, sus respuestas corales,
agolpáronse al pie de ígneos percances,
y airente amarillura conocieron los trístidos y tristes,
imbuidos
del metal que se acaba, del metaloide pálido y pequeño.
                    [The italics are mine.]

The miners came out of the mine
Climbing up their future ruins,
They bundled their health in explosions
And refining their mental functions
They closed the mineshaft
With their voices, in the form of a profound symptom.

Their corrosive dust was something to see!
Their oxides of altitude were worth hearing!
Wedges of the mouth and anvils of the mouth
And machines of the mouth
                    (It's impressive!).

The order of their tombs,
Their malleable inductions, their choral responses,
Crowded to the foot of fiery attributes,
And these wretched and wrale knew the wrathful yellowness,
Imbued as they were
With the diminishing metal, the pale and puny metalloid.

The miners emerge from the mines as the destroyers and the con-
structors of the new order, but also as the producers of the new
thought, a dialectical reason that is elaborated not only in their
work but through their collective action (their choral responses).
In Vallejo's book on *Rusia ante el segundo plan quinquenal*, there
is a passage which describes just such revolutionary thinking as
'a vast healthy and creative reaction against intellectualism and
the vice of abstract thinking for its own sake'; adding 'what is
needed in these times of struggle and concrete praxis is class
motivation, fervour and anger; conscious or instinctive values of
feeling. Revolutionary consciousness lives and is nourished by the
fire of passion and reason.'[13] And in his first book on Russia,
speaking of the role of work in the films of Eisenstein, he declares that labour is 'the great recreator of the world; the force
of forces, the act of acts. It is not the mass which is the most
important but the movement of the mass, the action of the mass;
nor is matter the matrix of life but the movement of matter.'[14]
In Vallejo's poem, the miners 'climbing up their future ruins' perform the perfectly dialectical function of closing the mineshaft as
'a profound symptom' – in other words it is they who close the
gulf between thought and action, between the subjective and the
objective, and between past and future, since their future comes
from the ruins of the past. The poem defines the miners in terms
of the kind of labour they do; so the destruction of the old system
must be by means of the 'corrosive dust' and the 'oxides' with
which they work and by means of which they produce. The
mouths (the organ of communication) are directly related to instruments of work, to 'wedges', 'anvils' and 'machines', so that the
mouth itself is a kind of tool in the general process. And thought
and behaviour are literally *mined out of the earth through work*,
are made visible in the 'order of their tombs, their malleable inductions', which are represented in dialectical conflict 'crowded
to the foot of fiery attributes'.

Vallejo creates a series of neologisms and alliterations – 'airente
amarillura conocieron los trístidos y tristes' – to convey the emotional impact of the exploited state which is, however, part of
pre-history by virtue of the fact that it is described in the past
tense. Compressed in the sentence are notions of anger (airente)
and suggestions of the withering of the old (metaloid) man.

In this poem, the puns and word-play which had abounded in

Trilce are replaced by a poetic language which is as complex, but which brings together work and language as the structuring principles of life. Thought and labour, theory and practice are united when man changes nature and himself:

> Craneados de labor,
> y calzados de cuero de vizcacha,
> calzados de senderos infinitos,
> y los ojos de físico llorar,
> creadores de la profundidad,
> saben, a cielo intermitente de escalera,
> bajar mirando para arriba,
> saben subir mirando para abajo.

> Craniumed with labour
> And shod with vizcacha pelts,
> Shod with infinite paths,
> And their eyes with a physical weeping,
> Oh creators of depth,
> They know, by the intermittent sky of the stairway,
> How to descend looking upward,
> They know how to ascend looking down.

The miners are 'craniumed' with labour both because thought is produced by their physical structure but also because their intellect is formed through work. Similarly, emotions are described in physical terms as a 'físico llorar'. Yet the miners are also related to the animal world; their feet covered in *vizcacha* skin (the *vizcacha* is a mole-like rodent) signal man's use of nature. The miner's activity is a *praxis* which unites the abstract and the concrete, the individual and the collective. In this social environment, the individual man's knowledge is an 'intermittent sky of the stairway', that is, an aspiration which is discontinuous (each man being a single step) and yet part of a total process which leads upward to a higher stage of humanity. The miners look upwards to the ideal as they go down their mines and they ascend with their eyes fixed below on the material world.

At this point, Vallejo breaks into a 'loor' or praise of the miners whose bodily organs never sleep, whose eyelashes he would have tempered like tools since it is their consciousness which brings into being the new man. They are the signs and portents of the future, organic and unalienated men whose language itself is to be organic and natural. 'May the grass, the lichen and the frog

grow in their *adverbs*, he writes, that is, in the part of speech
which indicates the mode in which an action is accomplished,
for it is in their activity that man and nature are reconciled. Ap-
propriately he wishes even their nuptial sheets to be 'felted with
iron' as if their very marriages forged the new man.

¡Loor a su naturaleza amarillenta,
a su linterna mágica,
a sus cubos y rombos, a sus percances plásticos,
a sus ojazos de seis nervios ópticos,
y a sus hijos que juegan en la iglesia
y a sus tácitos padres infantiles!
¡Salud, oh creadores, de la profundídad! . . . (Es formidable.)

Praise for their golden nature,
Their magic lantern,
Their cubes and rhombs, their malleable attributes,
Their great eyes with six optical nerves,
And for their sons playing in the church,
And for their silent, infantile fathers!
Your health! Oh Creators of depth! . . . (It's impressive.)

The miners are yellowish because they work underground, with
the 'magic lantern' that transforms nature, but they do so not in
any mystic fashion but by producing out of nature a geometry
and a destiny (percance) which cannot be separated from the
material world. Even the organ of perception, the eye, the 'ojazo'
(as if to emphasize their greater perception, something more
than mere *ojo*) has six optic nerves and is not some mystified
form of perception. So the 'silent, infantile fathers' of the past
have given birth to children who now can play in church, having
overcome the old religious and metaphysical view of man, having
created 'depths', the mineshaft of a new philosophy.

The Utopian dimension both in 'Los mineros' and in 'Gleba'
suggests the possibility of once again restoring power to speech.
Thus it is the *voice* of the miners which closes the separation of
one human being from another, their *voice* which both destroys
the old order and creates the new. As for the peasants to whom
orthodox Marxism had given a subordinate role, they are in
'Gleba' made into the ancestors of industrial man because they
have matured through suffering. They are 'hombres a golpes'
(men through beatings), wise elders with 'praised beards' and

'practical feet'. And once again, it is their *speech* which marks them out as different from the alienated intellectual:

> Hablan como les vienen las palabras,
> cambian ideas bebiendo
> orden sacerdotal de una botella;
> cambian también ideas tras de un árbol, parlando
> de escrituras privadas, de la luna menguante
> y de los ríos públicos! (¡Inmenso! ¡Inmenso! ¡Inmenso!) [15]

> They speak as words occur to them,
> And exchange ideas while drinking
> Priestly order of the bottle,
> They exchange ideas behind a tree, speaking
> Of private writings, of a waning moon
> And of public rivers! (Great! Great! Great!)

The directness of the peasant comes from an unmediated relationship with nature. He exchanges ideas 'while drinking', for the wine is his communion in every sense, being the product of his labour. Because the peasant's language refers to real things, there can really be an exchange of ideas and hence communication. The 'private writings, the 'waning moon', the 'public rivers' structure their very lives, defining private property, indicating the natural cycle and the water on which their very lives depend. But the genitive phrases also indicate the poet's own effort to produce a direct language which, in turn, involves a new structuring of reality. Thus the 'private writings' and the 'waning moon' seem to stand in opposition to the 'public rivers' which are not appropriated for private use. The peasant's strength also comes from nature and is summed up in the word 'palo' which means both 'tree' (and therefore refers to organic nature), 'stick' (and therefore suggests combat and aggression) and also has connotations of wooden or stupid (and therefore can refer to a stereotyped view of the peasant. Thus the 'palo' is an instrument of destruction and creation and is also the script with which the peasant writes his destiny; the 'gesto de palo, / acápites de palo, / la palabra colgando de otro palo' (Gesture like a stick, / Rubric of stick, / the words hanging from another stick).

All of this would seem to indicate an attempt to create a materialist poetry and a language that referred to man's experience as a worker. What remains problematic is the role of the poet himself. Indeed, in one of the poems of this period, 'Telluric and magnetic', the very process of composition reveals the difficulty of wedding this materialist poetry to his personal experience. For the *princeps* edition reveals that the poem originated as a hymn to the dialectics of nature, to the 'suelo teórico y práctico' (the theoretical and practical ground).[16] The first stage of writing produced twenty-two lines in which the personal adjective 'my' occured only twice. The specific references to Peru were all added during a further stage of composition. We may thus hazard the guess that Vallejo had first conceived a 'meditación agrícola' (the original title) which demonstrated the relation between the natural and the conceptual world. The revisions augmented both the personal and the Peruvian elements in the poem; for instance, the first line originally read 'Mecánica sincera y ascendida' and hence simply referred to nature as a system implying evolution. The final version reads '¡Mecánica sincera y peruanísima / la del cerro colorado!' thus converting nature into a Peruvian landscape and more specifically referring to the 'rosy hillside' of the poet's native Santiago de Chuco whose 'papales, cebadales, alfalfares', he also evokes in this section of the poem.

What 'Telúrica y magnética' represents, however, is a vast attempt to get back to the origins of thought itself, to relate conceptualization to labour and to man's conquest of nature. In this sense, it is a nostalgic poem, a work of reconstruction quite different from the destructive force of *Trilce*. Thus when in the opening stanza, the poet refers to:

> ¡Cultivos que integra una asombrosa jerarquía de útiles
> y que integran con viento los mujidos,
> las aguas con su sorda antigüedad!

> Plantings that an astonished hierarchy of tools now orders,
> And that the windy lowing of cattle
> And the dumbly ancient waters compose!

he is suggesting not only the interdependence of human, animal and vegetable life but also showing the very process by which, in separating himself from nature, man orders the world about him. Thus the key word is 'integrar' for the elements themselves – wind, earth and water – are not only meaningful because of their relation to human activity but are also the basic elements from which the human world is structured.

But perhaps the most striking feature of 'Telúrica y magnética' is the attempt to produce a demystified language which dispenses entirely with the myth of supernatural origins. Here we can see the influence of contemporary Soviet literature; and certainly the poem can be considered as an example of 'socialist realism'. For instance, when the poet recalls his origins, it is to retrace the evolution to its physical beginnings;

> ¡Cuaternarios maíces, de opuestos natalicios,
> los oigo por los pies cómo se alejan,
> los huelo retornar cuando la tierra
> tropieza con la técnica del cielo!
> ¡Molécula ex abrupto! ¡Atomo terso!

> Cuaternary maize, of nativities in opposition,
> I hear through my feet how they draw away,
> I smell them return when the earth
> Stumbles against the technics of the sky!
> Spontaneous molecule! Perfect atom!

We have to measure this passage against traditional 'lyrical' evocations of the native land. For Vallejo deliberately reminds the reader of the evolutionary history of corn, its birth in the quaternary era, its genetic structure and his own physical relationship to these origins which he 'hears with his feet'. He smells the return of these corn fields when 'earth / Stumbles against the technics of the sky' as if, in this apparently clumsy language, insisting on the accidental nature of the evolution process. Hence we have a disguised contrast with supernatural creation and the Christian account of the origin of man. The final line of the verse, which mentions 'the spontaneous molecule' and the 'perfect atom' suggest the common physical structures of the human being, of the animal and of nature. From this point onwards, the poem attemps to relate nature and more particularly the 'human fields' of Peru to the whole superstructure of social, intellectual and religious life.

> ¡Oh campos humanos!
> ¡Solar y nutricia ausencia de la mar,
> y sentimiento oceánico de todo!
> ¡Oh climas encontrados dentro del oro, listos!
> ¡Oh campo intelectual de cordillera,
> con religión, con campo, con patitos!
> ¡Paquidermos en prosa cuando pasan
> y en verso cuando páranse!
> ¡Roedores que miran con sentimiento judicial en torno!

¡Oh patrióticos asnos de mi vida!
¡Vicuña, descendiente nacional y graciosa de mi mono!
¡Oh luz que dista apenas un espejo de la sombra,
que es vida con el punto, y, con la línea, polvo
y que por eso acato, subiendo por la idea a mi osamenta!

O human fields!
Solar, nutritious absence of the sea,
And an oceanic sentiment of everything!
O climes within the gold, full of potential!
O intellectual field of the mountains,
With religion, and fields, and ducklings!
Pachyderms in prose when they pass
And in poetry when they halt!
Rodents gazing with judicial sentiment on all!
O patriotic asses of my life!
Vicuna, national and amusing descendent of my ape!
O light which is hardly a mirror's edge from shadow,
Which is life with the point, and, with the line, dust,
And which therefore I attend, climbing up the idea to my skeleton!

The 'solar, nutritious' absence of the sea and 'the oceanic sentiment of everything' refer us back to the great pre-Columbian
civilizations with their worship of the sun and their integration
of religion, state and work.[17] And this totality is reiterated later
on when he speaks of the 'intellectual field of the mountains', together with 'religion, and fields, and ducklings', thus sweeping
into one category the humble duck pond and intellectual and
religious life. These are the climes, 'within the gold, full of potential' – ready that is, for man in his totalizing activity. We have
here the exact poetic reproduction of Marx's notion of the 'uni-
versalizing' activity of man which is not simply life-activity as in
the animal but the labour which objectifies the species.[18] But
man does not relate himself only to inorganic nature but also to
the animal world; a series of animals – rodents, pachyderms, monkeys, vicunas – now come into the poem in order to illustrate the
scientific categorization of the animal world. They indicate a
taxonomy by which man orders the world around him and his
moral and intellectual life; so that the animals are not simply
there as elements of a perceptual field but are seen dialectically
in relation to man. So it is the structuring of consciousness itself
which underlies this section of the poem, and consciousness is
that 'light' which, he declares, 'is hardly a mirror's edge away
from shadow'. It is precisely this mirroring of the outer world –

in other words, man's capacity for reflecting on his own condition and relating it to the other – that makes him human. This is 'life with the point, and, with the line, dust' for this consciousness comes to an end at the full stop of death, after the linear journey of human life. Consciousness and conceptualization cannot be isolated from the body, and, reversing the Platonic hierarchy, Vallejo's idea *ascends* to his bone-structure rather than descending from the ideal into the material world.

This is as far as the first version of the poem took him. The facsimile edition shows that the last two-thirds of the poem were added later as pencilled additions to the first part. They appear to have been written in a different mood, and are half-humorous. And not only is creation demystified by the humour but also man's relation to nature. Now as he reviews the animals and the vegetable world of his childhood, of mother Peru whose hill-slopes are 'in fraganti' and to which he sardonically 'adheres', it is to separate nature into the consumable and the unconsumable. Thus the guinea-pig, no matter what its sex, is a delicacy to be eaten, while the condor is of no use to man:

> ¡Cuya o cuy para comerlos fritos
> con el bravo rocoto de los templos!
> (¿Cóndores? ¡Me friegan los cóndores!)

> Guinea-pigs to be eaten fried
> With the fierce *rocoto* of the temples!
> (Condores? Condores rub me the wrong way!)

Similarly the lichen can be saved since it is 'in formation', but the oak is there to be exploited. We recall here that the left-wing theorists of the time put the human being as firmly in the centre of creation as Christianity had done, not questioning the right to exploit nature. On the figurative plane of the poem, the use of metonymy and synecdoche suggests the organic relationship between the species and nature and not mere childhood associations. Thus nature and human life are brought into a meaningful totality even whilst the poet suggests that the human being's assumed sovereignty might be questioned. Yet it is precisely man's separation from nature which makes human experience whether in Peru or elsewhere universal. When the poet designates the native *llamas* by their scientific name, addressing them as 'Auquénidos

llorosos, almas mías', he both places them within a universal and
rational system and situates them in his own affective orbit. And
this relationship, in turn, is not arbitrary or given but has emerged
from reciprocal needs and functions. The poem ends on a personal
note. From the dialectics of nature, the origin of life and the
taxonomy of consciousness, the poet returns to his own past, to
the memory of the title-roofed houses of his native *sierra* with
allusion to himself as the citizen of two contrasting worlds:

> ¡Rotación de tardes modernas
> y finas madrugadas arqueológicas!
> ¡Indio después del hombre y antes de él!
> ¡Lo entiendo todo en dos flautas
> y me doy a entender en una quena!
> ¡Y lo demás, me las pelan! . . .
>
> Rotation of modern afternoons
> And rarified archeological early mornings.
> Indian after man and before him!
> I understand all, in two flutes,
> And I come to understand, in a *quena!*
> And the rest, oh they've got me going! . . .

Like Mariátegui, Vallejo places the Indian at the beginning of
human progress and also at its term since the collective form of
production provides a model for the future. The two 'flutes' by
which the poet understands perhaps represent this dual heritage
of Western thought and American practice, which he now in
turn communicates on his own native *quena*. The final flippant
line, '¡Y los demás, me las pelan! . . .' (And the rest, oh they've
got me going! . . .), marks the limit of conceptualization and
intuition alike. The poem himself and his 'flute' have become the
synthesis of the natural and the social, and represent species-man
acting and communicating on the universal level.

'Telúrica y magnética' is a poem which establishes through the
language itself a dialectic of humanity and nature. The energy of
nature is the universal force and man who is the only species that
has organized the forces of nature for means other than his immediate survival. This direct relationship is established by the
language which continually breaks with the pathetic fallacy in
order to show nature as the source of thought and feeling. Thus
the furrows themselves are 'inteligentes', the wood is 'Christian',

its trunk 'competent' not because these things are made vehicles
of human emotions but because the natural world has structured
human thought.

Thus the poet's nostalgia for origins reveals itself in that effort
to restore language to a source in nature itself.

Capitalism and alienation

'Los mineros', 'Gleba' and 'Telúrica y magnética' are related more
closely to *España, aparta de mí este cáliz* than to the rest of
Poemas humanos, most of which centre around the alienated individual and the reified products of modern society. However, it
is useful to contrast a poem such as 'Parado en una piedra' which
reflects the irrationality of capitalist society with the 'rationalism'
of 'Telúrica y magnética' since both use the figures of metonymy
and synecdoche but to opposite effect. The very figures which
in 'Telúrica y magnética' had suggested the interaction of man
and his environment, in 'Parado en una piedra' suggest the absence of a meaningful totality.

'Parado en una piedra' is a poem that epitomizes alienation. It
evokes the state of those 'fifteen million workers and their families', of that 'army without precedent in history' which Vallejo
had described in *Rusia en 1931.* Like many others at this time,
Vallejo believed that capitalist society was on the verge of breakdown, and lamented that the city which should be a 'social
hearth', the concrete realization of the ideals of co-operation, justice and universal happiness had become 'a cage of raw individualism'.[19] In his notebook of 1929–30, he speaks in similar
terms of the 'chaos and blind anarchy' of modern society.[20]

In 'Parado en una piedra', Vallejo takes the word 'parado' not
only in the figurative meaning of unemployed but literally as
someone who is motionless, as if humanity itself had been brought
to a halt by the economic crisis. The 'parado' is a specific kind of
man, the product of a capitalist society:[21]

> Parado en una piedra,
> desocupado,
> astroso, espeluznante,
> a la orilla del Sena, va y viene.
> Del río brota entonces la conciencia,

con peciolo y rasguños de árbol ávido:
del río sube y baja la ciudad, hecha de lobos abrazados.[22]

Completely stopped on a rock,
Out of a job,
Shabby and dishevelled,
On the bank of the Seine, he comes and goes.
Then consciousness erupts from the river,
With petioles and the outlines of an avid tree.
The city of wolves embracing rises from the river and sinks.

This ragged man reflects the horror of what has happened in a regime whose irrationality is reflected in the ebb and flow of the river (the economy goes up and down on the stock exchange). Capitalist society is one of 'wolves embracing', a Hobbesian organization based only on the need to control men's instinctual cruelty. The paradox is that a society which is inseparable from individualism reduces man to nothing:

El parado la ve yendo y viniendo,
monumental, llevando sus ayunos en la cabeza cóncava,
en el pecho sus piojos purísimos
y abajo
su pequeño sonido, el de su pelvis,
callado entre dos grandes decisiones,
y abajo,
más abajo,
un papelito, un clavo, una cerilla . . .

The stopped man watches it coming and going,
Monumental, carrying his fasts in his concave head,
His purest parasites on his breast,
And below,
His little noise, that of his pelvis,
Hushed between two great decisions,
And below,
Lower,
A little scrap of paper, a nail, a match . . .

The city is monumental, the individual concave, hungry, a host to lice, silenced between 'his two great decisions', and with 'his little noise, that of his pelvis' (the reproduction process). An individualistic society has trivialized man until all that can be said to be 'his' is his body. Below are 'a little scrap of paper, a nail and a match'; in other words, expression, suffering and consciousness are reduced to three products which represent useless detritus, reflecting the alienation and the atomization of the world.

For the poet this is the visible proof of the collapse of civilization, and he now addresses himself directly to his fellow workers, pointing to the tragedy of modern man:

> ¡Este es, trabajadores, aquel
> que en la labor sudaba para afuera,
> que suda hoy para adentro su secreción de sangre rehusada!

> This, workers, is that man
> Who sweated outward in his labour,
> Who sweats inward today his secretion of blood denied!

For to refuse man work is to refuse man's raison d'être, what makes a human being. Man is the producer of cannon, a weaver and builder of pyramids (and hence of hierarchical societies) and this very production is now turned against him because of the class nature of society.

> Fundidor del cañón, que sabe cuantas zarpas son acero,
> tejedor que conoce los hilos positivos de sus venas,
> albañil de pirámides,
> constructor de descensos por columnas
> serenas, por fracasos triunfales,
> parado individual entre treinta millones de parados,
> andante en multitud,
> ¡qué salto el retratado en su talón
> y qué humo el de su boca ayuna, y cómo
> su talle incide, canto a canto, en su herramienta atroz, parada,
> y qué idea de dolorosa válvula en su pómulo!

> The cannon founder, who knows how many claws are of steel,
> The weaver who knows the positive threads of his veins,
> Mason of pyramids,
> Builder of descents through serene
> Columns, through triumphant failures,
> One individual, stopped, among thirty million halted persons,
> Walking in a multitude,
> What a leap is depicted in his heel
> And what smoke, that of his fasting mouth, and how
> His figure coincides, line by line, with his atrocious tool, stopped short,
> And what an idea of dolorous valves in his cheekbone!

The worker as producer, as metal-worker, builder, weaver is subject to exploitation, symbolized by the 'claws' and the pyramid; he gives his labour and his blood, as the human opposite of the inhumanity of the system, he whose 'triumphant failures' consti-

tute a new consciousness. But he is also the unemployed individual among thirty million whose 'leap' into the collective future
is already 'depicted in his heel' since it is the worker's journey
into the future, his class-consciousness, which will revolutionize
society. (At the end of the poem, there will be a 'motor' in his
heel as if the very crisis accelerates him). The worker is not
simply the victim of the capitalist system but its destroyer, smoke
issues from his mouth, his body cuts, a valve beats in his cheek.
He is literally the motor force of the future, though paradoxically
at a standstill, along with the tools which should be used to
benefit society. And because nature is man's body, nature too
must come to a halt with crisis:

> También parado el hierro frente al horno
> paradas las semillas con sus sumisas síntesis al aire,
> parados los petróleos conexos,
> parada en sus auténticos apóstrofes la luz,
> parados de crecer los laureles,
> paradas en un pie las aguas móviles
> y hasta la tierra misma, parada de estupor ante este paro.

> Also stopped is the iron that stands before the furnace,
> The seeds with their submissive synthesis suspended in mid-air,
> Stopped are the connected petroleums,
> Stopped is the light in its authentic apostrophes,
> The laurels stopped from growing,
> The rapid waters halted on one foot,
> And even the earth itself, stopped in a stupor confronted with this
>   stoppage.

Nature is seen dialectically as a 'synthesis' of seeds, as the conflict
of molecules, a combustion of petroleum, though without human
labour the process is halted. It is not that nature is stopped but
that the dialectic of man and nature has been interrupted, and
hence history itself as the progress of man is in suspense. The
poem builds up to a climax of frustrations which are directly
related to the class system and the lack of social justice:

> ¡qué salto el retratado en sus tendones!
> ¡qué transmisión entablan sus cien pasos!
> ¡cómo chilla el motor en su tobillo!
> ¡cómo gruñe el reloj, paseándose impaciente a sus espaldas!
> ¡cómo oye degutir a los patrones
> el trago que le falta, camaradas,
> y el pan que se equivoca de saliva,
> y, oyéndolo, sintiéndolo, en plural, humanamente,

¡cómo clava el relámpago
su fuerza sin cabeza en su cabeza!
y lo que hacen, abajo, entonces, ¡ay!
más abajo, camaradas,
el papelucho, el clavo, la cerilla,
el pequeño sonido, el piojo padre!

What a leap is that depicted in his tendons!
What a transmission is boarded up in his one hundred steps!
How the engines in his ankles shriek!
How the clock grunts, walking up and down impatiently at his back!
How he hears the bosses guzzling
The drink that he lacks, comrades,
And the bread that chooses the wrong saliva,
And, hearing it, sensing it, in the plural, humanly,
How the lightning-bolt nails
Its headless strength into his head!
And what they are doing, down with it then, ay!
And down, comrades, with
The stinking scrap of paper, the nail, the match,
The little noise, the father louse!

In an earlier version of the poem, Vallejo had addressed the
'parado' as 'tú', referring to 'tus cien pasos', 'tu tobillo' etc. The
change is significant, because while putting the unemployed
worker on display, so to speak, as an example of the waste and
irrationality of the system, Vallejo's very protest is addressed to
a public, to 'workers' who in the course of the poem become
'comrades', thus indicating the way out of the impasse of individualism. Under capitalism everything is out of joint. Bread has
mistaken its saliva since it feeds the rich and not the worker,
who, nevertheless feels and hears in plural, 'humanly', and understands the irrationality of the disaster which like lightning strikes
blindly. So the poem comes full circle to the point where it
began, with the individual tragically reduced to nothing, left with
the fragments of his self, and his individualism, 'his nail' and his
'match', 'his little noise', the 'louse' that parasitically feeds on him
(as society does) and his 'papelucho', his great 'role' which is no
less than that of transforming society. The irony, however, lies in
the fact that 'clavo', 'papelucho' and 'cerillo' no longer have symbolic functions. They are parts without a whole, metonymy and
synecdoche divorced from cause and effect and from any totality. 'Parado en una piedra' thus stands as the reverse of 'Telúrica
y magnética' since in the former human products no longer belong

to the producer and can no longer be related to the totality of theory and practice. Against the 'cerro colorado', we have to set this city of 'wolves embracing'.

The negative dialectic

The only philosophy which can be responsibly practised in face of despair is the attempt to contemplate all things as they would present themselves from the standpoint of redemption: knowledge has no light but that shed on the world by redemption; all else is reconstruction, mere technique. Perspectives must be fashioned that displace and estrange the world, reveal it to be, with its rifts and crevices, as indigent and distorted as it will appear one day in the messianic light.   Adorno[23]

Since the *Poemas humanos* are in no way created out of a definitive aesthetics but rather represent a series of explorations, the dialectics of nature and of society which inform 'Telúrica y magnética' are themselves put in a critical perspective by other poems. Thus we have to be aware of the 'intertextuality' within the poems of this period since they constantly reflect back and forth over the fate of the individual. It is quite conceivable that even while Vallejo was writing a poem like 'Telúrica y magnética' the manipulation of nature implied in materialism came to seem suspect. The irony of 'cuya o cuy para comerlos fritos' and 'Me friegan los cóndores' suggest his awareness of a distorting *hubris*. And he subsequently wrote three apocalyptic poems, 'La rueda del hambriento' (The hungry man's rack), 'Los nueve monstruos' (The nine monsters) and 'Los desgraciados' (The unhappy ones) which turn, as it were, the full force of a negative dialectic on man. Two of these poems have received extensive attention from critics and cannot be discussed in detail here. Both 'La rueda del hambriento' and 'Los nueve monstruos' place the individual and society in that pitiless 'messianic' light (which Adorno mentions) to show them hyperbolically 'hungry'. In 'La rueda del hambriento', the hungry man is born out of his own mouth and comes 'shouting, pushing and defecating into the world'. 'My stomach empties out, so does my intestine, / Poverty extracts me from my own teeth, / Caught on a little toothpick by my shirt-sleeve.' This hungry man demands not bread but a stone, 'something on which finally to drink, to eat, to live and to rest upon'; thus his very emptiness requires an impossible satisfaction – impossible because he is born of emptiness itself. What he finds, however, is his own estranged self. 'I find a strange form, my shirt / Is very torn and dirty / And I have nothing, this is horrible . . .'.

It would seem that Vallejo considered alienation and absurdity as ontological categories. Plainly, separation from nature, the moment when the human being became 'parado', is the source of the hubris which distorts his relation with nature and sets him on a course in which further domination leads to even greater suffering. So, in 'Los nueve monstruos', suffering increases faster than time itself, 'at thirty minutes the second, step by step'. If this suffering has its origin in the 'duplication' and repetition inherent in the reproduction process, it is also clear that the division of labour increases alienation:

> Jamás, hombres humanos,
> hubo tánto dolor en el pecho, en la solapa, en la cartera,
> en el vaso, en la carnicería, en la aritmética![24]

> Never, human men,
> Was there so much pain in breast, coat-lapels, wallet,
> In glasses, in butcher-shop, in arithmetic!

'Breast', 'coat-lapels', 'wallet', 'glasses', 'butcher-shop', 'arithmetic' are all parts which suppose a system; indeed they imply a *social* system that produces commodities, shops and methods of calculation. Yet they are bonded only by suffering; thus, in so far as the health of individualistic society is shown in its domination of nature, the symptom of this is the increase in suffering:

> Jamás, señor ministro de salud, fue la salud
> más mortal
> y la migraña extrajo tánta frente de la frente!
> Y el mueble tuvo en su cajón, dolor,
> el corazón, en su cajón, dolor,
> la lagartija en su cajón, dolor.

> Crece la desdicha, hermanos hombres,
> más pronto que la máquina, a diez máquinas, y crece
> con la res de Rousseau, con nuestras barbas;
> crece el mal por razones que ignoramos
> y es una inundación con propios líquidos,
> con propio barro y propia nube sólida.

> Never, Mr Minister of Health, was health
> More mortal
> Or did migraines extract so much forehead from foreheads!
> And the chest had pain in its drawer;

The heart, in its drawer, pain;
The newt, in its drawer, pain.

Misfortune grows, brothers, men,
Faster than the machine, by ten machines, and it grows
With Rousseau's cow, with our beards;
Evil grows for reasons we do not know,
And it is a flooding of its own waters,
With its own mud and its own solid cloud.

'Mueble', 'corazón' and 'lagartija' represented items of a taxonomy which separates man from his products, feeling from expression and the human from the animal. Yet though these categories are plainly produced by humanity in the course of its history, they do not help us to understand or prevent the suffering which stems from that very separation. Thus paradoxically, suffering increases faster than the machine itself, increases moreover with the maturity of man (with his beard!) and with his socialization. The 'res de Rousseau' is a triple pun which combines *res* meaning head of cattle with *res* meaning thing but also refers to the *res publica* of Rousseau and hence conflates the notion that man is a social and 'reified' animal.

It would be wrong, however, to see the poem simply as a statement deploring human progress because it brings suffering in its wake. For the 'nine monsters' which plague man represent nature's vengeance on the human animal which has tried to escape from nature and dominate it through the machine. Nine is the number of gestation, a magic number which transforms triumphant man from hero into victim, from active into passive:

> y esta oreja da nueve campanadas a la hora
> del rayo, y nueve carcajadas
> a la hora del trigo, y nueve sones hembras
> a la hora del llanto, y nueve cánticos
> a la hora del hambre y nueve truenos
> y nueve látigos, menos un grito.

> And this ear tolls nine times at the hour
> Of lightning, and gives nine guffaws
> At the hour of wheat, and nine female sounds
> At the hour of weeping, and nine canticles
> At the hour of hunger, and nine thunderclaps
> And nine lashes, one shout till.

The very caesura in these lines marks both a discontinuity and repetition in which the main pattern is the number nine. The ear emits sound in response to certain events – 'the hour of wheat', 'the hour of weeping' etc. – a distortion of function which the repetition turns into hysteria or the obsessions of madness. And just as the madman projects his obsessions onto the outer world so the ear makes apocalyptic noises in response to all kinds of events and emotions. The nine is the biological programming that underlies all activity and one single cry alone can be subtracted from the cacophany since this is the cry that breaks the monotony, the cry of a new life.[25]

There is a difference between this, however and the ironies of *Trilce* for 'Los nueve monstruos' suggests a greater degree of desperation within a more concrete world. In *Trilce,* the instability of the sign had both concealed and revealed the truth which the poet, nevertheless, sought in and through language. Vallejo by no means loses this concern in *Poemas humanos* though the poems are now far more likely to bring together the randomness of objects juxtaposed within a single perceptual frame. The subject's being in the world is marked by fragments, perceptions in which objects of daily use are conceived as both discrete yet related to the individual by the suffering that bonds all things. Thus the pain of existence reaches into cinemas, 'nails us in gramophones / Un-nails us in our beds, falls perpendicularly / Onto our tickets, onto our letters'. Nor are these 'symbolic' objects charged with significance because of their place in the hidden design of a microcosmic poem but rather are things which because they are *used* conceal the fact that the user is also a part of nature. There is therefore an imbalance in the human condition which has turned it into nightmare, into the haunting dream of reason. 'The dream of reason engenders monsters' says Goya and the phrase could stand as epigraph of the poem.

When at the end of the poem, a subject appears, the strangely subdued 'I' can only claim that he is sad as a result of this universal suffering. Yet this sadness is specifically associated with the crucifixion of nature – of the humble turnip and onion, of cereal turned to flour, salt made dust and wine made into a 'ecce-homo' (into a powerless symbol). The relation of man and nature is thus one of domination not of communion. The individual consumes the products of nature, without redeeming them or himself. The conquest of nature, the organization of industry and the exploitation of man by man all represent an immense superstructure whose base is a humble creature haunted by the monsters created by his own consciousness.

Like Lorca's 'Poet in New York', apocalypse does not follow simply from the crisis of capitalism for this is only an extreme and distorted form of a major fault in human consciousness itself. With Horkheimer, Vallejo could have agreed that: 'this mentality of man as the master can be traced back to the first chapters of Genesis';[26] hence the urgency of tone in 'Los nueve monstruos' and 'Los desgraciados' both of which view the subject from the vantage point of desperation. It is this too which imbues the last line of the poem, 'Desgraciadamente, hombres humanos / hay, hermanos, muchísimo que hacer' with irony. For in reality, man is 'desgraciado' (or *without grace*) and precisely because of this, he cannot expect salvation; man alone can originate a change which has to go far beyond a five-year plan for industry or the socialization of the means of production.

It is worthwhile looking at 'Los desgraciados' in detail both because it projects this apocalyptic vision with extraordinary force and because it does so by means of a striking Cartesian separation between the speaking subject and the body.

Ya va a venir el día; da
cuerda a tu brazo, búscate debajo
del colchón, vuelve a pararte
en tu cabeza, para andar derecho,
Ya va a venir el día, ponte el saco.

Ya va a venir el día; ten
fuerte en la mano a tu intestino grande, reflexiona,
antes de meditar, pues es horrible
cuando le cae a uno la desgracia
y se le cae a uno a fondo el diente.

Necesitas comer, pero, me digo,
no tengas pena, que no es de pobres
la pena, el sollozar junto a su tumba;
remiéndate, recuerda,
confía en tu hilo blanco, fuma, pasa lista
a tu cadena y guárdala detrás de tu retrato.
Ya va a venir el día, ponte el alma.

Ya va a venir el día; pasan,
han abierto en el hotel un ojo,
azotándolo, dándole con un espejo tuyo . . .
¿Tiemblas? Es el estado remoto de la frente
y la nación reciente del estómago.

Roncan aún . . . ¡Qué universo se lleva este ronquido!
¡Cómo quedan tus poros, enjuiciándolo!
¡Con cuántos doses ¡ay! estás tan solo!
Ya va a venir el día, ponte el sueño.

Ya va a venir el día, repito
por el órgano oral de tu silencio
y urge tomar la izquierda con el hambre
y tomar la derecha con la sed; de todos modos,
abstente de ser pobre con los ricos,
atiza
tu frío, porque en él se integra mi calor, amada víctima.
Ya va a venir el día, ponte el cuerpo.

Ya va a venir el día;
la mañana, la mar, el meteoro, van
en pos de tu cansancio, con banderas,
y, por tu orgullo clásico, las hienas
cuentan sus pasos al compás del asno,
la panadera piensa en ti,
el carnicero piensa en ti, palpando
el hacha en que están presos
el acero y el hierro y el metal; jamás olvides
que durante la misa no hay amigos.
Ya va a venir el día, ponte el sol.

Ya viene el día; dobla
el aliento, triplica
tu bondad rencorosa
y da codos al miedo, nexo y énfasis,
pues tú, como se observa en tu entrepierna y siendo
el malo ¡ay! inmortal,
has soñado esta noche que vivías
de nada y morías de todo . . .[27]

Already the day is coming; wind
Up your arm, look under
The mattress, stand ready again,
In your head, to go straight,
Already the day is coming, put on your coat.

Already the day is coming; hold on
Tight to your large intestine, reflect
Before brooding, for it is horrible
When misery falls on one
And one's very teeth fall back into one.

You need to eat, but, I tell myself,
Don't bear this pain, it's not up to the poor,
This pain, this sobbing beside the tomb;

Pull yourself together, remember,
Trust your white thread, smoke a cigarette, go back over
Every link of your chain then put it behind your picture of yourself.
Already the day is coming, put on your soul.

Already the day is coming; they pass by,
They have opened one eye in the hotel,
Lashing it, holding it to a mirror of yours . . .
Are you shivering? It's that distant state, the forehead,
That newborn nation of the stomach.
And they are still snoring . . . ! What universe endures this snore!
But how your very pores bring it to judgment!
Among how many twos – ay! – you are so alone!
Already the day is coming, put on your dream.

Already the day is coming; I repeat this
Through the oral organ of your silence
And it impels you to go left with hunger
And to go right with thirst; in any case,
Refuse to be poor with the rich,
Stir up
Your coldness, because there my warmth is integrated, beloved victim.
Already the day is coming, put on your body.

Already the day is coming;
Morning, sea, and meteor follow
Your fatigue, with banners flying,
And, because of your classic pride, the hyenas
Move in step with the ass,
The baker's wife is thinking of you,
The butcher is thinking of you, feeling
The cleaver that imprisons
Steel and iron and metal; never forget
That during mass there are no friends.
Already the day is coming, put on your sun.

The day is coming now; double
Your breathing, triple
Your grudging good will
And elbow your fear, the nexus and emphasis,
For you, as one can see in your crotch, and evil
Being (ay!) immortal,
Have dreamed tonight that you were living
On nothing and dying of everything . . .

The voice which speaks during a wakeful, insomniac night proclaims the inevitable dawn; yet by constantly repeating, 'Ya va a venir el día', the 'day' comes to seem more than the end of night. It is as if every day were judgment day and apocalypse. Yet

clearly the usual sense of day as marking the awakening of consciousness as well as of the body is now displaced; awakening,
we normally forget the body. Here, however, the voice orders the
individual to wind himself up, to meditate on his intestine and
to stand on his head (thus reversing the priority of consciousness). He must also review his chain and hide it behind the portrait of his identity. Thus the opening of the poem puts into
reverse the kind of meditation that Saint Ignatius would recom-
mend in the *Spiritual Exercises* in which the devotee is taught
how to subdue and forget his body.[28] In Vallejo's poem, on the
contrary, the individual is told to meditate consciously on what
is normally forgotten and then to hide the chain which ties him
to the species behind his own identity.[29]

To awaken to the self is to awaken to this special awareness of
the body as a disparate set of functions which nevertheless form
the totality which is the individual. All that is comprehended between the 'remote state of the forehead' and the 'recent nation of
the stomach' belongs to that totaliy. Only in the fourth verse does
this self awaken to others and it is only now that 'they' are mentioned. 'They' pass by; 'they' have opened up an eye in the hotel
'lashing it, holding it to a mirror'.[30] Thus while the universe
snores, there is a wakeful element in the totality, something which
opens the eye of perception and keeps it open by punishing it
with a mirror. There is little doubt that Vallejo is here referring
to the narcissistic nature of consciousness. As Feuerbach had
implied, we are human beings precisely because of our consciousness of the other[31] and in Vallejo's poem the eye of consciousness
is kept awake through suffering inflicted by others.

The poem puts the relation between body and consciousness
into a new perspective which inverts the usual value systems.
Everything that in another context might suggest hope – morning,
the sea, the meteor (which occur as images in the poem) – are
here made into the mere aftermath of individuation. The notion
of an individual destiny thus comes to appear illusory and the
passage through life is depicted as a series of asinine footsteps
which are counted by scavenging hyenas. Man as individual is sac-
rificed by social man – by the baker and butcher whose thoughts
follow him. Thus man as victim is set against man as producer
for even though butchers and bakers are human beings, they are
here shown in their role as species-man.[32] Hence the poem subtly

indicates the part played by division of labour which, instead of saving the individual from his fate, only makes him a victim of his own kind. The ending of the poem, 'You dream that tonight you lived on nothing and died of everything' sums up the role of the individual since there is no basis for existence apart from the species. The Apocalypse for which the poem prepares the 'desgraciados' (literally, those without grace) is the immolation of the self. Only by recognizing the self as doomed can we really begin to conceive of a *human* race.

This poem whose energy stems from the sense of urgency transmitted by the repetition of 'Ya va a venir el día' creates the impression of spoken communication. As such, it represents a supreme effort to break out of the silence and solitude of print, to *utter* words and achieve that immediacy of communication which has been lost with the end of oral culture. This counterpoint between the solitude of print and the immediacy of the spoken word provides the *Poemas humanos* with much of their energy. Vallejo never read his poems aloud to large audiences as Neruda later did but the 'Sermon upon death' and many other of the *Poemas humanos* represent astonishing efforts to make print translate the presence of the human voice.

8

THE DESTRUCTION OF PROMETHEUS: *POEMAS HUMANOS*

Dicen que cuando mueren así los que se acaban,
¡ay! mueren fuera del reloj, la mano
agarrada a un zapato solitario.

They say that when those die who have come to an end,
ay! that they die outside the clock, their hand
holding tight a solitary shoe.[1]

Vallejo

The *Poemas humanos* are shot through with the sadness of the 1930s, when disasters were large and the human individual seemed of little account. Massed at Fascist rallies, standing in dole queues, shipped off to concentration camps, people were dispensable parts of a powerful system. Chaplin's little tramp, struggling to hold on to the shreds of dignity, had become the epitome of the lonely individual's tragi-comedy in a dehumanized world.[2] It was war – and first of all the Spanish Civil War – that paradoxically restored something of a sense of purpose, or at least gave individuals an intenser glow. For this reason Vallejo's 'Spain' poems are not only complementary to *Poemas humanos* but represent, so to speak, the apocalyptic backdrop against which man's obsession with the trivial is heightened to grotesque proportions, somewhat like Orwell's condemned man avoiding a puddle of water on the way to his execution.

The *Poemas humanos* and the 'Spain' poems are more than the schizoid halves in the poetic production of a Vallejo who had a public and a private personality. Rather they confirm that it was not possible for him to separate man from the society he had made and whose values he has internalized. Even Death and Birth are not grasped in terms of archetypal myth but rather in their specific manifestations, with man's allotted span reduced to a 'stumbling between two stars', a mere parenthesis between two moments of nonbeing, a losing battle in which he appropriates the objects of his environment only to find that they are in no sense really *his.* In the poem, 'Esto / sucedió entre dos párpados' (It / happened between two eyelids), which provides the epigraph to this chapter, the dying man holds tight to a solitary shoe which has been *produced* by human hand; something which the individual regards as *his* is no longer so. There can be no more exact image of reification[3] nor of man's alienation from others, trapped as he is in his lonely linear cage.

If death assumes supreme importance in these poems, it is because (to use a cliché) it is a moment of truth; though in capitalist society the lonely Passion of the cross is a less appropriate symbol than the conveyor belt to the grave. To diminish the importance of death is to lessen the importance of life; so that in a world of reified objects, man has no mirror in which to find a reflection of his dignity and worth. This 'fall' translates itself into this collection of poems, whose central devices are synecdoche and anti-climax, a poetry in which the subject is constantly forced to accept humble and tautological propositions about the self like 'I'm here because I'm here.'[4] In many of the poems, he is reduced to affirming his existence by touching himself:

> luego no tengo nada y hablo solo,
> reviso mis semestres
> y para henchir mi vértebra, me toco.[5]

> Then I have nothing and I talk to myself.
> I go over my semesters,
> And to swell my spine, I touch myself.

The poet, Narcissus-like, cannot get beyond the epicentre of the body, or rather can only get beyond with difficulty. The daily battle on this frontier of death is the main scenario of the *Poemas humanos,* one in which civilization has turned into a domesticity that is a kind of living death.

Summarized in this bald fashion, the bulk of the *Poemas humanos* seem out of keeping with the 'social poems' discussed in chapter 7, though they do not imply anything other than a materialist standpoint. Yet the loneliness of the subject who enacts their desperation makes even the project of a social animal appear Utopian and, more than this, would seem to make nonsense of any possibility of a language that truly communicates. What is at risk is both the future of man and the future of poetry insofar as poetry ideally supposes a language that binds men.[6]

The restatement of paradox

What immediately strikes a reader of the *Poemas humanos* is the setting of the trivial within the perspective of death, which recalls the poetry of the Golden Age. The traces are there in the use of rhetorical figures, in the binary patterns of imagery, whose opposing tensions are brought together in the *summa* at the end of the poem, in the recurrence of certain conventional metaphors like 'gold', 'snow', 'light'. Above all, paradox becomes of central importance, though it is not identical with seventeenth-century paradox which referred to an apparently untrue, outrageous or irrational statement which, in the light of Christian belief (or commonly accepted practice), could be seen to be true. The rich man, according to Christian doctrine, is really poor, for it is hard for him to enter the kingdom of Heaven. The poor man is spiritually rich. What at first reading seems to be a similar paradox in Vallejo's poems turns out to be very different, for there is no totalizing system to turn the paradox into common-sense:

> Ladrones de oro, víctimas de plata:
> el oro que robara yo a mis víctimas
> 　　¡rico de mi olvidándolo;
> la plata que robara a mis ladrones,
> 　　¡pobre de mi olvidándolo!

> Execrable sistema, clima en nombre del cielo, del bronquio
> 　　　　　　　　　　　　y la quebrada,
> la cantidad enorme de dinero que cuesta el ser probre . . .[7]

> Thieves of gold, victims of silver:
> The gold that I might rob from my victims
> 　　How wealthy I am if I forget it!
> The silver that I might rob from my thieves,
> 　　How poor I am if I forget it!

> Atrocious system, climate in the name of heaven, of bronchial
> 　　　　　　　　　　　　tube and bankruptcy,
> The amount of money it takes to be poor . . .

The lines occur in one of the many poems which begin on the edge of silence 'Por último sin ese buen aroma sucesivo . . .' (Finally, without this good successive aroma . . .) in which the poet makes an inventory of his life in the shadow of death, a moment which for the Christian permits the final truthful stock-taking and prepares the solemn transition to the next world. But here we have 'climate' instead of heaven. There is no ultimate system to which to refer and we have to read the poem in full awareness of this, knowing that in death the poet must be beyond both evil and good. Terms like gold and silver are no longer metaphors for the imperishable realms of the next world but simply degraded reminders that values are now dependent on exchange rather than use. 'Money', says Marx, is this *'overturning power* both against the individual and against the bonds of society etc., which claims to be *essences* in themselves. It transforms fidelity into infidelity, love into hate, hate into love, virtue into vice, vice into virtue, servant into master, master into servant, idiocy into intelligence and intelligence into idiocy.'[8] In the poet's account book, 'gold' and 'silver' represent the relative values which enable men to distinguish between moral actions, but they also reveal the absence of justice and equality in the world since there is no way of balancing gold with silver. Values like 'rich' and 'poor', moreover, are regulated by human beings within a system in which there are no longer absolutes, where there is no longer a possibility of expiation and redemption. This is, indeed, a climate of 'bronchial tube and bankruptcy' since each man is as unfortunate as the next; engaged in a complex of relationships with others, each man is poor since there is no ultimate satisfaction. The reified apparatus of values will survive but not the men within it.

Gold/silver, rich/poor are pairs and binary opposites which help to structure many of the poems (others are hot/cold, motion/rest) and whose point of intersection is man himself. But more than this, the group of values – 'gold', 'silver', 'poor' – is particularly evocative since it is not simply metaphorical but refers to the operation of a society based on capital whose intricate complexities are in inverse proportion to the well-being of individuals. 'The amount of money it takes to be poor' is not simply an eternal truism but refers quite specifically to a moment when material progress had failed most dramatically to supply the material and spiritual needs of man. The fact that gold is the alchemical metal, that into which base metal is transformed, also makes this figure the test for man's ability to transform himself and redeem the evolution process. Meanwhile what had appeared to be paradox turns out to be *contradiction* within reality itself.

The bleakness of many of the *Poemas humanos* is unquestionable, a bleakness, however, that is solemnized by a language whose appropriateness conditions derive from death. While, on the one hand, the colloquial demeans existence, confirming the automatic nature of our responses, heightened language makes life portentous. Where portentousness is inappropriate, poetry turns into hollow sound or parody. Who now takes Hugo's prophetic tones seriously? Vallejo's poems, however, function on a knife-edge between life and death and between tragedy and farce, for though he behaves as if every moment might be his last, he cannot, for all that, entirely rescue his life from triviality. A particularly fine example of this is the poem 'Escarnecido, aclimatado al bien . . .' (Ridiculed, acclimatized to good . . .), which like a seventeenth-century poem does not shrink from playing with words at the threshold of the grave.

Escarnecido, aclimatado al bien, mórbido, hurente,
doblo el cabo carnal y juego a copas,
donde acaban en moscas los destinos,
donde comí y bebí de lo que me hunde.

Monumental adarme,
féretro numeral, los de mi deuda,
los de mi deuda, cuando caigo altamente,
ruidosamente, amoratadamente.

Al fondo, es hora,
entonces, de gemir con toda el hacha
y es entonces el año del sollozo,
el día del tobillo,
la noche del costado, el siglo del resuello.
Cualidades estériles, monótonos satanes,
del flanco brincan,
del ijar de mi yegua suplente;
pero, donde comí, cuánto pensé!
pero cuánto bebí, donde llorré!

Así es la vida, tal
como es la vida, allá, detrás
del infinito; así, espontáneamente,
delante de la sien legislativa.[9]

Ridiculed, acclimatized to good, morbid, scorching,
I round the carnal cape and play cards,
Where destinies end up as houseflies,
Where I ate and drank from what is sinking me.

Monumental dram,
Numeral catafalque, that is my debt,
That is my debt, when impressively,
Noisily, lividly, I fall.

At bottom, then, it is time
To moan with the whole axe,
And thus it is the year of the whimper,
The day of the ankle,
The night of the ribs, the century of wheezing.
Sterile qualities, monotonous satans,
They bound from the side,
From the flank, of my substitute mare;
But, where I ate, how much I thought!
But how much I drank, where I wept!

Life's like that, just
As life is, over there, behind
Infinity; thus, spontaneously,
In front of the legislative forehead.

'Escarnecido . . .' is grounded in a paradox which occurs in
Trilce and which could be summed up by Borges's line 'Time is
the fire that consumes me but I am the fire.' But whereas in
Trilce 7 ('Rumbé sin novedad . . .') the search for essential
being is enacted (vainly) within the sexual encounter, in 'Escarnecido' the whole of the body becomes a playing-card in the
losing gamble with death. Yet the interest of the poem is in the
way that language itself is anchored to bodily experience, being
literally 'bodied forth'. And this is also true of values, so that
thought, emotion and sin are expressed as bodily acts. In *Trilce*,
the poet had asked, 'How can I speak of self when time destroys
any possibility of identity?' In *Poemas humanos,* the body *is* time,
is the perpetual game of chance with the grave as prize. The very
word which begins the poem, 'Escarnecido', combines the notion
of being punished and shamed in the flesh, for though etymologically it has no connection with *carne* (flesh), the context of
the poem makes us read the word as 'es-carne-cido'.

As in 'Por último . . .', the relativity of values is suggested by
'climate'; at the beginning of the poem, the poet describes himself as 'acclimatized to good', a notion that destroys any possibility of moral choice by suggesting natural adaptation to the
conditions of existence; but this is by no means a healthy state:
the poet also describes himself as 'mórbido' and 'hurente' (for
urente)[10] that is, as 'morbid' and 'scorching' (a term used to describe the physical symptoms of kidney and venereal diseases).
The attributes of the individual, 'escarnecido, aclimatado . . .
mórbido, hurente' all refer to his physical being. This mortally
sick individual rounds 'the carnal cape and plays cards' – an

activity that offers a minefield of possibilities. Vallejo had originally written, 'doblo el *golfo* carnal' but changed this to 'cabo'
probably because of the punning association with *acabar*, a verb
that appears in the next line. Rounding the carnal cape, the poet
plays with 'copas', a Spanish playing-card which bears the design
of a cup and is therefore associated with the eating and drinking
of the final lines of the stanza. The three figurative levels of life
as a journey (which ends with him sinking), life as a game of
chance and life as feast are meshed together by means of paronomasia, and anchor the only abstractions in the verse – 'bien' and
'destinos' – in physical reality. Man's limits are firmly prescribed
by the body, the 'cabo carnal' which has eaten and drunk of that
in which it drowns, i.e., of the food of this existence but not the
spiritual food of eternity. Vallejo turns upside-down the Golden
Age paradox which had made this life into a living death and
death into the ultimate reality; instead he asserts, 'where I *ate,*
how much I *thought!* / But how much I *drank*, where I *wept!*',
thus stressing the links between consciousness, suffering and
bodily survival.

The context makes it clear that, between the brackets of birth
and death, our notions of sin, guilt, time, emotion and thought
are man-created. Because there is no absolute, nobody can for-
give us our sins. Human beings have 'fallen' into the material
world not from God's spiritual emanation but because like all
other material things they are subject to the physical law of
gravity ('monumental adarme'). The 'fall' is not a Christian or
neo-Platonist fall but rather a fall in a conception of humanity,
from a position near the angels to one firmly on the ground. The
individual falls 'impressively', 'noisily', 'bruisedly' because of the
height of his former pretensions; and the 'noise' and 'bruise' are
physical traces of conflict with the world. Even duration is measured by the body, so that the poet refers to 'the year of the
whimper', 'the day of the ankle', 'the night of the ribs', 'the century of wheezing'. Because the individual's existence is thus
physical, he can do no more than conclude, 'life's like that', for
he cannot project beyond his own ephemerality. The last verse
of the poem ends with a catalogue in the manner of Golden Age
poems, yet offers no more unity than the *locus* of the poet's existence:

> Yace la cuerda así al pie del violín,
> cuando hablaron del aire, a voces, cuando

hablaron muy despacio del relámpago.
Se dobla así la mala causa, vamos
de tres en tres a la unidad; así
se juega a copas
y salen a mi encuentro los que aléjanse,
acaban los destinos en bacterias
y se debe todo a todos.

Thus at the foot of the violin lies the string,
When they talked of air, shouting, when
They talked quite slowly of the lightning-bolt.
Thus we doubled the point of bad cause, we go
Three by three to oneness; thus
The cards are played
And those who draw back come out to meet me,
Destinies end up as bacteria
And everything is owed to everyone.

The echo of the Lord's Prayer in the last line is ironic: it is clear that there can be no forgiveness for debts, only a total indebtedness. Since the body is our only card and one which we must lose, our fate is simply to join the dead and leave the 'todo' unaffected by our passage. By using a number of third person reflexive verbs – 'se acaban', 'se juega' – together with first person plural – 'vamos' – and the personal possessive adjective 'mi encuentro' – the poet suggests that this experience is both singular and plural, both apprehended as subjective and an objective fact of existence. Moreover, if 'everything' is owed to everyone at death, then this means that the removal of one individual neither affects the plenum nor changes the conditions for other individuals.

Clearly the heightened language of 'Escarnecido . . .' only underscores the devastating unimportance of the individual, and the loss of any hope of transcendence. Life is now lived on this side of infinity where destinies 'end up as bacteria' or 'as houseflies'; in other words, individuals return to nature which goes on creating and for whom the human being has no privileged position over micro-organisms.

The 'paradoxes' of the *Poemas humanos* do not seem to be different from those of *Trilce*, yet there is clearly a change in the language of the poem. The subject of *Trilce* is the butt of the species, engaged in a solitary struggle. In many of the *Poemas humanos,* the subject becomes the common denominator seeking the lost presence in the fragments of a once socially cohesive and meaningful text. Thus the vaguely Biblical echoes represent the traces left by a Logos which can no longer be marshalled to transmit a transcendental message. 'Escarnecido', 'satanes', and phrases like, 'Al fondo, es hora', 'se debe todo a todos' seem to lay claim to another context, to the context which the poet thrusts into the past of the prophets, 'when they talked of air, shouting, when they talked quite slowly of the lightning-bolt'. It is this we shall find in the poems, the nostalgia for voice and therefore for presence.[11]

Logos and words

There is no doubt a hankering after Logos although the *Poemas humanos* are in no sense Christian. There are references, it is true, to a 'someone' who 'has just passed by without ever having been',[12] to the 'bottle without wine' and the wine 'widowed of this bottle'.[13] Biblical allusion and quotation underscore the loss of Christian community, the transference of ritual from the Church as body of Christ to the human body as Holy Writ although the poems are often closer in spirit to parody than to nostalgia. To pray to 'mother soul' and 'father body' and to turn Saint Francis's songs to Brother Sun and Sister Moon into a savage hymn to 'Sister Envy' and 'Wifely Tomb' as Vallejo does in 'De puro calor tengo frío' (From sheer heat, I'm cold), is a form of pronouncing the end of any individual salvation. It follows that the prophetic tone can only be adopted as parody, as a demonstration too of the once performative language of God and Christ which can no longer actualize the command. If God's declaration 'Let there be light' no longer performs but only *says,* then the words turn into mere babble. This is precisely what occurs in the poem, '¡Ande desnudo, en pelo, el millonario!',[14] where the imperatives command though what they command cannot be performed. Further the commands range from the impossible Christian ideal, 'Ande desnudo, en pelo, el millonario' (Let the millionaire go naked in his skin), to 'Wash your skeleton every day', 'Let us die', 'Rain, rain', 'Don't take any notice of me'. In this way, the poet shows that moral commands, 'Woe to him who builds his death-bed with treasure', belong to the same grammatical category as the nonsensical command, 'Rain, rain' (for no human power can cause rain merely by commanding it). What the poem reveals is that human beings (and perhaps most particularly the poet-prophet) have aborgated God's language without the Creator's power:

sean los descendientes,
sea la codorniz,
sea la carrera del álamo y del árbol.

Let there be descendants,
Let there be quail,
Let there be a race between the poplar and the tree.

Words can only be performative when the speaker has the authority to have the command accomplished. What '¡Ande desnudo, en pelo, el millonario!' challenges is the very possibility of words to perform and, at the same time, it shows the ease with which the imperative category induces us to believe in the power of words.[15]

The irony, therefore, arises from the lack of appropriateness conditions which would allow the poet to set himself up as the creator or as the bringer of justice. Thus, in the poem 'Traspié entre dos estrellas' (A stumble between two stars), his distribution of blessings is not simply a parody of the Beatitudes but a demonstration of their total ineffectiveness.

¡Amado sea aquel que tiene chinches,
el que lleva zapato roto bajo la lluvia,
el que vela el cadáver de un pan con dos cerillas,
el que se coge un dedo en una puerta,
el que no tiene cumpleaños,
el que perdió su sombra en un incendio,
el animal, el que parece un loro,
el que parece un hombre, el pobre rico,
el puro miserable, el pobre pobre![16]

Blessed be the one who has bugs,
The one who wears a worn-out shoe in the rain,
He who watches over the corpse of a bread laid out between
        two candles,
He who catches his finger in a door,
He who has no birthday,
He who has lost his shadow in a fire,
The animal, who looks like a parrot,
He who looks like a man, the poor croesus,
The poor wretch, the poor poor!

The poet blesses those who are poor and deprived, those who are unlucky by accident, those who are not even men because they have no birthday and no shadow (and therefore no identity). The blessing includes the whole of creation and hence is tautological. Indeed, perhaps it is the poet himself who 'looks like a parrot', mouthing the vestiges of Christian moral ideals until they turn into mere chatter and the poem breaks off in despair, with 'Ay, so many, Ay, so few, ay, the others'.

The significance of these scriptural echoes, however, does not end here. For scriptures are words which have been *inscribed* not lost in the ephemeral speech act, words which because of being written down, proclaim a certain durability. Inscribing permits the 'message of smoke' to be recreated and hence re-experienced. Only in the Spanish Civil War was Vallejo able to conceive of a poetry having once again the force of the sacrificial act which gave rise to it, a 'poesía de pómulo morado, entre el decirlo y el callarlo'. When this condition was not open to him in the enforced superficiality of life in the Paris of the 1930s, then writing became a kind of torture. At best it might leave a trace of his passage through the world; at worst, it is tautological, the confirmation of human pettiness:

> Y no me digan nada,
> que uno puede matar perfectamente,
> ya que, sudando tinta,
> uno hace cuanto puede, no me digan . . .[17]

> Don't tell me,
> People can kill with perfect ease,
> Since, sweating ink,
> One does what one can, so don't tell me . . .

Writing is an alienating experience, a production process which is not entirely within the poet's control. So he writes, 'Quedéme a calentar la tinta en que me ahogo . . .' (I was left heating the ink in which I drown) for the ink (the undifferentiated blackness of non-being) is also the very material of the craft. Attempting to warm up the ink (with the passion of existence), cannot salvage him for the engulfing chaos. The culmination of this frustration is expressed in the sonnet, 'Intensidad y altura' (Intensity and height),[18] where the classic form of the sonnet is set against the notion that 'literature' can save individuals from their inglorious destiny. While Shakespeare could boast that 'in black ink' his love would 'still shine bright', Vallejo's attempt to assert his individuality by writing ends with his incorporation into the species until he is no longer Vallejo but species-man:

> Quiero escribir, pero me sale espuma,
> quiero decir muchísimo y me atollo;

no hay cifra hablada que no sea suma,
no hay pirámide escrita, sin cogollo.

Quiero escribir, pero me siento puma;
quiero laurearme, pero me encebollo.
No hay toz hablada, que no llegue a bruma,
no hay dios ni hijo de dios, sin desarrollo.

Vámonos, pues, por eso, a comer yerba,
carne de llanto, fruta de gemido,
nuestra alma melancólica en conserva.

¡Vámonos! ¡Vámonos! Estoy herido;
vámonos a beber lo ya bebido,
vámonos, cuervo, a fecundar tu cuerva.

I want to write, but foam spews from me,
There is so much I want to say, and I bog down;
There is no spoken cipher that is not a sum,
There is no written pyramid without a summit.

I want to write, but I sense I'm a puma;
To wreathe myself in laurels, but I simmer in a pot of onions.
There is no spoken cough that does not become mist,
There is no god nor son of god, without evolution.

So let's go, then, and feed on grass,
Flesh of lamentation, fruit of groaning sighs,
Our melancholy soul preserved in tins.

Let's go! Let's go! I am wounded;
Let's go drink what has been drunk already,
Let's go, friend crow, and fecundate your mate.

Instead of being the gateway to the beatific and timeless vision, poetry reveals the historical nature of language and the repetitive nature of human existence. The exigencies of the rhyme which produce strange images like 'puma' and 'me encebollo' lay bare the true process behind poetic production, which can escape neither the historical development nor the material nature of language. When the poet writes he finds 'foam' issuing forth, for there is no depth in a language which he conjures up as function. Yet on the other hand there is no fluency, because of the 'given' nature of spoken language which he describes as a 'cifra' (cipher) and which instead of holding the key to mysteries is merely a sum of historically accumulated meanings. The pyramid of written language has a heart, but it is significant that Vallejo designates this by the word 'cogollo', since the heart of a cabbage or a lettuce does not enclose a seed but is simply the centre of a number of layers. The implication is that while words have no ultimate point of reference, they do have layers of meaning and function. That is why language defies individual expression, for it can never be wholly appropriated by the individual who, when he tries to write, feels like a puma or a wild beast and simmers 'in a pot of onions' instead of earning a laurel crown. Plainly, the act of writing itself cannot free him from the material world or from nature. For the sign is material. However, it is also clear that he is not referring here to the primacy of the dialectics of nature as in 'Telúrica y magnética' but rather considering the paradigmatic aspects of language and historical development through time. For words carry with them the vestiges of their past which they introduce into the syntagmic chain. Speaking is a use of language which is immediate and ephemeral whilst writing facilitates development and historical continuity. The poem distinguishes speech which ends in mist and the 'desarrollo' which writing permits and which encourages the notion of a creator. 'There is no god nor son of god, without evolution', he writes. The final tercets of the sonnet, however, introduce a brusque change of tone, for the desire to write and hence to 'inscribe' his own individuality is now abandoned. Too much of an animal to immortalize himself in verse, the poet urges his fellows to keep the soul in preserve and accept the cycle of reproduction. The insistent repetition of 'vámonos' translates both the repetition of the cycle and the sense of process which we experience; individuals move on but the cycle is identical. By equating those he addresses with rutting crows, he lays bare the identity of human and animal reproduction which determines the superstructure of existence. Thus even while trying to liberate himself from mere reproduction by writing, the poet is betrayed by a language which cannot be freed from nature.

Unlike Neruda for whom the lost sense of communion between people might be recovered in the act of reading to an audience, Vallejo constantly discloses the gulf between discourse and the raw material of existence. For instance, in 'Un hombre pasa . . .' (A man passes by), he juxtaposes this raw experience with various kinds of discourse in a series of aphoristic couplets:

Un hombre pasa con un pan al hombro
¿Voy a escribir, después, sobre mi doble?

Otro se sienta, ráscase, extrae un piojo de su axila, mátalo.
¿Con qué valor hablar del psicoánalisis?
. . . . . .
Un albañil cae de un techo, muere y ya no almuerza.
¿Innovar, luego, el tropo, la metáfora?[19]

A man passes by with bread on his back.
Shall I write then about my double?

Another sits, scratches, removes a bug from his armpit and kills it.
How can I possibly speak of psychoanalysis?
. . . . . .
A bricklayer falls from the roof, dies, and does not eat his lunch.
How then to invent tropes and metaphors?

Vallejo is not writing here of man in the abstract but of social
categories from the humble beggar to the builder who falls from
the top of his own construction. The social miseries of human
beings, whether those of the beggar or the merchant, are set
against different forms of discourse – literary, scientific and so
on – as if the latter were irrelevant or a form of self-indulgence.
Literature is just one of the metalanguages at the poet's disposal
but like all metalanguages it comes between him and reality.

Vallejo often appears to share Bergson's distrust of conceptualization as the many taunting references to Rousseau, Descartes,
Newton and Voltaire reveal. 'If I thought with my nasal, funeral,
temporal, windows / Fraternally / Piously throw me to the philosophers', he writes, sardonically in 'Panteón', disposing of any
possibility of metaphysics. Intuition, however, is no alternative;
for, as with Horkheimer, his quarrel is with enlightenment itself
as *self*-consciousness. In 'Panteón', he has a moment of vision
when he understands the earth 'earthily'; yet the earth 'brutally
denies' *his* history since it takes no account of individuals. The
self is exiled, then, in such a manner that it can never find a
home. The poem is something 'exhumed' and his thinking though
it 'condemns to death' is his only solace, as the opening lines of
one of the *Poemas humanos* reveals:

> Al cavilar en la vida, al cavilar
> despacio en el esfuerzo del torrente,
> alivia, ofrece asiento el existir,
> condena a muerte.[20]

> Pondering on life, pondering
> Slowly on the force of the torrent,

> Existence comforts, offers a resting place,
> And condemns to death.

The shock effect in the lines derives from a delayed association of 'cavilar' with 'condenar a muerte'. The repetition of 'cavilar' in the first line had suggested that thinking slows down the onward rush of time, that pondering upon existence opens up a space in the torrent, a privileged area of consolation and relief. Yet it only does this because it also condemns to death. Its message cannot go against the current.

Even more than in *Trilce*, then, thinking, writing, documenting the passage of the individual through life are activities added to the basically simple structure. The main difference in the *Poemas humanos* is that these mediating activities add up to a social text by means of which humanity has ordered and made sense of life. Yet the entire complexity and rigour of human thought constitute a message which the silent body knows without need of language. There is a hyperbolic disproportion between the energy and complexity expended on social life and the simplicity of nature. 'Is it for this that we die so much?' he asks in the 'Sermón sobre la muerte', and in 'Otro poco de calma, comarada' (Comrade, a little more patience), he exclaims:

> ¡cuántos diplomas
> y poderes, al borde fehaciente de tu arranque!
> ¡Cuánto detalle en síntesis, contigo!
> ¡Cuánta presión idéntica, a tus pies!
> ¡Cúanto rigor y cuánto patrocinio!
>
> Es idiota
> ese método de padecimiento,
> esa luz modulada y virulenta,
> si con sólo la calma haces señales
> serias, características, fatales.
>
> Vamos a ver, hombre;
> cuéntame lo que me pasa,
> que yo, aunque grite, estoy siempre a tus órdenes.[21]

> So many diplomas!
> Powers of attorney, at the authentic edge of your career!
> How much detail in synthesis is with you!
> How much identical pressure at your feet!
> How much exactness and how much patronage!
>
> It's crazy
> This manner of suffering,
> And that modulated, virulent light,

When simply by being patient you make
Serious, characteristic and fatal signs.

Let's see man;
Tell me what's with me
For I, even when I protest, am always at your service.

The accumulation of words belonging to the discourse of law and of exact science – words such as 'diploma', 'power of attorney', 'exactness', 'pressure', 'synthesis' contribute to the 'virulent light' of consciousness and also to human suffering. Yet they are all part of a superfluous babble since the silent animal who transmits the will of the species is understood without need of words or calculation.

There is therefore an emptiness at the heart of discourse itself for it can never truly designate the wordless repetition which ensures the continuity of the generations. As Horkheimer has it, 'The distance between subject and object, a presupposition of abstraction is grounded in the distance from the thing itself which the master achieved through the mastered.'[22] But the master does not, for all this, achieve immortality, since words, the very instruments he uses to inscribe his 'being of smoke', sow doubts in his mind. The moving poem, 'Y si después de tántas palabras' (And if, after so many words . .) confronts the failure of script to rescue man from the triviality he has fallen into:

> ¡Y si después de tántas palabras,
> no sobrevive la palabra!
> ¡Si después de las alas de los pájaros,
> no sobrevive el pájaro parado!
> ¡Más valdría, en verdad,
> que se lo coman todo y acabemos!
> . . . . . .
> ¡Y si después de tánta historia, sucumbimos,
> no ya de eternidad,
> sino de esas cosas sencillas, como estar
> en la casa o ponerse a cavilar!
> ¡Y si luego encontramos,
> de buenas a primeras, que vivimos,
> a juzgar por la altura de los astros,
> por el peine y las manchas del pañuelo!
> ¡Más valdría, en verdad,
> que se lo coman todo, desde luego!
>
> Se dirá que tenemos
> en uno de los ojos mucha pena
> y también en el otro, mucha pena

y en los dos, cuando miran, mucha pena . . .
Entonces . . . ¡Claro! . . . Entonces . . . ¡ni palabra!²³

And if after so many words,
The word doesn't survive!
If after the wings of the birds,
The halted bird doesn't survive!
It would be better, truly,
If it were all swallowed up and let's be done with it!

. . . . . .

And if, after so much history, we give up,
Not to eternity
But to these simple little things, like being
At home or starting to split hairs!
And then if we suddenly
Discover that we're alive,
Judging by the height of the stars,
By a comb and the stains on a handkerchief!
It would be better, truly,
For it all to be swallowed up, right away!

Someone will say that we've got
A lot of sorrow in one eye
And in the other as well, a lot of sorrow
And in both, when they stare, a lot of sorrow . . .
Well . . . ! O.K. . . . ! Then . . . ! not a word!

'Tántas palabras' refers to a discourse which cannot be Logos
since words are represented as mere historical accumulation, the
product of 'tánta historia' which has not involved any qualitative
change, being simply a series of events. The only change has
been in man's evolutionary history, when the wings of the bird
atrophied and man became 'parado'. Words and history if divorced from any design are meaningless. Thus man succumbs
from the objects he himself produces and from existence (being
at home) and thinking since consciousness works not for individual survival but rather reveals ephemerality. People live for
objects like the 'comb' and the 'handkerchief' which are accoutre-
ments of civilization yet trivial as if the production process had
taken over, replacing the space religion had once filled.

   In the final verse, suffering is affected by the discontinuity of
existence; it is sensed first in one eye and then in the other and
in both eyes only when they are consciously looking (as opposed
to seeing). The poem ends in a stutter, 'Entonces . . . ¡Claro!
. . . Entonces . . . ¡ni palabra!', in which the repetition of the
word 'entonces' suggests the deferring of the empty conclusion,

and indicates the momentary postponement of that final silence when there will be 'not a word'. The 'ni palabra' which brings the poem to an end is one of the many colloquial expressions in the poem (like 'de buenas a primeras' and 'en verdad' or 'desde luego') which foreground the capacity of words for filling up silence with the appearance of meaning. Such phrases act as a destructive force, indicating the absence of Logos which would make civilization into something more than 'tántas palabras' and 'tánta historia'.

The analogy between birth and poetic creation no longer holds good in Vallejo's poems, for birth is a function of the species which poetry, in some sense, defies. Thus in the poem, '¿Y bien? ¿Te sana el metaloide pálido?' (And so you are cured by the pallid metaloid?) it is a hen which performs the act of creating by laying eggs which are described as 'smoking syllables'. God's 'let there be light' is repeated with each birth.

> Y la gallina pone su infinito, uno por uno;
> sale la tierra hermosa de las humeantes sílabas.[24]

> And the hen lays its infinity, one by one;
> The earth emerges beautiful from the smoking syllables.

In contrast, in 'Quedéme a calentar la tinta en que me ahogo' (I was left heating the ink in which I drown), the poet's hendecasyllable verses 'cleave the grass' on the way to the cemetery.[25] Thus poetry is more concerned with the ephemerality of human beings than with the reproduction of the species.

Several of the *Poemas humanos* foreground the functional aspects of language as if to emphasize the disappearance of Logos. In some of them, Vallejo separates nouns, adjectives, participles, demonstratives, adverbs and abstract nouns, grouping them together according to their grammatical function rather than making them part of a syntagmic chain or associating them for semantic reasons. These poems are symptomatic of the analogy he was now making between individual existence and language as functional. Unlike Neruda's poems which attempt to restore the sense of immediate communication permitted by the spoken words, these poems destroy the myth of presence, indeed reveal the process of selection which is behind each speech act. 'Terremoto', for instance, is a poem which shows how function and usage structure our perceptions and conceal both origins and ends from the speaker.

> ¿Hablando de la leña, callo el fuego?
> ¿Barriendo el suelo, olvido el fósil?
> Razonando,
> ¿mi trenza, mi corona de carne?
> (Contesta, amado Hermeregildo, el brusco;
> pregunta, Luis, el lento!)[26]

> Speaking of firewood, do I fail to speak of fire?
> Sweeping the ground, do I forget the fossil?
> Reasoning,
> My braided hair, my crown of flesh?
> (Answer, beloved Hermeregildo the Brusque!
> Ask, Luis the Slow!)

'Hablar', 'barrer el suelo' and 'razonar' all involve selection and imply the separation of the immediately functional from the irrelevant, the winnowing out of the useful from origins (fósil) and the ultimate destiny (fire). The bracketing of those whom the poet addresses represents a further process of selection and differentiation. Luis and Hermeregildo are differentiated by physical characteristics (one is quick, the other slow), by their names and by their different roles in the dialogue. What underlies the poem is the linguistic model itself since language operates through selection. But function is also the only web which holds the totality of binary opposites together:

> ¡Pregunta, Luis; responde, Hermeregildo!
> Abajo, arriba, al lado, lejos!
> ¡Isabel, fuego, diplomas de los muertos!
> ¡Horizonte, Atanacio, parte, todo!
> ¡Miel de miel, llanto de frente!
> ¡Reino de la madera,
> corte oblicuo a la línea del camello,
> fibra de mi corona de carne!

> Ask, Luis! Answer, Hermeregildo!
> Down, up, to one side, away!
> Isabel, fire, diplomas of the dead!
> Horizon, Atanacio, the part, the whole!
> Honey of honey, lamentation of the forehead!
> Reign of wood,
> A cut oblique to the line of the camel,
> Fibre of my crown of flesh!

What is needed here is a centre, something for the 'abajo, arriba', for the horizon and the diplomas to be related to. The poem destroys any sense of presence in order to replace this by relativity and function. What had been the centre of the Logos, the kingdom of Heaven, has now become the natural kingdom of wood to which both 'leña' and 'fuego' are related. Thus underneath function and relationship there is organic growth and the evolution process in which the individual with his crown (not of thorns but of ephemeral flesh) is both fibre and 'against the grain'. If we regard the tree as a metaphor for the species then the individual is an intersection, a layer in time, destined to become part of a single ring within the wood of the species.

The speech act

It is not only philosophy and literature, then, which are erected as superstructures by consciousness in order to hide the secret work of nature but even conversation and talk cannot be considered unmediated forms of communication. Indeed, spoken words also fill the sinister silences of life, monitoring trivial acts and giving them undue emphasis. In the poem, 'Hoy me gusta la vida mucho menos' (Today I like life much less), both speech and observation are something added to experience itself:

Me gusta la vida enormemente
pero, desde luego,
con mi muerte querida y mi café
y *viendo* los castaños frondosos de París
y *diciendo:*
Es un ojo éste, aquél; una frente ésta, aquélla . . . Y *repitiendo:*
Tánta vida y jamás me falla la tonada!
Tántos años y siempre, siempre, siempre!

Dije, chaleco, dije
todo, parte, ansia, dije casi, por no llorar.[27]

I like life enormously
Though, naturally,
With my beloved death and my café
And seeing the leafy chestnut trees in Paris
And saying;
It is an eye, this, that; a forehead this, that . . . And repeating:
So much life and I never forget the tune!
So many years and always, always, always!

I said vest, I said
All, part, anguish, I said almost, so as not to weep.

The words and the tune of life do not coincide. Whereas the tune
is programmed by the species, individual consciousness retro-
spectively passes what is happening in review. By speaking and
seeing, the poet is able to seize on a tiny section within the
boundlessness of nature and of time which is not eternity but a
continuum, a 'siempre, siempre, siempre'. Thus, he can speak of
my death, of *my* café and point to his own body as if affirming
its very existence in this way. But the totality he speaks is plainly
only the sum of scattered parts. 'I said vest, I said / All', he declares, showing that as far as the individual is concerned the part
is the whole. There is no way, then, for words to open up an area
of unmediated experience; no way the individual can grasp the
totality of life except through the grid of consciousness. At most,
language can be a form of solace, words uttered by the individual
'so as not to weep'.

There is no possibility of getting back to origins in *Poemas
humanos* because consciousness works through language which
is never immediate. Nor is there any essential man hiding behind
the shirt collar for human beings are defined by their clothing,
by what they have produced. Deprived of any aspiration to immortality even through literature or thought, the life of the individual is reduced to very modest proportions; it is revealed as
poverty-stricken when instead of a specific situation the poet tries
to communicate through what he has in common with others.
The paradox of individual consciousness is that in thus striving
for universality, it reduces existence to the common denominator
and hence to triviality. For civilization which separates species-
men from the animals because of the fact that they produce life
is also a flight from terror. The reified objects we produce are
alien, yet cushion us against a frightening universe. Nowhere is
this better expressed than in one of the last poems Vallejo wrote,
'Ello es que el lugar . . .' (It's just that the place . . .).[28]

> Ello es que el lugar donde me pongo
> el pantalón, es una casa donde
> me quito la camisa en alta voz
> y donde tengo un suelo, un alma, un mapa de mi España.
> Ahora mismo hablaba

de mí conmigo, y ponía
sobre un pequeño libro un pan tremendo.[29]

It's just that the place where I put on
My pants is a house where
I take off my shirt in a loud voice
And where I have a floor, a soul, a map of my Spain.
Just now I was talking
To myself about myself, and I put
A huge loaf of bread on top of a little book.

This is a poem predicated on a neuter pronoun – 'ello'. It is
this which provides the unity for the disconnected activities
which the poem monitors. This 'ello' is both a place and a house
and hence symbolizes identity and, more particularly, it is a place
in which the poet puts on and takes off the clothes which mark
him out as a civilized being. That he takes off his shirt *out loud*
suggests that he feels compelled to verbalize even this commonplace activity and, indeed, he may well be referring to poetry
itself in so far as poetry (or talking aloud) expresses feeling
about the world outside (the map of Spain). Thus the poet's
meditation within the house of identity is also an effort to enter
into dialogue, to overcome his solipsism through communion.
'Just now I was talking / To myself about myself, and I put / A
huge loaf of [communion] bread on top of a little book', he
writes. It is even possible that this 'little book' refers specifically
to the poems of *España, aparta de mí este cáliz* since these did,
in fact, represent a kind of poetry predicated on a new Logos.
But there is also a gulf between the aspiration to communion
and the tiny achievement which appears to have so little effect
on the world at large. For the poet quickly passes to those trivial
events which mark the daily round and which form the bulk of
our existence. 'Humming' (another reference to his poetry), he
transfers his existential account from the credit to the debit side
of existence. The account book metaphor was one he had often
used in *Trilce* to refer to that getting and spending of the gift
of life which adds up to the human economy system. In *Poemas
humanos,* however, this economy has become essentially social
and is reflected in the appurtenances of 'civilized' life which man
has himself produced:

Y he, luego, hecho el traslado, he trasladado,
queriendo *canturrear* un poco, el lado

derecho de la vida al lado izquierdo;
más tarde, me he lavado todo, el vientre,
briosa, dignamente;
he dado vuelta a ver lo que se ensucia,
he raspado lo que me lleva tan cerca
y he ordenado bien el mapa que
cabeceaba o lloraba, no lo sé.

Mi casa, por desgracia, es *una* casa,
un suelo por ventura, donde vive
con su inscripción *mi* cucharita amada,
mi querido esqueleto ya *sin letras,*
la navaja, un cigarro permanente.
De veras, cuando *pienso*
en lo que es la vida
no puedo evitar de *decírselo* a Georgette,
a fin de comer algo agradable y salir,
por la tarde, comprar un buen periódico,
guardar un día para cuando no haya,
una noche también, para cuando haya
(así *se dice* en el Perú – me excuso);
del mismo modo, sufro con gran cuidado,
a fin de no *gritar* o de llorar, ya que los ojos
poseen, independientemente de uno, sus pobrezas,
quiero decir, su oficio, algo
que resbala del alma y cae al alma. [The italics are mine.]

And I have, later, made the move, moved,
Wanting to *hum* a bit, the right
Side of life over to the left side;
Then later I've washed myself all over, my belly,
In a vigorous and dignified way;
I've turned around to see what is getting dirty,
I've scratched at what brings me so near
And I have put in good order the map
That was nodding or weeping, I don't know.

My house, unfortunately, is *a* house,
A floor by chance, where dwells
My beloved little spoon with its inscription,
My beloved now *unlettered* skeleton,
The straight-razor, and a cigar, permanently.
Truly, when I *think*
Of what life is,
It's impossible not to *tell* Georgette,
So as to eat something good, and then go out,
In the afternoon, to buy a good newspaper,
To save a day for when there are none,
And a night too, for when there are

(Sorry – *that's what they say* in Peru);
And similarly, I suffer with a great deal of care,
So as not to *shout* or weep, since one's eyes,
Independently of one's self, have their needs,
That is, I mean, their function, something
That slips from the soul yet falls to the soul.

Vallejo resorts to deliberate flatness, projecting the careful soul
of the petty bourgeois who debits time itself. Singing, speaking,
reading the newspaper, thinking, washing, tidying are activities
which publicly suggest his conformity, whilst also suggesting
secret desperation. The poet washes his belly 'dignamente', because there is nowhere else for human dignity to go except into
these activities by means of which he brings a certain routine
into his tiny universe. Nonetheless they do not affect the world
at large for the map of Spain 'was nodding or weeping' quite out
of his control. The one area of security – *his* house – now turns
out to be a very temporary shelter. '*My* house is . . . *a* house',
he declares for the 'I' is only the ephemeral possessor of the objects it has appropriated. He thus distinguishes between 'my
spoon' and 'my skeleton' and 'the straight-razor' and 'a cigar'.
What is truly his is what he has loved, the spoon on which he
has inscribed his identity and which symbolizes appetite and his
skeleton 'ya sin letras', that wordless frame which will outlast the
individual.

The triviality which invades daily life and which imbues all
that is usually considered essential – speaking, thinking, human
relations – becomes not simply a form of self-deception but a
palliative which alone permits him to live without shouting out
in despair. Again, the poet's bodily response is out of key with
consciousness which attempts to contain grief and channel it into
activities like buying the newspaper and talking to his wife. The
eyes, on the other hand, act independently, weeping whether he
wants them to or not. What is lacking is a Logos which would
make sense of suffering, but the only vestige of this is Sunday,
the day of rest:

Hoy es domingo y, por eso,
me viene a la cabeza la idea, al pecho el llanto
y a la garganta, así como un gran bulto.
Hoy es domingo, y esto
tiene muchos siglos; de otra manera,
sería, quizá, lunes, y vendríame al corazón la idea,

al seso, el llanto
y a la garganta, una gana espantosa de ahogar
lo que ahora siento,
como un hombre que soy y que he sufrido.

Today is Sunday, and therefore
The idea comes into my head, and sobbing into my breast
And my throat, like a great lump.
Today is Sunday, and this
Is centuries old; otherwise,
It would be Monday, perhaps, and the idea would come to
　　my heart,
To my brain, sobbing,
And to my throat, an astounding desire to choke back
What I feel now,
Like a man, which I am, and whom I have suffered.

The idea of Sunday is like an obstruction in the throat, it is a rest day which is no more than a tradition which has been there for centuries and for which there is now no justification. Sunday might perfectly well be Monday. Because Sunday no longer commemorates salvation, the other bodily organs function chaotically for they no longer are analogous to parts of a macrocosm. The heart thinks, the brain weeps and the throat suppresses instead of expressing feeling. The only response to the human condition should be a cry of terror. Instead of this, civilization acts as a control by socializing the animal in man.

Civilization and the silent animal

'How can I be / and exist without making my neighbour angry?'[30] Vallejo asks in one of his poems. The question is double-edged for what he calls the 'carbide of anger within the gum' is concealed by social activities; yet man is not yet enough of a social animal to have transcended the struggle for life. In these poems, civilization is epitomized by the comb, the overcoat and the cigarette, those superfluous products which are quite inessential to natural life. Often too, he describes people killing lice for this too is an activity which marks out civilized from primitive man though the action only suppresses the visible proof that man is part of an ecology system.[31] Microbes, bacteria, the very body itself, are a constant reminder of how superficial civilization is. Thus, in 'Fue domingo', the poet depicts himself as part of a

natural system, organically mediating so to speak between the
sun and inorganic nature whilst the statue of Voltaire, the philosopher of enlightenment, gazes at the city centre. Vallejo designates this empty centre by the word 'zócalo' which once referred
to a ceremonial centre and which like the 'Sunday' of the poem
indicates the empty place of religious belief:

> En su estatua, de espada
> Voltaire cruz su capa y mira el zócalo,
> pero el sol me penetra y espanta de mis dientes incisivos
> un número crecido de cuerpos inorgánicos.[32]

> Over his shoulder, with his sword
> Voltaire wraps his cape around and watches the square,
> But the sun pierces me and frightens from my incisors
> An increased number of inorganic bodies.

The natural cycle is constantly present, reminding the conscious
subject that he is a genotype, a poet of a system which has no
history or culture. It is this genotype whom Vallejo addresses as
the 'Señor esclavo' (in '¿Y bien? ¿Te sana el metaloide pálido?'
(And so you are cured by the pallid metaloid?).[33] The poet frequently addresses himself to this ever-present *tu* who is invariably
silent. In 'Pero antes que se acabe . . .' (But before it ends . . .),
he apostrophizes him thus:

> Me percibes, animal?
> me dejo comparar como tamaño?
> No respondes y callado me miras
> a través de la edad de tu palabra.[34]

> Do you perceive me, animal?
> Do you let me compare for size.
> You do not reply and silently you watch me
> From across the age of the word.

It is precisely this 'age of the word' which separates conscious
humanity from the silent unhistorical species. Like death, the
animal can only interject in the form of space or silence, in short
as the secret continuity across which the discontinuous act of
speech must cut. And thus it is that in death alone, are the conscious and the unconscious to be reconciled in the unity that has
no words and hence no human existence:

> y entonces oirás cómo medito
> y entonces tocarás cómo tu sombra es ésta mía desvestida
> y entonces olerás cómo he sufrido.

And then you will hear how I meditate
And then you will sense how your shadow is mine undressed
And then you will smell how I have suffered.

Plainly both speech and writing are instruments of divided
man, denying him the plentitude and the communion for which
he hankers.

Sermons upon death

But there are other kinds of silence. The species is mutely present
in the body which is the document of its evolution. But there is
also the silence of death which punctuates our very discourse
since pauses, breaks and interruptions are analogies for the death
which surrounds the space of every individual existence. Speech
can thus be regarded as the reverse of negation and emptiness
though pervaded through and through with the breath of absence.

One of the finest of the *Poemas humanos* is the 'Sermón sobre
la muerte' (Sermon upon death) which makes language itself
part of a dialogue with emptiness.[35] The poem is written in the
form of a sermon. In it, the poet uses traditional rhetorical devices such as anaphora, antanaclasis (repeating a word while
shifting from one of its meanings to another), auxesis (words
arranged in ascending order of gravity). These devices structure
the poem as if it were an argument (or a sermon) with the
speaker persuading the listeners of his very existence. It is an
argument, however, to which we are introduced at the moment
of summing up:

> Y, en fin, pasando luego al dominio de la muerte,
> que actúa en escuadrón, previo corchete,
> párrafo y llave, mano grande y diéresis,
> ¿a qué el pupitre asirio? ¿a qué el cristiano púlpito,
> el intenso jalón del mueble vándalo
> o, todavía menos, este esdrújulo retiro?[36]

> And, finally, passing on to the kingdom of death,
> Which functions as a squadron, the prior parenthesis,
> Key, and paragraph, large pointer, and dieresis,
> To what end the Assyrian desk? the Christian pulpit?
> The lively rod of the Vandal chattel
> Or, even less, this proparoxytonic retreat?

In this poem the poet and death as conflicting forces are drawn
up in opposing armies. Death's weapons are all silent – the

bracket, the paragraph, the key (which may be a typographical sign), the gesture and the dieresis. In other words, death uses the pauses and the discontinuities in speech and writing. In contrast, the poet's line of defence is cultural and material – the 'Assyrian' desk on which he writes, the Christian pulpit from which he speaks and the Vandal furniture (which is possibly a reference to the body, but more literally, that which is moveable) and 'este esdrújulo retiro' (his poetry).[37] Yet this struggle is in function of death itself and the next section of the poem is a gloss on the agonizing question, 'Is it for this that we must die so often?' For death's instruments – the bracket and the key – are now seen to be inseparable from the individual whose discontinuous experience is emphasized by the use of *anaphora*.

> ¿Y el párrafo que escribo?
> ¿Y el corchete deísta que enarbolo?
>
> Do we need to die at every instant?
> And the paragraph that I write?
> And the deistic parenthesis I raise high?

The bracket is 'deistic' precisely because it belongs to the given, to a creation from which the creator is absent. And the poet's eloquence is itself mere rhetoric, the very demonstration that talk cannot defer death nor the brain resist it.

The whole poem turns against the poet for he shows us that in raiding the domain of death through the writing of a poem, he can only grasp at the instrument of a language which is not his own but belongs to the given. This is strikingly illustrated in the involuntary conversion of defiant nonconformity into a demonstration of his role as a resigned beast of burden for the species. Through paronomasia and a set of associations, the poet passes from madness to resignation through the following chain: loco-lovo (lobo) – cordero (cuerdo) – sensato – (cabal) caballísimo.

> Loco de mí, lovo de mí, cordero
> de mí, sensato, caballísimo de mí.
>
> I'm wildly insane, wolfly woolly, lamb –
> Loony, lucid, hooting, horsily sage!

The one authentic moment of speech occurs at the moment of birth and death when the poet utters the primal cry. These are the two moments when he will defend his prey 'with the voice and with the larynx too and with the physical smell with which

I pray'. Utterance is here the clamour of existence uttered in the shadow of death, an analogue of the individual himself who at the end of the poem proclaims, 'For at the centre am I, and on the right hand too, and on the left, in the same way.' This apparently triumphant ending can only be read ironically for just as the sounds exist because of the silences against which they are uttered so the individual exists by virtue of the dialectic negation of death. The final lines are not a tribute to the glorious ego but indicate a self which fills the empty space by default.

Negation is an important part of *Poemas humanos*. In *Trilce* the zero, the left-hand sign, the minus and the process of subtraction were used as short-hand symbols which signalled the taboo word death. In *Poemas humanos,* death becomes as familiar a figure as the skeleton in mediaeval woodcuts. Yet clearly the end of the self is of little significance so that often what appears to be a poem on death is really a recognition of a plenum from which only the self is absent. By showing what death is *not*, life itself can be traced and defined as what has been left over:

> No. No tienen tamaño sus tobillos; no es su espuela
> suavísima, que da en las dos mejillas.
> Es la vida no más, de bata y yugo.
>
> No. No tiene plural su carcajada,
> ni por haber salido de un molusco perpetuo, aglutinante,
> ni por haber entrado al mar descalza,
> es la que piensa y marcha, es la finita.
> Es la vida no más; sólo la vida.[38]

> No. Its ankles have no size; it is not its gentle
> Spur which touches the two cheeks.
> It is simply life in dressing-gown and yoke.
>
> No. Its laughter has no plural,
> From having come out of the perpetual glutinous mollusc,
> Nor from having walked barefoot into the sea,
> It is life which thinks and journeys, it is the finite.
> It is just life, simply life.

Not-being is a unity, *not* plural, *not* linear; and life, in contrast, appears as all these things. From here, the poet goes on to discover another series of 'nothings' – nothing 'in front of or behind the yoke', 'no sea within the ocean' and 'nothing / In the grave pride of the cell / Only life. Thus; a very fine thing.'

The reader becomes enmeshed in these negations for what is

denied is not death but existence itself and the importance of
the individual in the universe:

> Pero aquello
> para lo cual nací ventilándome
> y crecí con afecto y drama propios,
> mi trabajo rehúsalo,
> mi sensación y mi arma lo involucran.
> Es la vida y no más, fundada, escénica.
>
> Y por este rumbo,
> su serie de órganos extingue mi alma
> y por este indecible, endemoniado cielo,
> mi maquinaria da silbidos técnicos,
> paso la tarde en la mañana triste
> y me esfuerzo, palpito, tengo frío.

> But that
> For which I was born ventilating myself
> And for which I grew with my own affection and my dream,
> This my work rejects,
> My feelings and my weapons turn inside out.
> It is life and that's all, established, theatrical.
>
> And in this direction,
> Its series of organs extinguishes my soul
> And from this unspeakable, demonic heaven,
> My machinery utters technical whistles,
> I spend my evening on a sad morning
> And I try, I touch myself, I am cold.

There is a sense of desolation in the last lines. The individual
drama in which the subject relates everything to himself so that
he can speak of '*my* work, *my* sensation, *my* arms' is in reality a
trick of the species which it is the poet's task to deny. Yet his
raison d'être as anything but an animal lies *only* in that denial.
For in reality life was already 'fundada' (given) before he came
onto the scene. His role is both determined and out of his control,
hence his sense of estrangement from the 'demonic heaven' from
which he was created and from his own 'machinery' with its
'technical whistles' which he cannot comprehend.

Comparing this poem with *Trilce* 1, we cannot but be struck
by the increased desolation and by what verges on his refusal of
the life lived on the terms of the species. Vallejo's original debt
to Schopenhauer has not decreased with the years yet he never
previously achieved such force in his depiction of the superfluous

nature of most of what passes for existence. It is not surprising to find that, in 'Va, corriendo, andando, huyendo . . .' (He goes, running, walking, fleeing . . .), the poet tries to escape from his very feet on their linear journey, nor that in 'A lo mejor soy otro' (Perhaps I'm another), he speaks of having 'exhumed' himself. For Vallejo, the individual does not live so much as survive. He is a prehistoric creature bearing the marks of evolutionary origins in arms 'that refused to be wings', a creature who, at the dawn of time, stood upright and uttered words and by these acts separated himself from nature and declared himself unique, a producer. Yet everything produced (except in function of continuation of the species) is superfluous; commodities, documents, poetry, buildings represent so many attempts to inscribe a passage through the world, to be something more than the beast of burden who patiently carries on life and disappears as new generations take his place. Each poem becomes an attempt to negate this role, to defer extinction. It is impossible to read the *Poemas humanos* and still doubt that Vallejo was profoundly concerned with the failure of both script and speech to replace the Christian Logos. Only in *España, aparta de mí este cáliz* is there any sense that a new kind of humanity and a new speech might emerge from the sacrifice of war.

9

THE MIRROR OF THE WORLD:
ESPAÑA, APARTA DE MÍ
ESTE CÁLIZ

In the Spanish people, America regards its own extraordinary destiny within human history, a destiny whose continuity consists in the fact that it has been given to Spain to be the creator of continents; today she is saving the entire world from nothingness.[1]

Vallejo

Vallejo spoke these words at the Second International Congress of Writers in Defence of Culture held in Spain just one year after the outbreak of the Civil War. Like most of the writers present at the meeting, he knew that he was the privileged witness of a decisive historical struggle. Like many of them, he would return home to dedicate himself, mind and body, to the Republican cause. But for him the war was more than a just cause; it was the razor's edge on one side of which was the possibility of human progress and on the other total regression to the childhood of humanity.

The last six years of Vallejo's life had been lived in full consciousness of the great political struggles of the time. He had returned to Paris from Spain in February 1932, at a dark moment in the history of the Western world, to find the unemployed deprived of the little human dignity they had once possessed, to read of the closing-down of factories in the big industrial cities and the triumph of Fascism in Germany. Before leaving Spain, he had written to his old friend, Juan Larrea, assuring him that political militancy had not changed 'his innermost concerns',[2] yet those innermost concerns were never entirely separated in his mind from the totality in which politics played an important part. However, his immediate problem on returning to Paris was economic. His income, as always, was irregular and he depended on journalism and teaching. Both he and his wife fell ill and the modest success he had enjoyed in Spain with *Rusia en 1931* and *El tungsteno* was never repeated. But this personal distress was made all the more acute by the world crisis, especially as it touched those places he knew best – Peru, France and Spain. In

VALLEJO

1933, he found himself signing a petition on behalf of his Communist party comrade Eudocio Ravines, sentenced to death by the government of Sánchez Cerro in Peru;[3] in 1934, when the right-wing party Action Française attempted to storm the Chamber of Deputies, Vallejo was out on the streets along with thousands of others.[4] How actively he was involved in the Communist party is hard to say, and it has been suggested that he was less than enthusiastic about their support of popular front governments.[5] Yet there is also plenty of evidence (including the 'Spain' poems) of his persuasion that the fight against Fascism took precedence over all other phases of the revolutionary struggle. Apart from his presence at the demonstration against Action Française, there was his work for Spain; and quite explicitly in an article he published in 1937 on the Axis treaty he stated his sense of the universal importance of the struggle between Fascism, which would 'elevate barbarism into a world order', and all the democratic forces of the world.[6] In mid-1937, offered the opportunity to return to Peru if he would modify his political opinions, he refused. 'Naturally I opted for my ideas', he wrote to Larrea.[7]

Intellectuals against Fascism

It was Henri Barbusse who took the initiative (possibly at the suggestion of Maurice Thorez, Secretary-General of the French Communist party) and organized a meeting of intellectuals against Fascism at Amsterdam-Pleyel in 1932, a meeting which the Spanish poet Rafael Alberti attended. A year later, the prominent Communist intellectual Paul Vaillant-Couturier founded the Association of Revolutionary Artists and Writers, while Louis Aragon, recently recruited to the party from Surrealism, became co-editor of its magazine, *Commune* and head of the *Maisons de la Culture*, the cultural centres which brought left-wing artists and writers into contact with a new public of workers.[8] In retrospect, it is not difficult to see this period as one of preparation for the inevitable world war for which each side was already marshalling its ideological cadres. Against the 'mass man' of Fascism, Communism proposed a new humanism which, in the immediate struggle, tended to be obscured by tactical and disciplinary issues. Not only the Surrealists but 'bourgeois' writers like

André Gide were opposed to subordinating their personal free-
dom merely because the long-term struggle demanded present
abnegation. In 1933 several Surrealists, among them André
Breton, Éluard and Benjamin Peret criticized Barbusse and
Romain Rolland for organizing the Amsterdam-Pleyel meetings,
saying that the notion of a united front of intellectuals against
Fascism directly conflicted with the notion of class struggle. For
this they were expelled from the Association of Revolutionary
Artists and Writers, and were then quick to point out that the
Communists in the name of humanism were in effect defending
bourgeois culture. Yet it is also true that the Communist party
had a sense of reality which writers like Breton with his insistence
on personal freedom could not perceive. Breton was to spend the
Second World War outside France in the United States, and so
escaped the occupation. Individual freedom interpreted in this
way as personal salvation was a far meaner prospect than the
collective goal proposed by the Communist party, though this
too, in practice, became distorted into authoritarian attitudes. It
is easy to condemn these attitudes of the 1930s, but equally ingenuous to suppose, as many critics now do, that cold-war politics give better hindsight. Romantic rebels and disciplined party
members were alike to meet death in Spain.

The conflict between individual freedom and party discipline
was only one of the problems of the time. Another less obvious
one (so that this became clear only in retrospect) was the party's
reverence for 'exemplary intellectuals' like Barbusse and Aragon
who were regarded as living examples of socialist humanism.
Once the Spanish Civil War broke out in 1936, there was added
reason for celebrating heroism and courageous action as a necessary preparation for battle. That the personality cult was to derive dangerously from this is now obvious. It is also true that we
cannot grasp the significance of writers like Neruda, Alberti and
Vallejo unless we understand their commitment as something
more than personality cult or a Utopian belief in the brotherhood
of man.

The notion of commitment in the 1930s went far beyond Barbusse's earlier appeals to the intellectuals. It owed something to
Soviet policy, but much to the hegemony of French culture which
the Communist party used skilfully to organize a world movement against Facism. Maurice Thorez, Secretary General of the

French Communist party, had visited Henri Barbusse in 1932, and in 1933 and 1934 had appealed to writers to make common cause against Fascism. The Comité de Vigilance des Intellectuels Antifascistes founded during the 1934 confrontations with the Action Française afforded an immediate rallying point. In the same year, Paul Nizan, Louis Aragon and Jean-Richard Bloch attended the First Congress of Soviet Writers and a year later were among the twenty-four signatories of an invitation to the First Congress of Antifascist writers and intellectuals which was held in France in June 1935. The Congress attracted delegates from thirty-eight countries and these included E. M. Forster (who had tried to prevail on Virginia Woolf to attend), Aldous Huxley, Heinrich Mann, Bertolt Brecht, Michael Gold, Waldo Frank, Alexei Tolstoy, Boris Pasternak and Ilya Ehrenburg. Vallejo's name is not on the list and in general Latin America was poorly represented, but he must have been alive to the debates and polemics which were published in *Commune* (edited by the French Committee for the Defence of Culture) and other journals.[9]

Despite the political struggles that rose to the surface during the Congress – Breton was not allowed to speak and Pasternak was almost denied the platform – there was constant reference to the dangers of Fascism, intensified by the presence of exiled German writers. The Communist party intellectuals and their sympathizers (including Barbusse, then at the end of his life) stressed that Fascism was the last ditch of the capitalist class, and to fight against Fascism was to fight for a class goal the achievement of which would make possible the liberation of the working class. Barbusse declared that by devoting themselves to this political fight, writers would overcome the original sin of individualism.

But suddenly it was Spain that was the mirror of the world. The defence of culture became the defence of Spain and commitment began to involve something more than listening to speeches.

Spain and the poets

The Spanish Popular Front came into power in March 1936 with Manuel Azaña as President. A government committed to reform, it faced a nation already bitterly divided, a nation emerging from the *bienio negro,* the low point of which had been the bloody crushing of the Asturias miners' strike. The election of the Popular Front government created an immediate revolutionary situation, with peasants seizing lands and Largo Caballero demanding the arming of the workers. There was violent reaction from the right and by July the assassination of two officers on the Republican side and the murder of the monarchist deputy Calvo Sotelo signalled the end of any possibility of peaceful coexistence. On 18 July 1936, the army rebelled. Spain was invaded from North Africa. The Civil War had begun. Within a few weeks García Lorca was dead, one among thousands of victims, another of whom would be Julio Gálvez, the young man who had in 1923 travelled to Europe in company with Vallejo. But if there were martyrs and deaths, there was also effervescence. Vallejo's friends, Alberti and Bergamín, had thrown themselves heart and soul into the struggle. Bergamín had helped to found the Spanish section of the Alliance of Intellectuals for the Defence of Culture. Alberti, who had long struggled to break down the barriers between literature and the people, organized poetry readings on the radio and at the Madrid front during the long defence of the city. The magazine *El mono azul,* the official organ of the Alianza de Intelectuales, counted among its contributors Manuel Altoaguirre, José Bergamín, Antonio Machado, Emilio Prados, Luis Cernuda and Vicente Aleixandre.[10]

Vallejo from the outbreak of the war had regarded it as a titanic struggle, one in which the Spanish people were in a 'state of grace'. He eagerly sought every bit of news from the front and would wait at the Gare Montparnasse for the latest information from Spain. He became one of the founder-members of the Comités de la defensa de la República española and helped publish (along with Pablo Neruda, David Alfaro Siqueiros, García Monge of Costa Rica and Aníbal Ponce) a mimeographed sheet, *Nuestra España.*[11] In December 1936 he was given permission to visit Barcelona and Madrid, spending about two weeks in Spain, which gave him enough time to observe something of the spontaneous reaction of the Spanish people that he so much admired.[12] His obsession with the day-to-day course of the war is clearly reflected in the poems of *España, aparta de mí este cáliz* which dwell in turn on each of the battlefronts of 1937 –

Madrid, the Ebro, Extremadura, the Basque country, Málaga, Bilbao and Teruel.

Early in 1937 José Bergamín, Max Aub, Rafael Alberti and María Teresa León were in Paris to help organize the second Congress of Writers in Defence of Culture, Neruda being delegated to help organize the invitations of the Latin Americans in Paris. Vallejo recorded the visit of the Spaniards in an article for the *Repertorio Americano* in which he expresses his enthusiasm for their commitment.[13] Arguing that the interests of the writer are in conflict with the goals of advanced capitalist and industrial societies, he explicitly states his belief that the writer can only have long-term effects on social change. The most exemplary artists are those who translate their conflict with society into public life. While it is beautiful and important to create a really revolutionary work 'in the silence of one's study' he writes, it is even more important to create such a work in the heat of battle, 'bringing it into being out of the deepest, warmest folds of life'.

The Second International Congress for the Defence of Culture opened in Barcelona on 2 July 1937, met in Valencia from 4–7 July and then closed in Madrid. There was a large French delegation which included Malraux, Julien Benda, André Chamson and Tristan Tzara.[14] Spender was there from England, Ehrenberg came from Russia, Neruda represented Chile, Jorge Icaza represented Ecuador, Juan Marinello and Nicolás Guillén represented Cuba, and José Mancisidor and Carlos Pellicer, Mexico. Vallejo attended as the Peruvian delegate. The Spanish delegation, naturally the centre of attention, included Bergamín, Antonio Machado, Alberti and Ramón Sender.

The delegates who swarmed onto the train from Paris were far from sinking their personal animosities, however. Vallejo travelled with his friend Vicente Huidobro, who was scarcely on speaking terms with Neruda, easily the most sought-after of the Latin Americans.[15] Once in Spain, there was a certain amount of competition for attention. Nevertheless, the war itself must have had a sobering effect. There were air-raid warnings during the meetings in Valencia, front-line mortar-fire could be heard in Madrid, and several delegates (including Vallejo) visited the Madrid front and heard eye-witness accounts of horrors. Vallejo was to bring back photographs of war victims, many of them children; and when he returned to Paris on 12 July, it was on the same

train as the body of Gerda Taro, 'a gentle newspaper photographer . . . who had died, crushed by a Fascist tank, on the
Brunete front'.[16]

In the general excitement of the Congress, Vallejo's presence
seems to have been almost overlooked, and indeed few of those
who attended could have been familiar with his poetry. In any
case, the main business was Spain and the celebration of the
authentic Spain, the Spain of the people. The Communist party
which dominated the proceedings set the tone, and Louis Aragon
in his opening address defended true nationalism and democratic
tradition against the false chauvinism of the capitalist class, now
resorting in its death agony to Fascism.[17] But it was the Catholic
writer José Bergamín whose words evidently had the deepest impact on Vallejo. Adopting a fervent, almost religious language, he
represented Spanish culture as one which had always had a secret
blood communion with the people, whose revolutionary will was
expressed in 'the invisible language of blood' and transmitted
through the word. Just as blood circulates in man, the word circulates in the people. It is 'born and dies in a breath, in air, in the
invisible bowels of the air, engendered in our breasts in order to
issue forth and die and be born again in our hearing'.[18]

There is no doubt that these words pulse behind the opening
poem of *España, aparta de mí este cáliz,* nor that this collection
is, in one sense, Vallejo's response to the closing resolution which
appealed to all writers to join actively in the struggle.[19] And when
it was his turn to speak at the Madrid session, he chose as his
topic 'The responsibility of the writer', predicting the 'horizontal'
union of the intellectual and the people, the breakdown of the
barriers between spirit and matter. He continued, 'Jesus said, "My
kingdom is not of this world". I believe that the moment has come
when the consciousness of the revolutionary writer might be expressed by a new formula . . . "My kingdom is of this world but
also of the next".' Writers, he declared are particularly responsible
because they control a powerful weapon, the Word, with which
they must now move the world. They are seldom heroic: nor do
they possess the spirit of sacrifice; yet it is when they feel the
guilt and shame of this most keenly that they are most truly
writers.[20]

Vallejo was saying and doing exactly what most of his fellow-
writers at the Congress were saying or doing. He does not stand

out as being original or different. Yet few others would be able
to translate opinions into poetic *praxis* as effectively as he. The
poetry of Auden, Spender and Neruda expresses the individual's
sense of shock at war and slaughter. For Vallejo, however, the
scenario of war and the collective spirit of the people had made
the individual more than ever superfluous. In his poems the individual word is clearly doomed or, at best, inadequate, though
now he sees the possibility of a different language, stemming out
of the social body, with the sacrifice of the Spanish people bringing about the 'consubstantiation' of word and action. Unlike
many of his contemporaries for whom 'inner' or 'individual' experiences were more 'profound', who felt themselves diminished
by 'society', Vallejo saw man's only hope as the union of individuals within a socially just 'body politic', that union through
sacrifice, that reconciliation of solitary man within the community of which Bergamín had spoken. That is why Spain became, for him, the matrix of a qualitatively different future, the
inventor of an America from which the new man could emerge.

Nothing he wrote is more revealing than his article on 'Los
enunciados populares de la guerra civil española' which might be
roughly translated as 'The people's message of the Spanish Civil
War'. Here it is plain that what he most admires is the spontaneity
of their sacrifice, for their body and brain have acted together not
for self-preservation but with a higher and nobler purpose.

Finally, for the first time, it is the people themselves, the man in the
street and not the military who, without coercion from the state, without captains, without military spirit or organization, without arms,
without uniform rush forth to meet the enemy and die in a clear, well-
defined cause, free of more or less inadmissible official obfuscations.
And since the people are in charge of their own struggle, it is easy
to understand that in this fight one senses the authentic human heartbeat of the people, an experience of extraordinary, unprecedented and
seminal scope.

In this article Vallejo mentions cases of individual heroism which
he was to use in his poetry – for instance Antonio Coll, who
faced and destroyed seven enemy tanks as a human grenade and
who was the subject of several Civil War ballads. Unlike the
'unknown soldier' of the First World War who acted under
orders, these Spanish fighters obey the 'direct, spontaneous, pas-
sionate impulse of the human being'. This kind of reflex-action

occurs when individuals defend their own possessions, but here it has occurred in defence of a *social* cause.

Men and women hastened along the roads of Somosierra and Extremadura in an intoxicated movement, in that inspired disorder of the epic of yore, to meet the rebels. A state of grace – we might say – seldom given to any people in history yet explicable because of the sensitive, direct and, as it were, Adam-like nature of the Spanish people which allowed these people to understand exactly, from the first, the true objectives of the Fascist insurrection which was to wipe out the few rights recently procured by the Spanish working-class, and then to extend the rule of force in the service of organized reaction, to the rest of the world.

This emphasis on the collective reflex-action against Fascism tells us a good deal about Vallejo's ideal of the whole man in whom thought and action are inseparably bound in the pursuit of a non-selfish end. Again and again, he stresses that the people took the initiative, sweeping their leaders along with them. 'And all this miracle is the sole work of the sovereign masses who are sufficient unto themselves and unto their insuperable future.'[21] The spontaneity would eventually come into conflict with Communist party discipline, but Vallejo had at least glimpsed unalienated man and he would not forget it. In applying the term 'Adam-like' to the Spaniards, he reminds us that this overcoming of alienation will apply to language too, for Adam had, according to Jacob Boehme, spoken the perfect language in which words really named things.

El mono azul, the magazine of the Spanish intellectuals against Fascism, from the first devoted its middle pages to war poetry, mainly to ballads, which had always offered Spanish poets a bridge between élite and popular culture. The Spanish ballad or 'romance' had recently been reinvigorated by García Lorca and Rafael Alberti. Now, at the outbreak of the war, both intellectuals and ordinary soldiers began to pour out new ballads, celebrating heroes like Antonio Coll and heroines like Lina Odena, (ambushed by the Fascists between Guadix and Granada) and recording the battles, the tragedies and the traitors. By 1937, in time for the Congress of Writers, Emilio Prados was able to collect three hundred of these poems in a *Romancero General de la Guerra de España.* The collection projects a whole range of new exemplary figures – the 'miliciano' and the Madrid workers, the peasants of Extremadura, the 'dinamitero', the fighters in the

international brigades. Above all, it shows a consciousness that
Spain was now the mirror of the world. 'Awake, awake Europe
to the rare example of Madrid', wrote one poet[22] and another
reminds his comrades that the whole world is applauding their
actions. The theme of sacrifice and resurrection, central to Vallejo's 'Spain' poems is a recurrent one, though it is often expressed as a simple transubstantiation of man and Spanish earth.
For example, Leopoldo Urrutia, addressing an unknown Asturian
miner who was killed in the Guadarrama, promises him resurrection as 'flesh of pine and scent of rosemary'.[23]

The enthusiasm of Alberti and the conviction that great actions
must give rise to great words undoubtedly helps to account for
this massive literary activity. Alberti, long a member of the Communist party, long convinced that the place of the poet was in
the streets, now appears consciously to create the kind of poetry
which will not record sacrifice but encourage it.

> Muchos no saben nada. Mas con la certidumbre
> del que corre al asalto de una estrella ofrecida,
> de sol a sol trabajan en la nueva costumbre
> de matar a la muerte, para ganar la vida.[24]

> Many know nothing. But with the certainty of
> Him who runs to seize an offered star,
> From dawn to dawn they work in the new habit
> Of killing death, to win life.

In 'Vosotros no caísteis', the dead are the seeds of 'furrows which
war opened':

> Se oye vuestro nacer, vuestra lenta fatiga,
> vuestro empujar de nuevo bajo la tapa dura
> de la tierra que al daros la forma de una espiga
> siente en la flor del trigo su juventud futura.[25]

> We hear your birth, your slow fatigue,
> Your new stirring under the hard cover
> Of earth which as it shapes you like a corn-stalk
> Senses your future youth in the flower of the grain.

'Matar la muerte' becomes one of the slogans of the time, implying that sacrifice will change the very nature of man. It is this
conviction that distinguishes the poems written by Spanish and

Latin American poets from those of many of the Anglo-Saxon writers who were appalled more than anything, by the waste of human life:

> Ask. Was so much expenditure justified
> On the death of one so young, and so silly
> Lying under the olive trees. O world. O death!

wrote Spender. Auden's 'Spain 1937', probably the best-known of the English war poems, makes the struggle a tedious interlude between a golden yesterday and a Utopian tomorrow. In contrast, Neruda's 'Voy a explicar algunas cosas' is a call to action against those who have attacked 'his' house and 'his' Spain. Vallejo's poetry is yet more radical. In *España, aparta de mí este cáliz*, Spain becomes a new Logos which is inscribed for all time in the history of the human race, marking a great change in the very notion of humanity.

Spain as text

The passion recorded in *España, aparta de mí este cáliz* is that of an entire people; the collection combines the messianic spirit of the Old Testament with the message of the New Testament that humanity can be saved from death. The fifteen poems include a hymn, a response, a prayer, a litany and a prophecy; in them, the Christian symbols which in *Trilce* and *Poemas humanos* had become empty vestiges now recover referential value. Bread once more refers to the bread of life and water to the water of grace though both life and grace are produced by the material world. When we recall how difficult the simple act of speaking and writing had been in some of the *Poemas humanos*, the tone of *España, aparta de mí este cáliz* is even more astonishing. Words like 'grandeza', 'llamar', 'grito', can now be used without irony for man finally lives up to the grandeur of language. The poet, meanwhile, does not assume the role of prophet but is simply a witness who bears the marks of a past which has been superseded by the events he describes:

> al no caber entre mis manos tu largo rato extático
> quiebro contra tu rapidez de doble filo
> mi pequeñez en traje de grandeza![26]

And since your long ecstatic moment will not fit into my hands
I break upon your double-edged speed
My tiny stature in its cloak of greatness.

The poet cannot be the prophet since it is not he who has made the leap into the future, not he who has produced the new text. The true creator is now the anonymous militiaman of 'Pequeño responso a un héroe de la República':

> Un libro quedó al borde de su cintura muerta,
> Un libro retoñaba de su cadáver muerto.[27]

> A book remained at the edge of his dead torso,
> A book sprouted from his dead body.

There is a world of difference between Vallejo's book and the dead heroes of Alberti's poems whose bodies return to earth and are metamorphosed as plants. This latter kind of immortality allows for no cultural transmission from one generation to the next whereas the 'libro' of the 'Pequeño responso' is both a cultural product and etymologically related to nature. The Latin *liber* derived from the same root as a tree bark;[28] hence it can readily be thought of as 'sprouting'. Yet the book is also separate from nature and no longer subject to its laws. Thus the analogy between the new man who overcomes death and the text which is born out of life but does not simply return to nature with the death of its creator is both exact and far-reaching. However its creator is irrevocably dead:

> Se llevaron al héroe,
> y corpórea y aciaga entró su boca en nuestro aliento;
> sudamos todos, el ombligo a cuestas;
> caminantes las lunas nos seguían;
> también sudaba de tristeza el muerto.

> Y un libro, en la batalla de Toledo,
> un libro, atrás un libro, arriba un libro, retoñaba del cadáver.

> They took away the hero,
> And bodily, fatefully his mouth entered into our breath;
> We sweated all, burdened with our navels;
> The wandering moons did follow us;
> And the dead man too sweated with sadness.

> And a book, in the battle of Toledo,
> A book, a book behind, a book above, sprouted from the body.

Plainly, the 'book' is different by its very nature from the sad
mortality of the hero whose death is sensed bodily by his com-
panions who as they breathe and sweat under the burden of life
receive into themselves the 'mouth' of their comrade. Like Neruda
becoming the voice of the dead in 'Alturas de Macchu Picchu',
the survivors here incorporate the dead man's mouth which is
the organ both of communion and of speech and hence a sign of
humanity. The common fate of all mortal men is indicated by a
series of images; the navel, the sign of a purely human origin, is
carried like a burden; the moons which follow the survivors indicate both the eternal cycle of nature and the transience of each
separate human being. The book, on the other hand, escapes the
purely mortal fate. Once the sacrifice is translated into the text,
it exists 'behind and above' the dead body; spatially it is removed
from its origins, separated from the death out of which it was
produced. The generous act of sacrifice not only raises the hero
above his own ephemeral fate but flowers into true poetry:

> Poesía del pómulo morado, entre el decirlo
> y el callarlo,
> poesía en la carta moral que acompañara
> a su corazón.[29]
> Quedóse el libro y nada más, que no hay
> insectos en la tumba,
> y quedó al borde de su manga, el aire remojándose
> y haciéndose gaseoso, infinito.

> Poetry of purple cheek, between speaking
> And silence,
> Poetry in the moral letter which should accompany
> his heart.
> The book and nothing else remained, for there are no
> Insects in the tomb.
> And the air remained at the edge of his sleeve, soaking
> Turning itself into vapour, infinitely.

The purple cheek 'between speaking and silence' suggests a poetry which is produced directly at the very moment of death;
a poetry that is inseparable from the common fate. Further, the
body itself transmits a message, a 'moral letter' since the sacrifice
of life is an act that betokens a moral choice of a high order.

Again and again, the poet uses words which denote a text –
'poetry', 'letter', 'book' – for that which survives the event of death

and transcends the struggle for life. The fact that the hero gives his life despite the fact that there is no personal survival is driven home by the grim lines, 'there are no / Insects in the tomb', and by the reference to limits of the decaying body beyond which is infinite air, the impersonal realm of nature. Alberti's comforting sense of the continuity of life is here expressly denied: only the book will survive. And the poet's role is merely that of witness, that of the survivor who observes the creation of the text out of the dead body:

> Todos sudamos, el hombligo a cuestas,
> también sudaba de tristeza el muerto
> y un libro, yo lo vi sentidamente,
> un libro, atrás un libro, arriba un libro
> retoño del cadáver exabrupto.[30]

> We all sweated, our navels on our backs,
> And the dead man sweated too with sadness
> And a book, I saw it with feeling,
> A book, a book behind, a book above,
> The abrupt budding of the corpse.

The abruptness with which the book and the hypallage (cadáver exabrupto) occur suggests the suddenness of the end. And the poem, far from diminishing the significance of death dwells on its horror, on its irreversability, on the burden of mortality. The reiteration of 'sudamos' and 'libro' turn these into the twin pivots of the poem – signifying the collective labour which does not allow the dead merely to die but ensures that the sacrifice will be inscribed in the lives of others.[31]

It is always interesting to take note of the erasures and changes which Vallejo made in these poems. In 'Pequeño responso a un héroe de la República', the second verse had originally spoken of a 'moral letter' and 'behind membranes of human stone / Christianity, good works, the great theme'. These lines refer back to a Christian ideal which had transcended individual egoism and which is expressed not only as a text but as 'membranes of human stone'. Bergamín's influence on these poems has already been noted and may have accounted for this first version since Bergamín was a Christian socialist. The suppression may have been dictated by the fact that 'stone' with its connotations of building and cathedrals distracted the reader from the important analogy between sacrifice and a text. The advantage of the metaphor of the text is that it does not oversimplify the notion of survival and resurrection since the text is not exactly analogous to human life, rather, it denotes a message which, until read, understood or in some way communicated is purely virtual. Nor do we need to take Vallejo's reference to a 'book' too literally. The thousands of war deaths which reveal the magnitude of the collective sacrifice constitute a message which need not be written down to be understood. The heroism of the militiaman, his generous sacrifice *speak.* That is why in the 'Himno a los voluntarios de la República', the supreme crime of the Fascists is to have destroyed everything that constituted human expression; they kill 'the old Adam who used to talk out loud to his horse' (an echo of those dialogues with the silent animal of the *Poemas humanos*); they kill the beggar who sang on the streets and they kill the book itself:

> ¡Matan al libro, tiran a sus verbos auxiliares,
> a su indefensa página primera!

> They kill the book, throw out its auxiliary verbs
> And its defenceless first page!

By throwing out the 'auxiliary' verbs, the Fascists destroy a part of the sentence which has no function in isolation but without which no sense is possible. Perhaps we might read this as a reference to the individual, to the 'defenceless first page' who can neither exist alone nor can be dispensed with.

The analogy of the text runs through several of the other poems and is used in a moving fashion in a poem addressed to the worker-martyr Pedro Rojas who left behind the mis-spelled message, '¡Viban los compañeros! Pedro Rojas'.[32] Vallejo himself had often in *Trilce* diverted himself with that common spelling mistake of writing *b* for *v.* Now the substitution of the *b* for *v* takes on a new significance. It is a *b* for buitre (for 'vulture' or 'buzzard'):

> ¡Viban con esta b del buitre en las entrañas
> de Pedro
> y de Rojas, del héroe y del mártir!

> Long libe with that b for buzzard in the guts
> of Pedro
> And of Rojas, of hero and of martyr.

What Pedro writes turns out not only to be a spelling 'error' but
also a direct sign of his exploited state. Yet another of the heroes
of this collection, the peasant Ramón Collar is exhorted to go out
and 'kill and *write*'.[33]

The analogy of the text had taken on particular significance
when he came to write the title poem 'España, aparta de mí este
cáliz' at a time when the Republican cause was threatened by
defeat. In this poem, 'mother Spain' has become a schoolteacher
who has absented herself from the classroom where the children
of the world are waiting to learn their lesson. The chance is that
she will fall and that the children will be left without her. Humanity will then slip back into ignorance:

> ¡Cómo va el corderillo a continuar
> atado por la pata al gran tintero!
> ¡Cómo vais a bajar las gradas del alfabeto
> hasta la letra en que nació la pena![34]

> How the lamb will then go on
> Being bound by a foot to the great inkwell!
> How you will go down the steps of the alphabet
> Until you reach the letter on which suffering was born!

Inkwell and alphabet are both signs of limitation for the 'great
inkwell' is the undifferentiated blackness of death and the letter
in which suffering was born must surely be the Alpha which
marks the beginning of consciousness itself – the moment when
man became upright and acquired consciousness; language was
the beginning of individualism which is only the primitive first
stage of human progress. The fall of Spain would wipe out from
the future any immediate possibility of going beyond this 'first
page' of human experience. 'Spain' would disappear and it would
then be up to the children of the world to seek her out again
and thus revive hope in the transformation of reality. This tragic
possibility is envisaged as an interruption of the lesson, a moment
when pencils are blunted and the text can no longer be written.
Even the poet absents himself:

> si tardo,
> si no veis a nadie, si os asustan
> los lápices sin punta, si la madre
> España cae – digo, es un decir –
> salid, niños del mundo; id a buscarla!

If I am late,
If you don't see anyone, if blunt pencils
Frighten you, if mother
Spain falls – I say, for the sake of argument –
Go out, children of the world; go out and look for her!

The image of 'teacher-Spain' thus suggests a didactic text written not by the poet but by events themselves.

It is often instructive to compare Vallejo with Neruda whom war introduced to the sufferings of the common people and who, soon afterwards, began to read his poetry aloud to a new public. The performance thus came to constitute a collective experience very different from the individual act of reading to which poetry had been very largely confined in the nineteenth century.[35] Vallejo, on the other hand, had always been obsessed by letters, by their strangeness, by the sight of print. He seems never to have read poetry aloud nor did he seem to have attached priority to the spoken over the written text. And even though *España, aparta de mí este cáliz* obviously owed much to Bergamín's speech at the Congress of Writers and his evocation of the word which 'is born and dies in a breath' yet mysteriously is communicated by the people themselves, from generation to generation, Vallejo's Logos is analogous to the book rather than to the spoken word. The written text opens up the possibility of inscribing human experience but only when that text emerges out of something other than individual experience.

The Utopia of the volunteers

The first poem of *España, aparta de mí este cáliz* is a hymn to the 'volunteers' of the Republic, those who had spontaneously rushed to defend Spain and who therefore epitomized the new man. Paraphrasing Bergamín for whom Spanish greatness had always sprung out of popular tradition, Vallejo relates the extraordinary sacrifice to the transmission of this folk spirit from generation to generation:

> (Todo acto o voz genial viene del pueblo
> y va hacia él, de frente o transmitido
> por incesantes briznas, por el humo rosado
> de amargas contraseñas sin fortuna).

(Each voice or act of genius comes from the people
And returns to them directly or communicated
Through unceasing blades of grass and the rosy smoke
Of bitter and unfortunate passwords)

Yet Vallejo makes this into something more than the transmission
of a 'Spanish spirit'. For what he sees in those very writers whom
Bergamín had mentioned as epitomizing the characteristic aspects
of Spain is a dualism which new men have now superseded. Thus
'Calderón asleep upon the tail of a dead amphibian', Cervantes
who had declared 'My kingdom is of this world and the other',
Quevedo described as 'instantaneous father of the sappers' (because of the destructive force of his wit and his literary excursions into hell in the *Sueños*), Goya and Saint Teresa – all were
unable to overcome that separation of the ideal from the real, of
the kingdom of Heaven from the kingdom of this world. In contrast, the new heroes – Lina Odena (a very different personality,
he points out, from Saint Teresa) and Antonio Coll 'in whose
Cartesian attack / The common footstep sweated cloud', exem-
plify the synthesis of the real and the ideal, of mind and body.
The description of Coll who had fought on the Madrid front and
had become a human grenade by strapping bombs to his body in
order to destroy enemy tanks stresses the conscious (Cartesian)
nature of the enterprise. The kamikazi converts the 'paso llano' of
ordinary men into the 'cloud'. The cloud is 'sweated forth' and
sweat is a word which Vallejo uses increasingly in this collection
to suggest the material production of a new consciousness.

The hymn is the longest poem Vallejo ever wrote and is closer
in spirit to 'Los mineros' and 'Gleba' than to most of the *Poemas
humanos*. Like those poems, it is addressed to an exemplary
group of people whose new form of consciousness is so superior
to that of the poet that he can only express his own inadequacy.
The tone is more akin to civic or public poetry and hence to
oratory and there is a self-conscious grandeur about the language
which can only be justified if we take into account the grandeur
of the events and the people that he is describing. Anyone reading the poem without sharing the poet's opinion of the magnitude
of the sacrifice might well find the tone exaggerated, though it is
consonant with Vallejo's entire poetics. If language had become
degraded, it was precisely because no speech could dignify a
sorry human fate when there was so little to distinguish the

human from the animal. Great speech could only be restored by a great humanity as it moved into a qualitatively different stage of its history. The word play that had characterized *Trilce* was not a liberation of the word so much as a sign of triviality. And the harmony and rhythm which he had found out of key with the disharmony and discontinuity of existence could only now be restored in a verse which once again beats with a rhythm:

> Voluntario de España, miliciano
> de huesos fidedignos, cuando marcha morir tu corazón,
> cuando marcha a matar con su agonía
> mundial, no se verdaderamente
> qué hacer, dónde ponerme.

> Volunteers of Spain, militiaman
> Of faithworthy bones, when your heart goes off to die,
> When it marches to kill in its universal
> Agony, I do not know, in truth,
> What I should say or where to put myself.

Possibly the 'faithworthy' bones of the militiaman are meant to suggest the (often inauthentic) relics of the saints. Certainly there is all the difference in the world between this purposeful advance in which the volunteers act universally and the disarray of the poet. Here we are reminded of certain traditional forms of poetry in which the singer doubts his ability to be able to describe adequately great or horrible events. Again like certain traditional singers, the poet breaks off to exclaim with wonder and admiration as he recalls the 'bienio trágico', the two years which had preceded the war when the Spanish people 'with elective hands' chose to overcome alienation and oppression, when the Spaniards had 'lit their captive matchlight' and 'prayed with anger'. Much of the poem consists in a 'naming' of the new man and a celebration of his qualities as 'worker', 'liberator', 'peasant', 'builder', whose sacrifices for the first time open up the space of the future and the end of all forms of alienation. Among these new men, Vallejo names the volunteers from outside Spain 'with their languages walking on their backs'.

The volunteer goes out to kill those who kill the past and the future, the killers of the 'book', while the poet can only cheer them on, seeing in them an idealized incarnation of his own wishes.

What immediately strikes anyone familiar with the rest of

Vallejo's poetry is the elimination of any sense of irony. Words once again spring forth from the essential unity of human experience in contrast to the aimless fragmentation that had characterized language of capitalist society:

> Liberador ceñido de grilletes,
> sin cuyo esfuerzo hasta hoy continuaría sin asas la extensión,
> vagarían acéfalos los clavos,
> antiguo, lento, colorado, el día,
> nuestros amados cascos, insepultos!

> Liberator girded with chains,
> Without whose efforts handles would not hold extension,
> Nails would wander without heads,
> The day remain old, slow and apoplectic,
> And our beloved helmets would go unburied!

Words like 'nail', 'handle', 'casco' (whether in its sense of helmet, skull or hoof) are familiar synecdoches in Vallejo's poetry. In *Poemas humanos,* they had represented vestiges with no system. But here a new and forceful language arises from the *praxis* of the worker. Now experience can once again be meaningfully structured, have 'handles'. Nails will recover their heads so that they can again fasten and hold things; 'helmets' (or hoofs) can now be buried since they belong to an animal and aggressive past. Not only does the synecdoche once more belong to a greater whole but figures such as oxymoron and paradox can be used in a new way no longer to harness irreconcilable differences but to indicate synthesis. 'Frenetic harmony', 'methodic violence', 'theoretical and practical chaos', 'to love . . . your enemy' need no longer remind us of the fact that there is no Christian Logos which would remove the paradox since there is a new Logos inscribed in the book of history by the actions of the militiamen. The consequences for the poet can be grasped in the 'Utopian' sections of the poem. Here, Vallejo refers to the volunteers as the 'rural, civil and warrior-builders of ant-busy eternity' whose role is not simply that of changing society but more profoundly of removing alienation from existence. In that era 'even gold . . . will be gold', he writes:

> Unos mismos zapatos irán bien al que asciende
> sin vías a su cuerpo
> y al que baja hasta la forma de su alma!
> ¡Entrelazándose hablarán los mudos, los tullidos andarán!

¡Verán, ya de regreso, los ciegos
y palpitando escucharán los sordos!
¡Sabrán los ignorantes, ignorarán los sabios!
¡Serán dados los besos que no pudisteis dar!
¡Sólo la muerte morirá! ¡La hormiga
traerá pedacitos de pan al elefante encadenado
a su brutal delicadeza; volverán
los niños abortados a nacer perfectos, espaciales
y trabajarán todos los hombres
engendrarán todos los hombres,
comprenderán todos los hombres!

The same shoes will fit both him who ascends
Without tracks to his own body
And him who descends to fit the form of his soul!
Embracing one another, the dumb will speak, the lame will walk!
On their way home, the blind will see
And trembling the deaf will hear!
The ignorant will know; and the wise will not know!
The kisses which you could not give will be given!
Only death will die! The ant
Will carry pieces of bread to the elephant chained
To its brutal delicacy; aborted
Children will again be born perfect, spatial
And all men will work!
All men will procreate!
All men will understand one another!

It is unmistakably Vallejo's paradise and best read in conjunction
with 'Traspie entre dos estrellas' with its ironic parodying of the
Beatitudes. The change from *Poemas humanos* is marked by the
conversion of the alchemic metal gold from a token of exchange
that has debased all human relationships into its rightful role
within nature. From this all other forms of dealienation stem.
Soul and body, ideal and real once more come together; the blind
see and the deaf hear. It is particularly significant, however, that
Vallejo is not content simply to envisage unalienated forms of
production. Now he can dream of a more profound reconciliation
of body and soul. In a striking image, he has the ant which is a
social and working insect feeding the captive elephant, a beast
which appears to be one of those many symbols of the species.
The communion between ant and elephant suggests that even the
breach between social and producing man and species-man might
be healed.

This Utopian vision recurs in the first part of poem 2, addressed

to 'man of Extremadura',[36] with its humorous references to fighting 'so that the individual may become a man / So that gentlemen
may become men and so that everybody may become a man'.
Even the animal kingdom, he foresees, might become men, 'the
vulture, an honest man, / The fly a man and the olive tree a
man / And even the river-bank a man / And the very heaven a
perfect little gentleman'.

Perhaps, as Adorno suggests, it is necessary to view things from
the standpoint of Utopia, if only to make the present strange and
untenable. We have to bear in mind too that for Vallejo the
present *was* untenable and that only a holocaust would save it.
At the end of 'Hymn to the volunteers of the Republic', he appeals on behalf of the 'illiterate man for whom I write and for
the barefoot genius and his lamb', and thus he implicitly disassociates himself from an élite. Yet for a poet of Vallejo's convictions a problem remains which the 'Himno' does not quite
solve; how to write a poetry which goes beyond individualism
without laying false claim to being a poetry of the people. Vallejo
was too scrupulous to represent himself as the mouthpiece of the
illiterate soldier and there was no folk tradition available to him.
He laid hold therefore on what *was* available – the tradition of
public oratory and of the sermon. And like the Christian sermon,
the effectiveness as far as the reader is concerned must then depend in part on faith. Gold may once more be really gold but
the poem is read in a present when this is not so, when words
are still debased and manipulated. Hence the project of writing
the hymn is itself an act of faith in the Utopian outcome.

Like one of those 'reptiles with imminent eyelashes' who appear at the end of the poem crawling behind the marching militiamen, Vallejo's only possible role is that of audience in an event
in which he cannot participate. It is the ultimate irony for a poet
whose politics depend on the notion of *praxis* and of human transformation through struggle. For the struggle is elsewhere – in the
hands of those militiamen who have good on their side:

Marcha hoy de vuestra parte el bien ardiendo,
os siguen con cariño los reptiles de pestaña inmanente
y, a dos pasos, a uno,
la dirección del agua que corre a ver su límite antes que arda.

Good marches at your side today burning,
Reptiles with imminent eyelashes follow you affectionately

And, two steps behind you, or one,
The direction of water which runs to see its limit before burning.

The final image is one of grace and purification and will recur uneasily in other poems when Vallejo attempts to justify slaughter in a good cause from other kinds of killing.[37]

The disasters of war

Many poems in this collection deal with the accidental victims of war – the peasants of Extremadura, the people of Guernica, Madrid and Bilbao who faced bomber-raids, the victims of the fall of Gijón and those who made the horrifying retreat from Málaga. Apart from the Italian campaign in Abyssinia, it was the first large-scale modern war to involve the civilian population, and newspapers of the time were full of horrified eye-witness accounts. In Extremadura, one foreign correspondent described the exodus of peasants 'driving their pigs and goats, women dragging their children behind them'. The fall of Málaga was described by another reporter as a 'tragic calvary'.

Corpses piled up at the roadside. In the midst of a staccato noise and under mortar-fire and bomb attacks, a bloody herd advanced, having lost all human appearance. The panic gave rise to collective madness and individual heroism. Many who could not take one more step killed their children so that they would not fall into Fascist hands and then threw themselves under the wheels of cars and trucks. Others tore open and bit into their own arms and finally shot themselves.[38]

Vallejo recorded in his notebook one incident that filled him with particular horror – the sealing of a mine in Gijón in which hundreds of fleeing workers had taken refuge.[39] He dedicated sections of *España aparta de mí este cáliz* to the fall of Gijón, the bombing of Guernica and to the flight from Málaga.[40] In the latter, what caught his attention was the loss of the identity of a city and he plays on the name until it turns into 'Mal haga', into a curse.

Some time, possibly in November 1937, Vallejo read his wife a poem that began, 'Cae agua de revólveres lavados' (Water falls from washed revolvers). On 15 December 1937, the Republicans launched an attack on the Aragon front which resulted, after a long battle fought in bitter cold, in the capture of the town. The victory came on 7 January 1938 shortly before Vallejo's final ill-

ness and when he had supposedly written his last poem.[41] It
seems likely that he simply changed the title of 'Después de la
batalla' which he had originally given to 'Cae agua de revólveres . . .' to 'Invierno en la batalla de Teruel'. Though there
are no specific references to the Teruel campaign, except the
phrase, 'in Aragon' (which was added when he revised the
poem), the fact that the poet asks in the fourth verse, 'Who goes
there beneath the snow?' suggests that he knew the story of
Teruel's hero, Juan Marcos who, earlier in the war had been ambushed by Loyalists when they had given the Republican pass-
word and thus penetrated the lines.[42] Thus the poem might have
been composed before the battle of Teruel though it was evidently revised during the course of the battle and only weeks
before he died. It is one of the bleakest poems he wrote:

¡Cae agua de revólveres lavados!
Precisamente,
es la gracia metálica del agua,
en la tarde nocturna en Aragón,
no obstante las construídas yerbas,
las legumbres ardientes, las plantas industriales.

Precisamente,
es la rama serena de la química,
la rama de explosivos en un pelo,
la rama de automóviles en frecuencias y adioses.

Así responde el hombre, así, a la muerte,
así mira de frente y escucha de costado,
así el agua, al contrario de la sangre, es de agua,
así el fuego, al revés de la ceniza, alisa sus rumiantes ateridos.

¿Quién va, bajo la nieve? ¿Están matando? No.
Precisamente,
va la vida coleando, con su segunda soga.

Y horrísima es la guerra, solivianta,
lo pone a uno largo, ojoso;
da tumba la guerra, da caer,
da dar un salto extraño de antropoide!
Tú lo hueles, compañero, perfectamente,
al pisar
por distracción tu brazo entre cadáveres;
tú lo ves, pues tocaste tus testículos, poniéndote rojísimo;
tú lo oyes en tu boca de soldado natural.

Vamos, pues, compañero;
nos espera tu sombra apercibida,

nos espera tu sombra acuertelada,
mediodía capitán, noche soldado raso . . .
Por eso, al referirme a esta agonía,
aléjome de mí gritando fuerte:
¡Abajo mi cadáver! . . . Y sollozo.

Water is falling from cleaned revolvers!
It is precisely
The metallic grace of water,
In the nocturnal dusk of Aragon,
Notwithstanding the constructed grasses,
The burning vegetables, the industrial plants.

It is precisely
The serene branch of chemistry,
The branch of explosives in a hair,
The branch of automobiles in frequencies and good-byes.

Thus man answers death – thus! –
Thus he looks straight ahead and listens at his side,
Thus water, unlike blood, is of water,
Thus fire, contrary to ash, tempers its ruminants stiff with the cold.

Who goes there beneath the snow? Are they killing? No.
Precisely
Life goes on, wagging its tail, with its second rope.

And war is horrendous, it rouses,
It stretches you out, fills you with cheesy holes;
War tumbles into tombs, it makes for falling,
It makes for the making of a strange, anthropoid leap!
You smell it perfectly, friend,
As you tread on your own arm
Distractedly among the corpses;
You see it, for you felt for your testicles, blushing bright red;
You hear it in your own natural soldier's mouth.

Let's go then, friend;
Your shadow has been tipped off and awaits us,
Your shadow is quartered and awaits us,
Captain midday, foot-soldier night . . .
Therefore, in referring to this agony,
I draw away from myself, loudly shouting:
Down with my body! . . . And I sob.

This is a poem where the image deliberately obscures unpleasant
implications as if Vallejo were dealing with matters that were
dubious even to himself. The setting is darkness and a winter of

bleak destruction without the usual lyrical solace of nature's rebirth and the coming of warmth and spring. Death-dealing revolvers are described as washed, that is, *purified*. They bring
grace, a grace that is not miraculous for water is simply water
and destruction cannot be represented as anything other than
destruction. Yet, in order to show that Republican destruction is
different in kind from that of the enemy, chemistry, explosives
and the dynamics of the engine have to be shown as the technological harnessing of nature as against the 'constructed grasses,
burning vegetables' and the 'industrial plants' which can only
flourish in a world at peace.

Images of fire and water recur throughout the poems of this
collection, signifying salvation and purification, grace through
destruction. Now fire tempers even the ruminants, turning the
peaceful into fighters.[43] Yet when the poet calls out, 'Who goes
there?', it is life itself which is found beneath the snow, 'wagging
its tail, with its second rope'. This grotesque image is followed by
two lines in which the alliterated *d* mimes the sound of war guns.

> *da* tumba la guerra, *da* caer,
> *da dar* un salto extraño de antropoide! [The italics are mine]

The suggestion is that war is 'man-like', that there is something
horribly human about it. This reading is supported by the final
verses in which the poet addresses a comrade who 'treads on his
own arm distractedly among the corpses'. The very fact of mortality makes both the killing and the risk of death paradoxically
human. Yet it is hard for Vallejo to humanize technological war-
fare or to persuade us that one side may bring 'grace' rather
than simply destruction. And this is all the more difficult when
the poet himself is horrified by his own mortality, at his own
shrinking from death, as he reveals in the final 'Down with my
body' of the last line of the poem. *España, aparta de mí este
cáliz* creates a rhetoric of commitment though at a price. The
poet can no longer afford irony or doubt though it is difficult for
him to celebrate the war in full consciousness of death and destruction. Based on a socialist realist aesthetic, the poems celebrate
exemplary heroes, collective bravery or disaster in a manner that
recalls other Communist writing of the time. If Vallejo was willing to accept a socialist poetics, it was because he considered that
the collective spirit of the Spanish militiamen represented a qual-

itative leap beyond individualism. That is why, even when he foresaw the defeat of the Republican side, he could not really countenance it in his poetry. To do so would have been to cross the limits into the realm of the unthinkable.

10
THE INVENTION OF VALLEJO

Al cabo, al fin, por último,
torno, volví y acábome y os gimo, dándoos
la llave, mi sombrero, esta cartita para todos.
Al cabo de la llave está el metal en que aprendiéramos
a desdorar el oro, y está, al fin
de mi sombrero, este pobre cerebro mal peinado,
y, último vaso de humo, en su papel dramático,
yace este sueño práctico del alma.

At the end, finally, at last,
I go back, returned and finish and lament you, giving up
The key, my hat and this small letter to everyone.
At the end of the key is the metal on which we learned
To tarnish the gold and there, at the end
Of my hat, this poor brain badly combed
And, last cup of smoke, on its dramatic paper,
Lies this practical dream of the soul.[1]

Vallejo

Vallejo said farewell to the world not once but many times before
he died, always leaving behind an inventory of possessions – a
shirt, a spoon, his café, and now, in 'Despedida recordando un
adios' (Farewell remembering an adios), 'his' hat, 'this' letter,
'the key'. We cannot simply take these possessions as 'charged
symbols', elements in a poetic universe which constitutes his
personal vision and is reproduced with every reading. For the
poet is somehow getting at the contingency of the symbol-making
process itself. The hat, the key and the letter belong to the poet's
empirical self, though he would also like to give them universal
significance. Yet this very project is somehow thwarted by the
nature of the objects and by his own knowledge and experience
of them which takes away their mystery and suggestiveness. Even
the emphatic opening line with its syntagmatic variations on the
theme of 'at the end' is firmly anchored in material reality, for we
discover that 'al cabo', 'el fin' and 'por último' are not simply
markers in discourse, part of the rhetoric which ushers in the last
act of his drama but refer quite literally to the limits between the

material and the immaterial. Each item in the inventory is presented as discrete, though they also extend individual existence, so to speak, by giving the self temporary empire over what is immediately beyond the body. Yet, precisely because these objects are man-made but not unique to the poet, they have acquired meaning beyond their use value – the hat signifies civilized man, the key suggests revelations beyond the immediately apparent, the letter communication. Vallejo's legacy is a cultural transmission, and one whose significance is not entirely determined by him; for the hat hides a brain which, being 'badly combed' resists civilizing influence; the key ends in metal, delivering a mute message of man's debasement of the raw material, his tarnishing of the true value of gold by turning it into cash; the 'small letter', the communication made possible by poetry itself, that 'practical dream of the soul', is discovered to be merely a 'cup of smoke'. As he had often done in the past, Vallejo caps the moment of solemnity with a pun. The 'practical dream of the soul' lies on 'its dramatic paper' but also in its dramatic *role* since the word 'papel' may mean either. So the line synthesizes very clearly the notions of poetry both as a dramatic projection and as an inscription on the blank paper of silence and death.

The finality of death does not preclude the wretchedness of man but rather throws it into relief. There is irony in the fact that *things* remain behind (even if not for long) as the poet's alibi and that, though man-made, they are only lightly touched with his personal imprint. In 'Paris, Octubre 1936', his possessions and surroundings speak as the mute witness of his contingency:

> Y me alejo de todo, porque todo
> se queda para hacer la coartada:
> mi zapato, su ojal, también su lodo
> y hasta el doblez del codo
> de mi propia camisa abotonada.

> I leave behind everything, for everything
> Remains as alibi;
> My shoe, its lacehole and the dirt,
> Even the elbow of my buttoned shirt.[2]

It is as if these objects are captured at the very moment of betrayal when, just as he claims them as 'his alibi', as the witnesses of his passage over the face of the earth, they become reified, strange, rejecting his possession of them, and remaining, not to speak of Vallejo, but of a civilization which produces shirts and shoes but lets man slip away into silence.

This Vallejo, obsessed by the pathos of his own disappearance (of the disappearance of any individual) caught people's imagination when the *Poemas humanos* were first published. For many he became the poet who foresaw his own death when he wrote:

> Me moriré en París con aguacero,
> un día del cual tengo ya el recuerdo.[3]

('I shall die in Paris with the rain, / A day which I already remember.')

Yet this invented Vallejo, fed on scraps of text, deflects the reader from the very matter that really interested the poet, that verbal exercise in humility which is the beginning of wisdom. In his notebooks, he had written, 'The death of one person is not a misfortune. The misfortune lies elsewhere.'[4] His insistent question was, 'Why the chord, then, if the tune is so simple? Why the chain, if iron exists on its own?'[5] Indeed, the estrangement which is so marked a feature of his poetry is produced by this godless paradox – that the complexity behind the production of a shirt or a human being or a poem which we accept as a given, is a baffling superstructure raised on the simplest of bases, on triadic and linear foundations which represent the skull beneath the skin. In the chord, a number of different notes are played simultaneously. In a chain, a number of smaller links succeed one another in linear fashion. But if there is no purpose other than the continuation of life, then we may well ask, as Vallejo does, whether we amount to nothing more than wasteful aberrations of nature and acquire consciousness only the better to observe our own antics.

Vallejo is the poet of wretchedness and poverty precisely because he strips his verse down again and again to these elementary postures (an approach so different from Neruda's generous all-inclusiveness which somehow leaves the reader no other role than that of mere observer). If Vallejo chose to represent himself as the wretched scapegoat of mankind, however, it is not because he wished to call attention to Vallejo the personality but rather because he had come to believe it was more 'profound and poetic' to write 'I' – always, of course, taking this as the symbol of all men.[6] To speak of all men means becoming the lowest common denominator, the most wretched of men, in order to force the reader to contemplate his mirror-image, to inculcate a Christian humility without Christianity. And this in turn means that there is nothing further from the cult of personality than these poems where the 'I' adopts such a lowly status and in which the new man can only arise out of the ashes of the holocaust or as the partner in the lonely game of death. Only out of loneliness has he the right to seek solidarity:

> olvídame, sosténme todavía, compañero de cantidad pequeña,
> azotado de fechas con espinas,
> olvídame y sosténme por el pecho,
> jumento que te paras en dos para abrazarme;
> duda de tu excremento unos segundos,
> observa cómo el aire empieza a ser el cielo levantándose,
> hombrecillo,
> hombrezuelo,
> hombre con taco, quiéreme, acompáñame . . .[7]

> Forget me, hold me still, comrade of small quantity,
> Flayed by dates of thorns,
> Forget me and hold me by the breast,
> Beast of burden, standing two-fold to embrace me;
> Doubt your excrement for a few seconds,
> Observe how the air begins to rise again to become heaven,
> Little man,
> Great man,
> Man with a heel, love me and come with me . . .

The difference between Vallejo's poetry and much of the left-wing poetry of his contemporaries is that his verse does not gloss over the terrible loneliness of human existence but accepts this as the foundation on which to work. If man can doubt his excrement for a few seconds, if he can forget the absurd economic system which makes the products of his individual body mere waste, then he might perhaps become a human being. And if he does so, it will not be to remember the poet but to forget him, not to carry the poet on his anonymous back in order to save him for posterity, but to carry on the collective genius through love and action.

That the notion of celebrating his personality was repugnant to Vallejo is illustrated by the poem 'Al revés de las aves del monte' (Unlike the birds of the hills), a poem dated 20 November 1937, in which, exceptionally, he uses allegorical figures to dramatize the conflict within the self. The framework of the

poem puts it outside the mere struggle for existence, represented
by the 'birds of the hills who live off the valley'. Yet the Orphic
power which the poet fleetingly experiences when 'the Sincere',
'the Pallid', 'the Incarnated' and 'the Intoxicated' 'plaited the
colts' manes / And the tresses of the powers', when 'the workers
sang' and he was happy cannot be separated from the outside
world.

Pues de lo que hablo no es
sino de lo que pasa en esta época, y
de lo que ocurre en China y en España, y en el mundo
(Walt Whitman tenía un pecho suavísimo y res-
piraba y nadie sabe lo que él hacía cuando lloraba en su comedor).[8]

For what I speak of is only
Of that which happens in our time, of that
Which is happening in China and in Spain, and in the world
(Walt Whitman had the softest of breasts and bre-
athed and nobody knew what he did when he wept in his dining-room.)

What was happening in China and Spain was Fascism and Mili-
tarism; for the Japanese were advancing on Nanking and the
Spanish rebels were driving towards the Mediterranean. In the
face of these events, the poet seems powerless. Even Whitman's
generous, collective vision is only that of a private individual.[9]
By implication, Vallejo suggests the inadequacy of poetry, of the
rhetoric of sincerity or grandeur or mad intoxication. Seeing, as
he explains, that 'man is evil-born, wicked alive, wicked dead and
wicked dying', the 'sincere' and the 'intoxicated' (now demoted
from allegorical figures to mere abstract nouns) depart, leaving
only the pallid one who will be 'pallid for some reason', for that
reason is fear of death. Though the allusions are veiled, the poem
suggests that the rhetoric of poetry founders on the monstrous
truth of the times. Vallejo's notebooks for the period, indeed,
suggest that he was concerned not only with the heroism and
sacrifice which he had translated into *España, aparta de mí este
cáliz* but also with the intractable pettiness of human beings even
in the midst of cataclysm.[10] We do not deduce from this that he
believed in some eternal human nature but rather that he realized
how brutally difficult change was and how little the sincerity of
the vision of poetic utopias could prevail. He could neither elevate his individual opinions and style to the status of prophecy
nor would he simplify the horrifying dangers that faced the

human state. In this sense, Keat's 'negative capability' would apply perfectly to him, standing as he does on that exposed point from which he could envisage both the total defeat of man, the reversal of evolution and the great leap forward into collective life.

The making of the legend

The irony is that this poet whose life-work was to destroy the spurious images that men worshipped, whose poetry resisted solace and simplicity, that he should so speedily be made into a cult and a legend that was to stand awkwardly between readers and his poetry. But perhaps it would be more correct to say 'legends', for there were many.

He fell ill on 13 March 1938. One of his last messages had been a letter to Luis Alberto Sánchez outlining plans for an international campaign on behalf of civil rights in Peru.[11] When he took to his bed, it may have seemed like nothing more serious than fatigue, but he was soon delirious and running a high fever. Even when transferred to the clinic, the Villa Arago, the doctors had trouble diagnosing the illness, and the death certificate gave the cause of his death as acute dysentery. All deaths are mysterious, all 'causes' of death absurd, and Vallejo's was more so than most, since no one seemed to be able to put a name to what was wrong. A doctor later suggested that it might have been a bout of malaria. The myth-makers would decide on tuberculosis, syphilis or, more figuratively, 'hunger' or grief for Spain.[12] The thirty-four days of his dying coincided with the collapse of the Republican resistance in Spain, and Spain obsessed him in his delirium. On 29 March he was said to have dictated to his wife the words, 'Whatever the cause I have to defend before God and beyond death, I have one Defender, God', words to which no weight can be attached, though they helped to sustain the myth of subliminal Christianity.[13] In reality, all that was there in his delirium were the ragged traces of preoccupations in phrases released haphazardly by the fever. The tragedy is that they would be given more weight than the poetry he had laboured over; and each witness of the agony – his wife, Juan Larrea, the Peruvian Gonzalo More – would read into these traces what they wanted to read. His wife asserted that he lived in Spain his deathbed, and 'we should admire such disinterestedness and stoicism'.[14] Another witness declared he had called for his mother and loved ones; his final words, according to one observer were, 'I am going to Spain.' Georgette Vallejo says they were 'Palais-Royal'.[15]

He died on the morning of 15 April, which happened to be Good Friday. The photographer was there at the deathbed, and a death-mask was made. If Vallejo's dead soldier had created a book, the poet was to suffer a more ambiguous fate, being abruptly reincarnated as Vallejo–Christ (he died on Good Friday), as Vallejo–Martyr (he had died for Spain), Vallejo–Militant and Vallejo–Prophet. The occasion was ripe for myth-making and the first to contribute was the Communist party itself, which had developed a secular ritual for its glorious dead. The funerals of Barbusse and of Vaillant-Couturier had become mass demonstrations, a communion of the intellectual and the masses, the assurance of a posterity with a place on the positive side of the balance-sheet of humanity. Vallejo's funeral followed the pattern. Though arranged and paid for by the Peruvian Legation, the details were organized by the Communist party. His body was transferred to the Maison de la Culture to await the funeral; there was a lying-in-state and bodyguards in half-hour shifts. Soon the left was attributing his death to Spain, and in a letter communicating the event to their members, the International Association of Writers paid 'pious homage to a man who, tormented by the tragic events in Spain, could not resist so much suffering'.[16] The left-wing press published obituaries, and the funeral held at Montrouge Cemetery on 19 April was attended by the leading Communist intellectuals and sympathizers – Jean Cassou, Louis Aragon, André Malraux, Tristan Tzara and Jean-Richard Bloch; among the Latin Americans was the Cuban poet, Nicolás Guillén. The funeral speeches were delivered by Louis Aragon in the name of the International Association of Writers in Defence of Culture, Antonio Ruiz Villaplana for Republican Spain and Gonzalo More for the Peruvian Communist party. Aragon, who could hardly have known much about Vallejo's poetry, appeared more concerned with the party line than the poet's actual achievements, for he stressed Vallejo's synthesis of the language of the *conquistador* and the tradition of the Incas, a curious evaluation, even if we only take *Trilce* into account. He added 'and the miracle was that this should have been synthesized in that modern faith in a better world which had made of Vallejo not only a poet but a fighter on behalf of socialism'.[17] The political turn that the funeral took, apparently at the suggestion of the French Communist party, was intensified by Gonzalo More's speech which stressed that Vallejo had 'lived and died as a revolutionary'.[18]

The legend was already becoming remote from Vallejo the poet, whose militancy had never consisted in the unquestioning acceptance of a party line, who had accepted popular front politics (which now triumphantly asserted themselves at his funeral) with reluctance and had entertained some sympathy for Trotskyism. If his poetry means anything at all, it means the confrontation of difficulty and complexity, not their submersion in the reductionism of tactics. But far worse was to come. For far more misleading than the myth of the revolutionary Vallejo which has at least the merits of corresponding to his poetry, were the legends of Vallejo–Christ, Vallejo–Martyr, which distorted the whole sense of his attacks on the *hubris* of Western man. The obituary notice in *El Comercio* of Lima was only too symptomatic. The writer who had been with Vallejo at the end spoke of his 'tormented face', the growth of beard which 'gave him the impressive aspect of the Nazarene'. This Christlike figure was somehow also a *poète maudit*: 'For a quarter of an hour, I felt the warmth of those hands which had caressed the flasks of sin, but also knew the harshness of the bread of poverty. Beautiful hands which had written poems of Biblical simplicity and grandeur.' 'The dead man', wrote this fervent witness, 'inspires confidence . . . Those of us who have followed his tormented agony, day by day, are already tranquil. The legend begins.'[19]

The publication of his books would provide more material for the legend. The title *Poemas humanos*, given to an edition of his unpublished writings which includes the *Poemas en prosa* and *España, aparta de mí este cáliz* as well as the rest of his unpublished verse, was to give encouragement to those who now began the *identikit* criticism of Vallejo's poetry, searching beneath his words for the man or, to use Spitzer's term, for the 'spiritual radiography'. It was as if the poems were the transplant organs in a literary resurrection job whose sole purpose was the rediscovery of the authentic Vallejo. More than anyone else, Vallejo's old friend Juan Larrea contributed to this sentimentalization, to this use of the poetry as a window through which to view the man. In 1940, he had written an introduction to a Mexican edition of *España, aparta de mí este cáliz* which he called 'Prophecy of America'. This, together with a later book, *César Vallejo o Hispanoamérica en la cruz de su razón*, turned Vallejo into the suffering Messiah of the Spanish world 'martyred by our existential Cainism, by our practical hatred of our brother', martyred too by the sadism latent in the human condition 'which only understands the glory of life through the destruction and frustration of others'.[20]

The problem with the myths is that they absolve us from reading the poetry, from confronting the treachery and incompetence of language, from exploring the difference between the ironbound and necessary and what it is in our hands to change. Vallejo knew that with every automatic word and gesture man contributes to his own damnation and imprisonment. His great achievement as a poet is to have interrupted that easy-flowing current of words which is both a solace and the mark of our despair, to have made each poem an act of consciousness which involves the recognition of difficulty and pain. The poems do not demand that we use Vallejo as a scapegoat in order to release ourselves from experience, but that we take up the challenge of the text. 'There are', he once declared, 'questions without answers' and these constitute 'the spirit of science and of common sense translated into problems. There are answers without questions', and these constitute 'the spirit of art and the dialectical conscience of things'.[21] If art has no questions, it is surely because it deals with areas too dense for reductionist formulations. The least we can do is to put the myths aside, to abstain from seeing the poet as surrogate sufferer and take on the difficulties and conflicts as our own.

GUIDE TO TEXTS AND CRITICISM

The texts

The text used throughout this book has been the *Obra poética completa* (*OPC*) which was published by Francisco Moncloa Editores in 1968. The edition includes facsimiles of the *Poemas humanos* either in Vallejo's handwriting or in typescript with Vallejo's own alterations. This edition begins with *Los heraldos negros:* it includes a foreword by Américo Ferrari and Georgette de Vallejo's 'Apuntes biográficos sobre *Poemas en prosa* y *Poemas humanos*'. Poems not included in *Los heraldos negros* and belonging to his earliest period have been reproduced by Luis Mario Schneider, 'Comienzos literarios de Vallejo', *Aproximaciones*, I, 137–81. Original versions of some poems from *Los heraldos negros* and *Trilce* are included in Juan Espéjo Asturrizaga, *CV. Itinerario del hombre* (see below), pp. 179–92. Stories and novels have been collected in *Novelas y cuentos completos* (Moncloa, Lima, 1970). There is no complete collection of articles, as far as I know, and I have not been able to see *Desde Europa* edited by Jorge Puccinelli and apparently published by the Instituto Raúl Porras Barranechea (Lima, 1969). *Literatura y Arte* (Ediciones del Mediodía, Buenos Aires, 1966) includes only edited selections and not complete articles. The collection, *Artículos olvidados,* edited by Luis Alberto Sánchez and published by the Asociación Peruana por la Libertad de la Cultura in 1960 includes only articles published in *Mundial* and none published after 3 June 1927. A selection of articles on 'Estética, literatura y arte', including articles published in *El Comercio,* are included in *Aula Vallejo,* nos. 1 and 3. Letters by Vallejo are to be found in *Aula Vallejo,* in *VP,* no. 4 and Espejo Asturrizaga, *CV.* His *Cartas a Pablo Abril* were published by Rodolfo Alonso Editor (Buenos Aires, 1971). Vallejo's thesis for the title of Bachiller in the Facultad de Filosofía y Letras de la Universidad de la Libertad, Trujillo, 1915, was published in Lima in 1954 as *El Romanticismo en la poesía castellana* by Juan Mejia Baca &

P. L. Villanueva. The two first editions of *Trilce* are both worth consulting since they have interesting introductions. *Trilce* (Lima, 1922) was printed in the printing shop of the Penitenciaría and has an introduction by Antenor Orrego; the second edition, *Trilce* (Cía Iberoamericana de publicaciones, Madrid, 1931) has an introduction by José Bergamín. Most easily available editions of Vallejo's poem are unreliable and need to be checked against the *OPC*. *Los heraldos negros, Trilce, Poemas humanos* and *España, aparta de mí este cáliz* are published as separate titles by Losada of Buenos Aires. The useful, *Poesías completas* (1965) edited in Casa de las Americas in La Habana with a prologue by Roberto Fernández Retamar is, unfortunately, difficult to obtain. James Higgins has an introduction to the poetry of Vallejo and a selection, *César Vallejo* (Pergamon Press, Oxford, 1970) and a new *Obra poética completa* with revised 'Apuntes biográficos' by Georgette de Vallejo was published in 1974 by Mosca Azul, Lima, Peru as the third volume of the *OC*. Other work by Vallejo includes *Rusia en 1931; Reflexiones al pie del Kremlin* (Ediciones Perú Nuevo, Lima, 1959); *Rusia ante el segundo plan quinquenal* (Editorial Gráfica Labor, Lima, 1965). In 1973, two volumes of *Obras completas de CV* (Mosca Azul, Lima), appeared. The first volume *Contra el secreto profesional* includes various reflections on life and art, some of which are to be found embedded in his articles, though there is also much unpublished material. There is also a brief *carnet* of jottings from the years 1929–37. In the second volume, *El arte y la revolución*, there is much material previously published elsewhere together with some unpublished fragments of discussion on art and revolution, a *carnet* for the years 1929–37 and 'apuntes para un estudio', notes for a study of art and revolution. Vallejo's projects for plays which were formerly in the possession of Mould Távora are now in the Biblioteca Nacional of Lima, though I have not yet been able to consult them. There is a useful note on this unpublished material in José Miguel Oviedo, 'Vallejo entre la vanguardia y la Revolución', *Hispamerica*, II (6 April 1974), 3–12.

Translations of Vallejo come up against the problems discussed in the introduction. A selection of poems in French translated by Georgette Vallejo and with an introduction by Américo Ferrari was published in Paris in 1967: *César Vallejo* (Poètes d'aujourd'-

hui, no. 168). Translations in English include Clayton Eshleman, *Poemas Humanos*. *Human Poems* (Grove Press, New York, 1968); Gordon Brotherston and Ed Dorn, *César Vallejo* (Penguin Books, London, 1975); David Smith, *Trilce* (New York, 1973); Robert Bly (ed.), *Neruda and Vallejo* (Boston, 1972); Clayton Eshleman and José Rubio Barcia, *Spain Take this Cup from Me* (New York, 1974).

I have found the following *bibliographies* particularly useful: Elsa Villanueva de Puccinelli, 'Bibliografía selectiva de CV', *VP*, no. 4, pp. 58–65; *Aproximaciones*, II, 429–42; Alfredo A. Roggiano, 'Mínima guía bibliográfica' *Revista Iberoamericana*, XXXVII, no. 75 (January–March 1971), 269–97. On Peruvianisms in the poetry, see Angeles Caballero, *CV. Su obra* (Lima, 1964).

Critical works on Vallejo

Vallejo's poetry received little serious attention during his life-time except for the preface to the first edition by Antenor Orrego and to the second by José Bergamín. For the rest, the only serious discussion of his work was to be found in José Carlos Mariátegui's essay, 'Proceso de la literatura peruana', included in *Siete ensayos de la realidad peruana* (1928, 9th edition, Biblioteca Amauta, Lima, 1964). After his death, the first serious biographical study was that of André Coyné, *CV y su obra poética* (Editorial Letras Peruanas, Lima, 1957); Juan Espéjo Asturrizaga, *CV. Itinerario del hombre, 1892–1923* (Librería-Editorial Juan Mejía Baca, 1965) has much useful material relating to the years before he left for Paris; Ernesto More in *Vallejo en la encrucijada del drama peruano* (Librería y Distribuidores Bendezú, Lima, 1968) collects reminiscences of friends. The second number of *Aula Vallejo*, 2-3-4, included further biographical material. Georgette de Vallejo, 'Apuntes biográficos sobre *Poemas en prosa y Poemas humanos*', *OPC*, pp. 489–96 and *VP*, no. 4, pp. 169–92 (the latter with annotated responses to critics and facsimiles of documents), is indispensable for the Paris period. There is a succinct summary by Angel Flores 'Cronología de vivencias e ideas', *Aproximaciones*, I, 27–128.

One of the most serious early studies to combine biography with criticism was Luis Monguió, *CV (1892–1938): Vida y obra*,

bibliografiá, antologiá (Hispanic Institute, New York, 1952).
Xavier Abril, in *Vallejo, ensayo de aproximación crítica* (Ediciones Front, Buenos Aires, 1958) and in *CV o la teoría poética* (Taurus, Madrid, 1962), is particularly concerned with the influence of Mallarmé and of Quevedo. Juan Larrea, in *CV o Hispanoamérica en la cruz de su razón* (Córdoba, Argentina, 1957), makes Vallejo the archetype of the 'new Hispanoamerican humanity'; Antenor Orrego, in 'Vallejo, el poeta del solecismo', *Cuadernos Americanos*, XVI, no. 91 (January–February 1957), 209–16, starts from a different approach, Vallejo's 'solecisms' which makes him the mediator and interpreter of the Americas. Many scholarly studies of Vallejo have tended to be stylistic and existentialist. The two are not incompatible since Spitzerian stylistics is directed towards the discovery of the 'spiritual radiography' of the poet. Giovanni Meo Zilio, *Stile e poesia in CV* (Liviana, Padua 1960), makes a close examination of 'Himno a los voluntarios de la República' linking up the images with those in other Vallejo poems; James Higgins, *Visión del hombre y de la vida en las últimas obras poéticas de CV*, siglo xxi (Mexico, 1970), considers the poems thematically and stylistically, relating these to Vallejo's 'vision'; Roberto Paoli in 'Alle Origini de *Trilce:* Vallejo fra Modernismo e Avanguardia', *Annali*, series II, vol. I (Facoltà di Lengua in Verona, Università di Padova, 1966–7) has a good discussion of the two poles of expression in Vallejo's early poetry. Eduardo Neale Silva has a number of articles with close readings of the poems and these are mentioned in the appropriate places in the text. These form part of a substantial book which will be published shortly. Among structuralist interpretations of Vallejo, there is Américo Ferrari, 'Sobre algunos procedimientos estructurales en "Poemas humanos"', *Amaru*, no. 13 (Lima, October 1970). The same author has a thesis on Vallejo presented at the Universidad de San Marcos, Lima, which I have been unable to see, and a book, *El universo poético de CV* (Caracas, 1972). A further structuralist interpretation is offered by Enrique Ballón Aguirre in *Vallejo como paradigma: un caso especial de escritura* (Instituto de Cultura, Lima, 1974). Another recent book is that of Alberto Escobar, *Como leer a Vallejo* (P. L. Villanueva Editor, Lima, 1973), which presents a number of close readings of poems from *Los heraldos negros* to *España, aparta de mí este cáliz.* Two

extended essays on Vallejo are of interest. Saul Yurkievich, in *Fundadores de la nueva poesía latinoamericana* (Barral, Barcelona, 1971), had three essays on Vallejo including one on 'CV y su percepción del tiempo discontinuo', pp. 39–51. Julio Ortega is concerned with the nature of the poetic *persona* in two essays, '*Heraldos negros*. La poética de la persona confesional' and '*Trilce:* cuestionamiento de la persona', both of which are included in *Figuración de la persona* (Edhasa, Barcelona, 1971). Astonishingly, there has been little good Marxist criticism of Vallejo, the notable exception being the indispensable article by Noël Salomon, 'Algunos aspectos de lo "humano" en *Poemas humanos*' included in *Aproximaciones*, II, 191–230. And recently, there has appeared some interesting criticism on Marxist structuralist and semiotic lines in *Séminaire Césaire Vallejo* (Travaux de synthèse, Université de Poitiers, October 1972 and 1973).

There are several major collections of critical works which are mentioned frequently in the footnotes of this book. *Aula Vallejo* published by the University of Córdoba has published four volumes, which include papers on Vallejo's life and work, and much interesting documentary material. Indispensable to any student of Vallejo's poetry is Angel Flores (ed.), *Aproximaciones a CV*, 2 vols. (Las Américas, New York, 1971), which includes most of the important Vallejo criticism. The *Revista Iberoamericana*, vol. XXXVI, no. 71 (April–June 1970) devoted an entire number to César Vallejo.

However, I am most indebted of all to three books which in very different ways pose the problems set by the sensory and social aspects of language itself. I refer to Gerald L. Bruns, *Modern Poetry and the Idea of Language* (Yale University Press, 1974) which, as far as I know, is unique in confronting the questions of instransitive speech, negative discourse and hermetic poetry. It was this book which led me to discover two critics of widely diverging views. They are Walter J. Ong, S.J., author of *The Presence of the Word* (Yale University Press, 1967) and Jacques Derrida, author of *De la grammatologie* (Paris, 1967). The dialectic of these two works motivated much of my thinking in the present study.

NOTES

1. POETRY AS A MODE OF EXISTENCE

1 In 'Los Caynas' included in *Escalas melografiadas* (1923), a collection of stories included in *Novelas y cuentos completos* (Lima, 1970), pp. 46–54.
2 José Carlos Mariátegui, 'Esquema de la evolución económica', *Siete ensayos de interpretación de la realidad peruana* (Lima, 1964).
3 Antonio Raimondi, *Notas de viaje para su obra, El Perú* (Lima, 1943), vol. II, has a description of Santiago at this period.
4 Antenor Orrego, preface to *Trilce* (Lima, 1922), p. xi.
5 Angel Flores in 'Cronología de vivencias e ideas', *Aproximaciones a CV* (New York, 1971), I, 27–128, synthesizes the facts of Vallejo's life from his correspondence and articles and from previous works on Vallejo, especially André Coyné, *CV y su obra poética* (Lima, 1957) and his more recent *CV* (Buenos Aires, 1968): and Juan Espejo Asturrizaga, *CV. Itinerario del hombre 1892–1923* (Lima, 1965).
6 Ernesto More, *Vallejo en la encrucijada del drama peruano* (Lima, 1968), p. 20.
7 Ciro Alegría, 'El CV que yo conocí', *Cuadernos americanos*, III, no. 6 (November–December 1944), 175–91.
8 André Coyné, *CV y su obra poética*, p. 37.
9 Espejo Asturrizaga, *CV. Itinerario del hombre*, p. 26 and p. 30. *Aproximaciones*, I, 28 only mentions Quiruvilca.
10 Peter F. Klaren, *Modernisation, Dislocation and Aprismo. Origins of the Peruvian Aprista party 1870–1932* (University of Texas Press, Austin and London, 1973).
11 *Ibid.* p. 39. Artemio Zavala from Santiago de Chuco helped form a trade union in the 'Roma'.
12 *NCC*, pp. 279–84.
13 For some early manifestations of his 'poetic temperament', see Francisco Izquierdo Ríos, *Vallejo y su tierra* (Lima, 1949).
14 *Aproximaciones*, I, 29.
15 Espejo Asturrizaga, *CV. Itinerario del hombre*, pp. 31–5.
16 Macedonio de la Torre's reminiscences of Trujillo are included in More, *Vallejo en la encrucijada del drama peruano*, p. 73.
17 *El Romanticismo en la poesía castellana* (Lima, 1954), p. 50.
18 Manuel González Prada, 'La poesía', *Nuevas páginas libres* (Santiago, 1937), p. 71.
19 Espejo Asturrizaga, *CV. Itinerario del hombre*, p. 37.
20 Luis Mario Schneider, 'Comienzos literarios de Vallejo', in *Aproximaciones*, I, 143–5.

264

21 Espejo Asturrizaga, *CV. Itinerario del hombre*, pp. 33–4.
22 E. Haeckel, *The History of Creation*, 2 vols. (New York, 1892).
23 E. Haeckel, *The Riddle of the Universe* (New York and London, 1900), pp. 14–15.
24 *NCC*, pp. 46–54.
25 *The Riddle of the Universe*, pp. 381–2.
26 Espejo Asturrizaga, *CV. Itinerario del hombre*, p. 32.
27 *Ibid.* p. 34.
28 Klaren, *Modernisation, Dislocation and Aprismo;* Luis Alberto Sánchez, *Haya de la Torre y el Apra* (Santiago de Chile, 1950).
29 Luis Monguió, *La poesía postmodernista peruana* (Mexico, 1954), p. 49; Espejo Asturrizaga, *CV. Itinerario del hombre*, p. 44.
30 Espejo Asturrizaga, *CV. Itinerario del hombre*, pp. 44–58, has a variety of anecdotes about these affairs – Vallejo's brief desire to commit suicide over Mirtho, the café life and parties.
31 Preface to Alcides Spelucín, *El libro de la casa dorada* (Trujillo, 1926).
32 The letter is dated 2 May 1915, and is included in *Aproximaciones*, I, 30.
33 Alegría, 'El *CV* que yo conocí', p. 180.
34 *Ibid.* p. 103.
35 *Aproximaciones*, I, 33. The quotation is from an article in *La Industria*.
36 The article signed J.V.P. was by Julio Víctor Pacheco. See *Aproximaciones*, I, 36.
37 *Ibid.* p. 37. Clemente Palma, son of Ricardo Palma, author of the famous *Tradiciones peruanas*, was apparently responsible for the criticism.
38 *Ibid.* p. 35.
39 An anthology of this early poetry by Luis Mario Schneider is included in *Aproximaciones*, I, 137–81. These lines are from 'Sombras', p. 156.
40 'En desdén mayor', *Ibid.* p. 160.
41 *Ibid.* p. 153.
42 *Aproximaciones*, I, 38.
43 *Aula Vallejo*, no. 2, p. 118 includes Orrego's account of the early poetry. For a list of authors Vallejo read, see Espejo Asturrizaga, *CV. Itinerario del hombre* and *Aproximaciones*, I, 34 and note.
44 Sánchez, *Haya de la Torre y el Apra*, pp. 29–30.
45 The anthology, *La poesía francesa moderna* (Madrid, 1913) included translations by the poet, Juan Ramón Jimenez and Martínez Sierra (Azorín) among others.
46 Julio Herrera y Reissig, 'Sylabus', *Poesías completas* (Madrid, 1961), p. 715.
47 *Aula Vallejo*, no. 2, published a selection of texts from Cervantes including manifestoes of the Ultraist movement. It also included, 'Dada 1919' by Tristan Tzara and the Cansinos Assens translation of Mallarmé's 'Un coup de dès'. The influence of Mallarmé on

Vallejo has been exhaustively dealt with by Xavier Abril in *CV o la teoría poética* (Madrid, 1962) though critics generally agree that this influence has been greatly exaggerated.

48 Luis Alberto Sánchez, *Valdelomar o la belle époque* (Mexico, 1969).

49 José Carlos Mariátegui, 'El proceso de la literatura', *Siete ensayos de la realidad peruana*, p. 282.

50 Details of the lecture tours are included in A. Angeles Caballero, *Valdelomar conferenciante* (Ica, 1962).

51 *Aproximaciones*, I, 38.

52 *Ibid.* p. 40.

53 *Ibid.* pp. 38–9.

54 'Con el Conde de Lemos' published in *La Reforma* (18 January 1918) is included in Espejo Asturrizaga, *CV. Itinerario del hombre*, pp. 213–15.

55 'Abraham Valdelomar ha muerto', *La Prensa* (4 November 1919) is included in Espejo Asturrizaga, *CV. Itinerario del hombre*, pp. 220–1.

56 Eugenio Chang Rodríguez, *El pensamiento político de González Prada, Mariátegui y Haya de la Torre* (Mexico, 1957), p. 85.

57 *Aproximaciones* I, 38.

58 Klaren, *Modernisation, Dislocation and Aprismo*, pp. 95–105.

59 Espejo Asturrizaga, *CV. Itinerario del hombre*, pp. 225–31.

60 *Aproximaciones*, I, 42–3.

61 Luis Monguió, *CV: Vida y obra, biografía, antología* (New York, 1952), p. 24. A. Coyné, *CV y su obra poética* pp. 27–8.

62 The best documented account of the incident is to be found in Espejo Asturrizaga, *CV. Itinerario del hombre*, pp. 237–43.

63 Two scenes of the first act were published in *Letras*, no. 56–7 (Lima, 1956), pp. 5–18. The second scene is included in 'Homenaje internacional a CV', *VP*, no. 4.

64 Letter to Oscar Imaña, *Aproximaciones*, I, 47.

65 Espejo Asturrizaga, *CV. Itinerario del hombre*, p. 157.

66 'Palabras prologales', *Trilce* (Lima, 1922).

67 Espejo Asturrizaga, *CV. Itinerario del hombre*, pp. 126–7.

68 *Ibid.* p. 109.

69 *Ibid.* p. 110.

2. THE ALIENATED ROMANTIC:
Los Heraldos Negros

1 M. H. Abrams, *Natural Supernaturalism. Tradition and Revolution in Romantic Literature* (New York, 1971).

2 Keith A. McDuffie, *The Poetic Vision of CV in Los heraldos negros and Trilce*. Unpublished dissertation (Pittsburgh University, 1969).

3 Espejo Asturrizaga, *CV. Itinerario del hombre*, pp. 174–6, lists poems published in periodicals and indicates poems written in

Trujillo and Lima, though the source of his information is not always clear.

4 This is borne out by the paring away of anecdotal elements as Vallejo revised his poems. See McDuffie *The Poetic Vision of CV*, pp. 181–203. As late as June 1929, he is still writing to ask his brother Víctor to have a mass said for him. See Espejo Asturrizaga, *CV. Itinerario del hombre*, p. 204.

5 Ricardo Jaimes Freyre, *Leyes de la versificación castellana* (Buenos Aires, 1912).

6 The poem 'El poeta a su amada' is from 'De la tierra' and is included in *Obra poética completa* (Lima, 1958), p. 76.

7 *Aproximaciones*, I, 36.

8 Enrique A. Carrillo, 'Ensayo sobre José María Eguren', *Colónida*, no. 2 (1916), p. 7.

9 F. Max Müller, *Natural Religion* (London, 1907), especially pp. 51–2. In this work Müller studies primitive religions.

10 Abrams, *Natural Supernaturalism*, especially the section 'Forms of Romantic Imagination', pp. 169–95.

11 José Martí (1853–95) was known at this period chiefly for two collections of poems and essays such as 'Nuestra América'. The quotation that follows is from a review of 'El poema del Niágara', the celebrated Romantic poem by the Venezuelan poet Juan Antonio Pérez Bonalde. The essay had been included in a popular selection of Martí's work, *Flor y lava*, published in Paris around 1910 and this may well have been read by Vallejo. The editor Américo Lugo had, in the introduction, quoted Martí's statement that 'in every word, there must be an act. The word is an abominable coquette when it is not in the service of honour and love.' In Martí's review of 'El poema del Niágara', we find some key images which Vallejo was also to adopt – for instance 'gold' (as inner treasure and external wealth); the 'wing' as symbol of the ideal and 'feet' as a metonymic figure for the laborious journey of life. So, poets are said by Martí to be unsuited for foot-slogging and solid ground. 'Filled with memories, winged, they seek their broken wings, poor poets.' Vallejo's debt to Martí has not gone unnoticed by critics; see Cintio Vitier, 'En la mina martiana' in Iván A. Schulman and Manuel Pedro González, *Martí, Darío y el Modernismo* (Madrid, 1969), pp. 17–18.

12 'El poema del Niágara' is included in José Martí, *Obras completas* (La Habana, 1964), VII, 223–38.

13 Mariátegui, 'El proceso de la literatura' *Siete ensayos de la realidad peruana*, pp. 312–13.

14 Manuel González Prada, 'La muerte y la vida', *Páginas libres* (Lima, 1966), pp. 215–23. Rafael Gutiérrez Girardot in his essay 'La muerte de Dios' included in *Aproximaciones*, I, 335–50 indicates the importance of González Prada's essay and discusses the motive in Vallejo's poems.

15 Victor Hugo, *Cromwell*, first published in 1827. I consulted the Paris, 1881 edition, p. 18.

16 Izquierdo Rios, *Vallejo y su tierra*, pp. 31–2.
17 Enrique Diez-Canedo and Fernando Fortún included in their anthology *La poesía moderna francesa* many poems which dealt with family scenes – for instance, Rodenbach's 'Le dimanche est toujours'. McDuffie, *The Poetic Vision of CV* comments extensively on the two poles of poetic expression in *Los heraldos negros* originally suggested by Roberto Paoli, 'Alle origine de *Trilce*: Vallejo fra Modernismo e Avanguardia', *Annali* (Università di Padova series II, vol. 1 (Verona, 1966–7)). The two poles are represented by the literary language derived from Modernism and colloquial or homely language. He has some interesting points to make on the sense of intimacy produced by metonymic figures. However he also shows that there is no clear movement in *Los heraldos negros* from literary expression to a more intimate language.
18 Müller, *Natural Religion*, especially pp. 131–65.
19 F. Nietzsche, 'On Truth and Falsehood in their Extra-Moral Sense', included in Warren A. Shibles (ed.), *Essays on Metaphor* (Wisconsin University Press, 1972).
20 Arthur Symons, *The Symbolist Movement in Literature* (New York, 1908), p. 8.
21 Abraham Valdelomar, 'Consideraciones sobre el ritmo', in 'Belmonte el trágico', *Obras completas* (Lima, 1947), pp. 173–83.
22 Julio Herrera y Reissig, 'El círculo de la muerte', *Poesías completas*, pp. 678–93.
23 *Aproximaciones*, I, 38, in a letter to his Trujillo friends.
24 'Impía' *OPC*, p. 80.
25 A. Schopenhauer, 'On the Suffering of the World' (from the *Parerga*) and included in Richard Taylor (ed.), *The Will to Live. Selected Writings of Arthur Schopenhauer* (New York, 1967), p. 223.
26 *Ibid.* p. 223–4.
27 'En suma, no poseo', *OPC*, p. 379.
28 Valdelomar, *Obras completas*, p. 175.
29 See 'Les fenêtres,' a poem included as 'Las ventanas' in the Diez-Canedo and Fortún anthology.
30 *Romanticismo en la poesía castellana*, p. 27.
31 Mario Praz, *The Romantic Agony* (Oxford University Press, 1951).
32 'Linda Regia', in *Aproximaciones*, I, 151–2.
33 This is one of Teufelsdroch's definitions in Carlyle's *Sartor Resartus* (New York, 1838), p. 176.
34 For the poetic subject, see Julio Ortega's discussion of *Los heraldos negros*, 'La poética de la persona confesional', *Figuración de la persona* (Barcelona, 1971), pp. 15–43.
35 *Romanticismo en la poesía castellana*, p. 20.
36 'Amor Prohibido', *OPC*, p. 115.
37 For instance, Coyné, *CV y su obra poética*, p. 77.

38 Schopenhauer, 'Human Nature', in *The Will to Live*, pp. 273–93.
39 González Prada, 'La muerte y la vida', *Páginas libres*, p. 216.
40 Abrams, *Natural Supernaturalism*, pp. 199–252.
41 Ana Maria Pucciarelli, 'Polimorfismo del pan', *Aproximaciones*, I, 282, points to sources in the *Psalms* for much of the Biblical language.
42 González Prada, 'La muerte y la vida', *Páginas libres*, p. 220. Rafael Gutiérrez Girardot has dealt extensively with the influence of this essay by González Prada in 'La muerte de Dios', *Aproximaciones*, I, 335–50.
43 Esteban Pavlevitch, 'El paso de V. por los Andes Centrales del Perú', *Aproximaciones*, I, 129–33.
44 K. McDuffie, 'Babel', *Aproximaciones*, II, 51–64.
45 Gaston Bachelard, 'House and Universe', *The Poetics of Space* (Boston, 1970), pp. 38–73.

3. THE BODY AS TEXT: NATURE AND CULTURE IN VALLEJO'S POETICS

1 'Lomo de las sagradas escrituras' is included in *OPC*, p. 271.
2 In chapter 5, I discuss the significance of punning in *Trilce*.
3 The original version is included in *Aproximaciones*, I, 166.
4 The original version read:

> Porque antes de la Droga, que es hostia hecha de Ciencia,
> está la hostia, Droga hecha de Providencia;
> y antes de no ser nada ser lágrima y sufrir . . .

> For before the Drug which is the host made by Science,
> There is the host, which is the Drug made by Providence;
> And it is better to be tears and suffering than to be nothing . . .

5 *OPC*, p. 134. 'Hay soledad en el hogar sin bulla, / sin noticias, sin verde, sin niñez.'
6 Paul Ricoeur, *Freud: una interpretación de la cultura* (Mexico, 1970) has an illuminating discussion of Freud's treatment of this game in which the mother hides from the child and then reappears. The game has a cognitive function in that the child thus learns that the mother who disappears and the mother who reappears are one and the same.
7 Georgette de Vallejo, 'Apuntes', p. 176.
8 Included in *NCC*, pp. 23–9.
9 I refer to the well-known sonnet, 'Ay de la vida! Nadie me responde', a forceful expression of Quevedo's Christian 'desengaño'.
10 In the essay, 'La muerte y la vida', *Páginas libres*.
11 According to the now famous essay by Ferdinand de Saussure in *Cours de linguistique générale* (Paris, 1968), especially pp.166–9.
12 In *Trilce* 1, islands (associated with guano) are contrasted with the 'peninsula' which stands up (a sign of human existence) at

the end of the poem. There is a similar association of islands and guano in poem 25.

13 The 'comb' and 'combed hair' are signs of social man in *Poemas humanos*. Weaving, on the other hand, sometimes refers to the silent work of the species as it fabricates the warp and woof of life with its 'unending' thread (cf. *Trilce* 66).

14 Because of the acoustic similarity of *b* and *v* in Spanish, there is no way of adequately rendering these lines into English.

15 The most obvious example of this euphemism is poem 35.

16 '¡Tánta vida y jamás me falla la tonada!' in 'Hoy me gusta la vida mucho menos', *OPC*, p. 307.

4. THE END OF THE SOVEREIGN ILLUSION: *Trilce*

1 *Aproximaciones*, I, 50. Letter to Antenor Orrego quoted by José Carlos Mariátegui in *Siete ensayos de la realidad peruana*.

2 Laforgue's poem is quoted by Michael Hamburger in 'Lost Identities', in *The Truth of Poetry* (London, 1969), p. 51.

3 *Páginas de Gonzalo Zaldumbide* (Quito, 1959), I, 117.

4 Kant separates intentions from actions, stating that nothing in the world can be conceived as good without qualification, except a good will. 'It is good in itself, and considered by itself is to be esteemed much higher than all that can be brought about by it in favour of any inclination, nay, even of the sum total of all inclinations.' Kant, *Selections* (New York, 1957), p. 271. Kant also describes the ego as the highest point on which the possibility of the logical form of all knowledge necessarily depends. *Ibid.* pp. 80–1.

5 'Que la vitre soit l'art, soit la mysticité', says Mallarmé in 'Les fenêtres'.

6 *OC*, II, 161. In his own personal list of 'ismos', he includes himself with Neruda under 'Verdadismo'.

7 Nietzsche in Shibles (ed.), *Essays on Metaphor*, p. 5.

8 *Ibid.* p. 8.

9 'Guitry, Flammarion, Mangin, Pierre Louys', *Mundial* (24 July 1925); *Aproximaciones*, I, 57.

10 Other critics, especially Vallejo's friend Juan Larrea, read the poem differently. See, for instance, his book, *CV o Hispanoamérica en la cruz de su razón* (Córdoba, Argentina, 1958). For good close readings of the poem, see McDuffie, *The Poetic Vision of CV*, and Alberto Escobar, 'El paraíso perdido', *Como leer a Vallejo* (Lima, 1973). On *Trilce*, see Julio Ortega, '*Trilce*: cuestionamiento de la persona', *Figuración de la persona* (Barcelona, 1971) and Saul Yurkievich, 'CV y su percepción del tiempo discontinuo', *Fundadores de la nueva poesía latinoamericana* (Barcelona, 1971), pp. 39–51. Américo Ferrari, *El universo poético de CV* (Caracas, 1972).

11 González Prada, 'La muerte y la vida', *Páginas libres*, p. 223.
12 'Excrementido' may, according to A. Coyné in 'Carta a Carlos Milla sobre *El tungsteno y Poemas humanos*', VP, no. 5 (June 1970), p. 58, be a misprint. However, the second edition of *Trilce*, which Vallejo may have supervised and which was published in Madrid in 1930, has the same spelling and Vallejo was, of course, perfectly capable of having invented the verb ending.
13 González Prada, 'La muerte y la vida', *Páginas libres*, p. 223.
14 Xavier Abril, 'Trilce XIX', *Aproximaciones*, II, 131–45 sees the poem in rather more positive terms as a moment when man has left the prisonhouse of contradiction. As I pointed out in chapter 1, Vallejo had at least read Max Müller at this point. Later on, he will mention Feuerbach. See, for instance, the poem 'En el momento en que el tenista', *OPC*, p. 267. Feuerbach had defined man as a passive being with needs and had seen religion as a human invention in response to needs.
15 Samuel Taylor Coleridge, *Biographia Literaria* (London, 1967), especially pp. 145–6.
16 *The Orphic Voice* (London, 1961).
17 I. A. Richards, *Principles of Literary Criticism* (London, 1967), p. 189.
18 Octavio Paz, *El arco y la lira* (Mexico, 1956), pp. 107–8. After *Signos en rotación* (1965) Paz introduced the notion of the free-play of the sign into his aesthetics, but he considers irony essentially destructive and counter to the central responsibility of poetry. See *Children of the Mire*, tr. Rachael Phillips (Harvard University Press, 1974).
19 Gerald L. Bruns, *Modern Poetry and the Idea of Language* (Yale U. P., 1974).
20 Ortega, '*Trilce*', *Figuración de la persona*, pp. 51–2 sees the Venus de Milo as announcing a new attitude to time and beauty. See also McDuffie, *The Poetic Vision of CV*, pp. 256–63, who declares that the non-existence of the arms suggests the possibility of perfection.
21 'Ortivos nautilos' and 'todaviiza' offer impossible tasks to the translator. 'Orto' is an astrological term referring to the rising of planets. Nautilus can mean either a mollusc or the name of the Argonaut's ship. 'Todaviiza' is one of the lexical inventions discussed in chapter 5.
22 Edmund Husserl, *Ideas. General Introduction to Pure Phenomenology.* (Collier Books, London, New York, 1972), pp. 98–9.
23 Bruns, *Modern Poetry*, p. 77 discusses this aspect of Formalist thinking. His chapter 'From Intransitive Speech to the Universe of Discourse' is particularly helpful for the discussion of hermetic poetry.
24 Valdelomar, 'Consideraciones sobre el ritmo', in 'Belmonte el trágico', *Obras completas*, pp. 173–83. For Vallejo music implies succession since it is based on the scale. See *OC*, I, 22.

25 Ferrari, *El universo poetico de CV*, pp. 55–6.
26 'Entre Francia y España', *Mundial* (1 January 1926), reprinted in *Artículos olvidados* (Lima, 1960), pp. 62–3.
27 Alberto Escobar has a more detailed discussion of the poem. See 'El paraíso perdido', *Como leer a Vallejo*, pp. 106–14.
28 Kenneth Burke, *A Grammar of Motives* (Berkeley and Los Angeles, 1969), pp. 506–7. Roman Jakobson and Morris Halle, *Fundamentals of Language* (The Hague, 1956).
29 For a useful discussion of this figure, see Jaime Alazraki, *La prosa narrativa de Jorge Luis Borges* (Madrid, 1968), pp. 200–25.
30 César A. Angeles Caballero, *CV. Su obra* (Lima, 1964), p. 116 gives two definitions of *ajiseco;* it is the colour of dried chile pepper and also refers to fighting cocks of this colour.
31 *Los signos en rotación y otros ensayos* (Madrid, 1917), especially pp. 332–3.
32 *Children of the Mire*, p. 74.

5. THE DISCOURSE OF THE GIVEN : *Trilce*

1 *Aproximaciones*, I, 63. It occurs in an article, 'Las pirámides de Egipto', *AO*, p. 75.
2 André Coyné, 'Vallejo y el Surrealismo', in *Revista Iberoamericana*, XXXVI (April–June 1970), 243–301, makes the point that Vallejo nowhere shared the Surrealists' sense of the marvellous. Vallejo, like the Surrealists, however, worked within the tradition that goes back to German Romanticism and hence not surprisingly, they share common concerns.
3 This is particularly evident after reading entries in the *carnets* at the end of volumes I and II of *OC*.
4 E. Neale Silva, 'The introductory poem in Vallejo's *Trilce*', *Hispanic Review*, XXXVIII, no. 1 (January 1970), 2–16, regards the poem as a statement on the artist's need for freedom.
5 Ricoeur, *Freud*, p. 253.
6 Words like 'grupada' which is here translated as 'squall' are not rich in associations. This is what helps to give the poem its opaque quality. For a categorization of the lexical elements in *Trilce*, see Estela Dos Santos, 'Vallejo en *Trilce*', *Aula Vallejo*, no. 3, pp. 22–46.
7 There is much in these attitudes that recalls Freud's view of language. See Ricoeur, *Freud*.
8 Ferrari has amply documented this in *El universo poético de CV*, especially pp. 260–5.
9 De Saussure, *Cours de linguistique générale*, especially pp. 36–9.
10 See especially Ferrari, *El universo poético de CV*. He also discusses Vallejo's habit of conflating words. See chapter IV.
11 On this aspect of Vallejo's poetic language, see Antenor Orrego, 'Vallejo, el poeta del solecismo', *Cuadernos Americanos*, XVI, no. 91 (January–February 1957), 209–16.

12 Thus music implies sequence in its very use of scales. See *OC*, I, 22.
13 Ricoeur, *Freud*, p. 34.
14 S. Freud, *Three Case Histories* (Collier Books, New York, 1972), p. 37.
15 S. Freud, 'Mistakes in speech', *Psychopathology of Everyday Life*, tr. A. A. Brill (Mentor Books, New York), pp. 37–58.
16 Roman Jakobson's definition of poetry in which 'the poetic function projects the principle of equivalence from the axis of selection onto the axis of combination' appeared in an essay on 'Linguistics and poetics', in Thomas A. Seboek (ed.), *Style in Language* (New York and London, 1960), p. 358.
17 Though de Saussure, *Cours de linguistique générale*, pp. 101–2, points out that even onomatopeia is not completely unarbitrary.
18 The anthology of Futurist poetry appeared in *Cervantes* in 1919. Valdelomar's interview was published as 'Breves instantes con Santos Dumont', *Colónida*, no. 3 (Lima, 1 March 1916).
19 Interview in *Caretas* (Lima, 22–31 March 1971), pp. 17–21.
20 *OC*, I, 99.
21 Hegel, 'Love', in *On Christianity: Early Theological Writings* tr. and ed. T. M. Knox and Richard Kroner (New York, 1961), pp. 307–8.

6. ART AND REVOLUTION

1 'El duelo entre dos literaturas', *OC*, II, 94 (*Aula Vallejo*, no. 3, pp. 85–7).
2 *Aproximaciones*, I, 122.
3 Vallejo's economic difficulties and his efforts to get a scholarship to study in Spain can be followed in his letters to the diplomat Pablo Abril de Vivero. Abril served in the Peruvian Legation in Madrid during the 1920s. See CV, *Cartas a Pablo Abril* (Buenos Aires, 1971).
4 More, *Vallejo en la encrucijada del drama peruano*, p. 153 and *Aproximaciones*, I, 51 ff.
5 *Aproximaciones*, I, 55. Selections from the articles have appeared in *LA*, though these are much abbreviated. *AO* includes only the *Mundial* articles up to 3 June 1927. I have not seen *Desde Europa* (Lima, 1969) included in Elsa Villanueva de Puccinelli's 'Bibliografía selectiva de CV', *VP*, no. 4, pp. 58–65, which gives a list of his articles. See also 'Sobre estética literatura y arte', *Aula Vallejo*, no. 3, pp. 47–87, which includes his articles from *El Comercio*.
6 Dated September 1925 and included in *Aproximaciones*, I, 58–60.
7 His *carnets* for this period are included in *OC*, I. Vol. II, *El arte y revolución*, included a series of articles which Vallejo had originally intended to publish under this title.
8 José Carlos Mariátegui, 'La realidad y la ficción', *El artista y la época*; in *Obras completas*, VI (Peru, 1959), 25.

9 According to Pablo Neruda in *Confieso que he vivido. Memorias* (Mexico, 1974), p. 182.

10 Vicente Huidobro, 'La poesía', *Obras completas*, I (Santiago 1964), 655.

11 Henri Barbusse in *La lueur dans l'abîme* (Paris, 1920) published the manifesto of the *Clarté* group with the epigraph, 'Nous voulons faire la révolution dans les esprits.'

12 Henri Barbusse, *Manifeste aux intellectuels* (Paris, 1927).

13 'El apostolado como oficio', *Mundial* (9 September 1927).

14 In an article on Remarque's novel, *All Quiet on the Western Front*, 'Un libro sensacional sobre la guerra', *El Comercio* (11 August 1929).

15 'Autopsía del surrealismo', *Variedades* (26 March 1930), *Nosotros* (Buenos Aires, March 1930), *Amauta*, no. 30 (April–May 1930).

16 Soon after arriving in Paris, he also published several articles in the Trujillo paper, *El Norte*, which I have been unable to see.

17 'Sensacional entrevista con el nuevo Mesías', *Mundial* (21 October 1927).

18 'El más grande músico de Francia', *Variedades* (24 July 1926).

19 *OC*, II, 53.

20 *Approximaciones*, I, 68. The article was also published in *Amauta*, no. 3 (November 1926).

21 'Arte, revolución y decadencia', *El artista y la época*, pp. 18–22. Mariátegui also castigates the emptiness of much avant-garde experiment, seeing it as a sign of decadence and the absence of a cohesive social myth.

22 *LA*, pp. 21–3. The manifesto also appeared in *Amauta*, no. 4 (December 1926).

23 'Contra el secreto profesional', *LA*. p. 35.

24 Raul H. Castagnino, in 'Dos narraciones de CV', *Revista Ibero-americana*, XXXVI, no. 71 (April–June, 1970), 321–39, surveys some of the early narratives. On the prose poems, see Escobar, 'El paraíso perdido', *Como leer a Vallejo*, pp. 197–208 and Ferrari, *El universo poético de CV*. Vallejo's narratives are collected in NCC.

25 Limitations of space prevent me from considering these prose poems in detail. Of special interest is 'Cesa el anhelo', *OPC*, p. 261, which projects a Kantian separation of art from life.

26 'No vive ya nadie', *OPC*, p. 255.

27 'Hallazgo de la vida', *OPC*, p. 247.

28 This vitalist current is particularly clear in 'Los ídolos de la vida contemporánea', *Mundial* (22 April 1927) and *AO*, pp. 183–5; 'Los artistas ente la política', *Mundial* (31 December 1927) and *LA*, pp. 49–53; 'Literatura a puerta cerrada', *Variedades* (26 May 1928) and *LA*, pp. 63–5.

29 'Los escollos de siempre', *Variedades* (22 October 1927) and *LA*, pp. 47–8 (in a much abbreviated form).

30 'Los artistas ante la política', *Mundial* (31 December 1927) *LA*, pp. 49–53.

31 'El apostolado como oficio', *Mundial* (9 September 1927).

32 *Cartas a Pablo Abril*, pp. 47–8.
33 'La consagración de la primavera', *Mundial* (23 March 1928); *Aproximaciones*, I, 89.
34 'Literatura a puerta cerrada', *Variedades* (26 May 1928); *Aproximaciones*, I, 90.
35 'Literatura a puerta cerrada', *Variedades* (26 May 1928); *Aproximaciones*, I, 92.
36 'Obreros manuales y obreros intelectuales', *Variedades* (2 June 1928).
37 *Aproximaciones*, I, 93.
38 'El pensamiento revolucionario', *Mundial* (3 May 1929); *Aproximaciones*, I, 100. See also the essay entitled, 'Función revolucionaria del pensamiento', *OC*, II, 11–20.
39 'El espíritu polémico', *Mundial* (2 November 1928); *Aproximaciones*, I, 93–4.
40 'Una gran reunión latinoamericana', *Mundial* (18 March 1927).
41 'Oriente y occidente', *Mundial* (27 May 1927).
42 Ideological lines were not so clearly drawn at this time. Mariátegui's editorial in *Amauta*, no. 17 (September 1928) emphasizes that American socialism should not be a mere copy of European socialism.
43 See his letter to Mariátegui dated 1 December 1927 in *Aproximaciones*, I, 72–3.
44 Ricardo Martínez de la Torre, *Apuntes para una interpretación marxista de la historia social del Perú*, 2nd ed. (Lima, 1968), II, 328 and 329–35, includes letters and documents of these meetings, most of them signed by Vallejo. The programme of the Paris cell included the expropriation of the landowners and the arming of the workers.
45 *Aproximaciones*, I, 97.
46 Martínez de la Torre, *Apuntes para una interpretación marxista*, II, 329–35.
47 'Las lecciones del marxismo', *Variedades* (19 January 1929); *Aproximaciones*, I, 98–9. He also reviewed the life of Lenin in 'La vida de Lenin', *Mundial* (4 October 1929).
48 *El Comercio* (6 May 1929); *Aproximaciones*, I, 100–1. With some modifications this is the same as 'La obra de arte y el medio social', *OC*, II, 47–9.
49 *OC*, II, 137.
50 *Ibid.* p. 138.
51 *Ibid.* p. 141.
52 *Aproximaciones*, I, 114. It was published in Lima, 1965.
53 *Rusia en 1931*, 3rd ed. (Lima, 1965), p. 8.
54 *Ibid.* p. 163.
55 'La vida de Lenin', *Mundial* (4 October 1929).
56 *Rusia en 1931*, pp. 89–90.
57 *Ibid.* pp. 219–25.
58 *Rusia ante el segundo plan quinquenal* (Lima, 1965), p. 92.
59 *Ibid.* p. 111.

60 His writings under this topic have now been published as 'El arte y la revolución', *OC*, II.
61 'Una gran consulta internacional', *Mundial* (31 May 1929); *Aproximaciones*, I, 102–3.
62 Georgette de Vallejo in 'Apuntes' has a facsimile of the expulsion order from the French Ministry of the Interior.
63 *Aproximaciones*, I, 112.
64 *Ibid.*
65 *OC*, II, 70.
66 'Las lecciones del marxismo', *Variedades* (9 January 1929); *Aproximaciones*, I, 99.
67 *OC*, I, 85.
68 His first article on 'El pensamiento revolucionario' appeared in *Mundial* (3 May 1929) and gave Darwin, Freud and Marx equal weight as revolutionary thinkers. See *Aula Vallejo*, no. 3, pp. 63–5; 'Función revolucionaria del pensamiento', *OC*, II, 11–20. On Bolshevik art, see 'Ejecutoria del arte bolchevique', *OC*, II, 26–7. On socialist art, 'Existe el arte socialista?' *OC*, II, 37–42 and 'Ejecutoria del arte socialista', *OC*, II, 28–9.
69 Parts of the plays Vallejo wrote during these years have been gradually appearing in various periodicals in Lima. However, any discussion of them would have to take into account the collection of Federico Mould Távara in the Biblioteca Nacional of Lima. There is a description of the plays and of this collection in José Miguel Oviedo, 'Vallejo entre la vanguardia y la revolución', *Hispamérica*, no. 6 (Maryland, April 1974), p. 312.
70 *El tungsteno* is included in *NCC*, pp. 151–250. It was first published by the Editorial Cenit in Madrid in 1931.
71 The story is included in *NCC*, pp. 107–13. It was first published in *Amauta*, no. 8 (1927).
72 Henri Barbusse, *Jesus*, tr. Solon Librescot (New York), made Christ into a revolutionary figure.
73 *OC*, I, 63–6.
74 *NCC*, pp. 253–71.
75 For his interest in cinematic technique, see *OC*, I, p. 76 as well as his remarks on Eisenstein already referred to. He was intensely interested in Chaplin and one of his projected plays was inspired by Chaplin. See Oviedo, 'Vallejo entre la vanguardia y la revolución', *Hispamérica*, no. 6, p. 312.
76 *Colacho hermanos* is included in *VP*, no. 4 (July 1969) pp. 283–321.
77 'Duelo entre dos literaturas', *Universidad U.M.S.M.* II (1 October 1931), included in *OC*, II, 94–9 and *Aula Vallejo*, no. 3, pp. 84–7.

7. THE DIALECTICS OF MAN AND NATURE

1 CV, 'Sicología de los diamanteros', *Mundial* (4 May 1928).

2 According to Georgette Vallejo, 'Apuntes', p. 169, the dates give a wrong impression because they refer to the revised version and not to the date Vallejo originally wrote the poem. Nor is there any clue as to how final he considered these revisions to be. Forty-seven of the *Poemas humanos* in the *OPC* are dated between September and November 1937 although according to his widow only about twenty-five were actually composed at this time. I do not know whether there is any significance in the fact that the September poems are sometimes dated 'Set' sometimes 'Sept' as if they were added by different people or whether Vallejo was simply inconsistent in his abbreviations. At all events, the dating of the poems is extremely risky. See, for instance Clayton Eshleman, the Translator's Foreword to *Poemas humanos* by Clayton Eshleman, *Human Poems by César Vallejo* (Evergreen editions, New York, 1969), pp. xvi–xviii. See also Ferrari, *El universo poético de CV*, pp. 269–78.

3 Georgette Vallejo, 'Apuntes', p. 18. The title *Poemas humanos* may possibly have been suggested by Luis Alberto Sánchez's comments on Vallejo's poetry. See note 5. We know that he intended at one point to publish a third collection of poems and, when he died, his widow and some of his friends brought out an edition to which they gave a title *Poemas humanos* which he himself had once proposed. This 1939 edition included fifteen poems later published separately as *España, aparta de mí este cáliz*. Editions of *Poemas humanos* have usually included the poems in prose which date from the 1920s and other poems written during these early years in Paris. For my present purpose, I have chosen to consider the *Obra poética completa* of 1968 as the master text.

4 For an interesting contrast, see Alfonso Reyes, *Diario 1911–1930* (Guanajuato, 1969). Reyes was in charge of the Mexican legation in Paris during the 1920s and thus represented the official literary world, of which Vallejo never became a part.

5 Luis Alberto Sánchez, 'Nuevos versos de Vallejo', *Mundial* (18 November 1972).

6 *OC*, I, 13. The poem has been commented on intensively by Enrique Ballón in *Vallejo como paradigma* (Lima, 1974) in which the author applies a structuralist methodology. Though undoubtedly a very thorough application of structuralism, the conclusions reached do not seem to spring out of the method.

7 *OPC*, p. 266.

8 Zawar Hanfi (ed. and trans.), *The Fiery Brook: Selected Writings of Ludwig Feuerbach* (New York, 1972), p. 103.

9 Karl Marx 'Private property and Communism', *The Economic and Philosophic Manuscripts of 1844*, ed. Dirk J. Struik (New York, 1964) especially p. 137.

10 Noël Salomon, 'Algunos aspectos de lo "humano" en *Poemas humanos*', included in *Aproximaciones*, II, 191–230. For a discussion of Vallejo's Marxism, see especially pp. 218–220.

11 *Rusia ante el segundo plan quinquenal*, p. 148.
12 Noël Salomon, in *Aproximaciones*, II, 222, comments on changes to 'Los mineros' and particularly on the addition of exclamations of praise ('loor' etc.) which are a feature of Soviet poetry of the time. Translations of Soviet poetry had been appearing in *Commune* at this time.
13 *Rusia ante el segundo plan quinquenal*, p. 148.
14 *Rusia en 1931*, pp. 219–20.
15 *OPC*, pp. 300–1.
16 *OPC*, pp. 298–9.
17 This reading is also suggested by his substitution of 'pirámides' in the third line of the poem (which is not characteristically Peruvian) for 'el monolito y su cortijo'. The 'monolith with its court', on the other hand, is a closer description of pre-Columbian Peruvian ceremonial centres.
18 Marx, 'Estranged Labour', *Manuscripts of 1844*, p. 112.
19 *Rusia en 1931*, p. 19.
20 *OC*, II, 142.
21 James Higgins, 'La sociedad capitalista en los *Poemas humanos* de CV', *VP* no. 4, pp. 68–74.
22 *OPC*, p. 335.
23 Theodore Adorno, *Mínima moralia* (London, 1974), p. 247.
24 *OPC*, pp. 320–3.
25 For a different reading, see James Higgins, 'Los nueve monstruos', *Aproximaciones*, II, 305–312.
26 The quotation comes from the *Eclipse of Reason* (New York, 1947) and is quoted by Martin Jay, *The Dialectical Imagination* (Boston, Toronto, 1973), p. 258.
27 *OPC*, pp. 380–3.
28 One of the spiritual exercises consists of seeing 'all my corruption and foulness of body' and then looking 'upon myself as a sort of ulcer and abscess . . .' (Joseph Rickaby, S.J. *The Spiritual Exercises of St. Ignatius Loyola* (London, 1923), p. 34).
29 See also, Alain Sicard, 'Los desgraciados', *Aproximaciones*, II, 274–83.
30 *Ibid.* p. 278.
31 *The Fiery Brook*, p. 98.
32 The baker is feminine in the original but 'female baker' or 'bakeress' sounds awkward. The division into masculine and feminine is deliberate since it also signifies sexual differentiation as well as division of labour.

8. THE DESTRUCTION OF PROMETHEUS:
Poemas Humanos

1 'Esto/sucedió entre dos párpados', *OPC*, p. 315. The poem is dated 23 September 1937.
2 Vallejo had begun work on a play which was tentatively called

'Charlot contra Chaplin' and he mentions Chaplin in his articles. See 'La pasión de Charlie Chaplin', *Mundial* (9 March 1928) and references in *OC*, I, 91.

3 Américo Ferrari, 'CV. Trajectoire du poète', preface to the Poètes d'aujourd'hui anthology, *CV* (Paris, 1967), p. 39 discusses the shoe as one of those words like spoon which Vallejo uses to indicate emptiness.

4 This form of closure could be seen as a parody of the traditional closures discussed by Barbara Herrnstein Smith in *Poetic Closure. A study of how poems end* (University of Chicago Press, 1968).

5 *OPC*, p. 315. For the numerous commentaries on the *Poemas humanos* by Américo Ferrari, Alberto Escobar, James Higgins, Alain Sicard and others see the Guide to texts. It is useful, as Clayton Eshleman attempts to do in his translations of the *Poemas humanos*, to try and arrange the poems according to the order of composition. However because of the difficulties discussed in chapter 7, this kind of effort must be tentative.

6 Gerald L. Bruns' work, *Modern Poetry and the Idea of Language*, which I have frequently mentioned gives a very good introduction to this problem.

7 *OPC*, p. 339.

8 Marx, 'The power of money in bourgeois society', *Manuscripts of 1844*, p. 169.

9 *OPC*, p. 401. The poem is dated 7 October 1937.

10 The Spanish is *urente* but Vallejo often adds *h* to words beginning in a vowel, for comic effect.

11 For a discussion of this point, see Jacques Derrida, *De la grammatologie* (Paris, 1967).

12 *OPC*, p. 359.

13 *OPC*, p. 389.

14 *OPC*, p. 423.

15 On performatives in non-literary discourse, see J. L. Austin, 'Performative-constative', in J. R. Searle, *The Philosophy of Language* (Oxford, 1971), pp. 13–22.

16 *OPC*, p. 405.

17 *OPC*, p. 377.

18 *OPC*, p. 347. Américo Ferrari has commented on this poem in *El universo poético de CV*, pp. 196–8.

19 *OPC*, p. 417.

20 *OPC*, p. 317.

21 *OPC*, p. 313.

22 Max Horkheimer and Theodore W. Adorno, *Dialectic of Enlightenment*, p. 13.

23 *OPC*, p. 371.

24 *OPC*, p. 399.

25 *OPC*, p. 357.

26 *OPC*, p. 285. See also Américo Ferrari, *El universo poético de CV*, pp. 312–319.

27 *OPC*, pp. 306–7. The italics are mine. The earlier version of the last line reads, 'en fila a bastonazos' which suggests the linear nature of existence. According to Georgette de Vallejo, 'Apuntes', p. 171, the poem dates from around 1931. See also Mercedes Rein, 'Hoy me gusta la vida mucho menos', *Aproximaciones*, II, 285–96.

28 Georgette de Vallejo states definitely that Vallejo's last poem was written on 21 November 1937 which is the date of this poem. See chapter 9 for a possible later dating of 'La batalla de Teruel'. The image of the weeping map of Spain also occurs in Rafael Alberti; see *Poesías completas* (Buenos Aires, 1961), p. 414. Alberti's poem '18 de julio' reads, 'Sufre el mapa de España, grita, llora'.

29 *OPC*, p. 433.

30 'Guitarra', *OPC*, p. 331.

31 See, for instance, 'Un hombre pasa . . .', *OPC*, p. 417.

32 *OPC*, p. 297.

33 *OPC*, p. 343. See also 'A lo mejor, soy otro', *OPC*, p. 407. The association of this other with the species is clearly shown in one of his stories as was pointed out on page 143.

34 *OPC*, p. 303.

35 *OPC*, p. 327.

36 For a more extensive analysis of this poem, see my *Poetry and Silence. CV's 'Sermon upon Death'* (London, 1973).

37 'Esdrújulo' refers to a word which is accented on the antepenultimate syllable and since such words are less common in Spanish than those accented on the final or on the penultimate syllable, the 'esdrújulo retiro' suggests a language that is removed from ordinary language, hence literary language or poetry.

38 *OPC*, p. 311.

9. THE MIRROR OF THE WORLD:
España, Aparta De Mí Este Cáliz

1 'La responsabilidad del escritor', *El Mono Azul*, no. 4 (Madrid 1939), pp. 103–6, included in Willy Pinto Gamboa, *CV en España* (Lima, 1968), pp. 173–7.

2 *Aproximaciones*, I, 116. Originally published in *Aula Vallejo*, no. 3, pp. 372–3.

3 Pinto Gamboa, *CV en España*, p. 166.

4 Georgette de Vallejo, 'Apuntes', p. 171.

5 *Ibid.*

6 'Hispanoamérica y Estados Unidos ante el tratado Nipo-Alemán-Italiano', *Repertorio Americano*, 831 (San José, Costa Rica, 18 December 1937).

7 *Aproximaciones*, I, 121; *Aula Vallejo*, no. 2, p. 139.

8 David Caute, *Communism and the French Intellectuals 1914–60* (London, 1964).

9 *Ibid.* In a letter to Virginia Woolf urging her to attend, E. M. Forster wrote, 'But I have no doubt as to the importance of people like ourselves *inside* the conference. We do represent the last utterances of civilisation'. Quentin Bell, *Virginia Woolf* (London, 1973) II, 188.

10 A. R. Rodríguez Moñino, 'Origen y formación del *Romancero de la Guerra de España*', in *Romancero General de la Guerra de España* (Madrid–Valencia, 1937).

11 Georgette de Vallejo, 'Apuntes', pp. 171 and 183. His name continued to appear on editions of *Nuestra España* for several editions after his death.

12 Georgette de Vallejo, *ibid.* p. 80, includes the facsimile of a paper issued by the Republicans of Catalonia which gave him permission to visit the region 'excepto fronteras y zonas de guerra'. The document states that he was on an information tour on behalf of the propaganda department of the Spanish Embassy in France.

13 'Las grandes lecciones culturales de la guerra española', *Repertorio Americano*, 796 (San José, Costa Rica, 28 August 1937).

14 *Commune*, nos. 48 and 49 (Paris, August and September 1937) published extensive accounts of the Congress and reprinted many of the speeches, including those of Nicolás Guillén, González Tuñón and Carlos Pellicer.

15 *Commune*, no. 49 mentioned Neruda in its editorial on the Congress. In his autobiography, *World within World* (London, 1951), Spender mentions Neruda, Malraux and Alberti as the foci of interest at the Congress and comments on the 'kind of hysterical conceitedness' which 'seized certain delegates' (p. 243). Neruda's autobiography, *Confieso que he vivido. Memorias* (Mexico, 1974), pp. 180–5, is disappointing; he seems far more concerned with stressing his own central role as organizer than in the ideological significance. And even at some distance in time, he could not resist telling a damaging anecdote about Huidobro.

16 Georgette de Vallejo, 'Apuntes' p. 172. The photographs of Spanish children are included in *VP* no. 4, pp. 252–71. Some of Gerda Taro's photographs are included in Robert Capa, *Death in the Making* (New York, 1937).

17 See Louis Aragon's speech in *Commune*, no. 48, pp. 1411–21.

18 *Commune*, no. 49, pp. 7–12.

19 *Commune*, no. 48, pp. 1409–10.

20 Pinto Gamboa, *CV en España*, pp. 173–7.

21 Included in Juan Larrea, *CV o Hispanoamérica en la cruz de su razón* (Córdoba, Argentina, 1957), pp. 165–75.

22 *Romancero General de la Guerra de España*, p. 54.

23 'Elegía a un minero asturiano muerto en la sierra de Guadarrama', *Ibid.* pp. 94–6.

24 Alberti, *Poesías completas*, p. 410.

25 'Vosotros no caísteis', *ibid.* p. 411.

26 'Himno a los voluntarios de la República', *OPC*, pp. 439–45. The

poem has been analysed in detail by Giovanni Meo Zilio, *Stile e poesia de CV* (Padova, 1960). The facsimiles in *OPC* show extensive reworking of the poems, which confirm the observations made by McDuffie, *The Poetic Vision of CV*, with regard to *Los heraldos negros* and *Trilce* of a clear desire to compress and to remove, in doing so, the anecdotal elements. But there is also, in the reworking, a tendency to fix the poem historically, as for instance in 'Invierno en la batalla de Teruel' where the poet added the words 'en Aragón'. Salomon, in *Aproximaciones*, II, 199n. observes with respect to modifications made in one of the *Poemas humanos* that there is 'la voluntad de actualización histórica'.

27   *OPC*, p. 467. Dated 10 September 1937.

28   *OPC*, p. 466. The third line of an earlier version made the material nature of the book explicit, for it read, 'libro con rango de honda fibra o filamento'.

29   The word 'moral' is important and occurs in an earlier version of poem 3 which had dealt with Irún. In this poem he had referred to 'pómulos morales' suggesting that the living body in its fight for survival represents the moral imperative.

30   Vallejo changed the final lines which had read 'retoñaba exabrupto del cadáver', and in which 'exabrupto' had clearly modified 'retoñar' so as to make the line more ambiguous. 'Exabrupto' is normally used as a noun, but in the revised version, takes on adjectival function.

31   The crucial theme of bodily resurrection also occurs in two other poems of the collection: 'Masa' and 'Miré el cadáver'; in both of these the poet insists on the death of the individual though in the first he suggests the possibility of a kind of immortality through the collective will.

32   Vallejo plays on the word 'red' (since Rojas is a 'red') which is a symbol of vitality and of revolution. An early version of this poem which was extensively rewritten is included in *VP* no. 4, p. 181. The facsimile and the revised text are included in *OPC*, 454–5.

33   *OPC*, p. 465.

34   *OPC*, pp. 479–81.

35   Walter Ong in *The Presence of the Word* deals extensively with this.

36   *OPC*, p. 447.

37   See below p. 248. This is not to diminish Vallejo's achievement. However poetic predictions are not absolved from historical judgment. The Spanish Civil War was an appalling event but in retrospect it was only the first stage of a world struggle.

38   Juan García Oliver, 'El calvario trágico de un pueblo entre Málaga y Almería', *Nuestra España* (9 March 1937) and in *Repertorio Americano* (1 May 1937).

39   *OC*, II, 157.

40   It is possible that Vallejo had originally conceived the collection

as a diary. Early versions of the section, 'Batallas', dealt with the first battles of the war in Extremadura, Irún and the fall of Toledo. 'Retrocediendo desde Talavera' had followed a section on the fall of Toledo (which occurred in September 1936). Málaga fell in February 1937. Poem 6 is a lament for the fall of Bilbao which occurred on 19 June 1937. Gijón, which is the subject of poem 7, fell on 20 October 1937, and poem 13 refers to Durango captured in April 1937. An earlier version of poem 3 had described the crossing of the Bidasoa at Irún in an armoured train. However, if Vallejo did intend to write a war diary, it did not survive these early versions.

41 Information on the dating of the poems is based on Georgette de Vallejo's 'Apuntes'. For some discrepancies, see, Ferrari, *El universo poético de CV*, p. 276.

42 'Tres romances de Juan Marcos', *Romancero General de la Guerra de España*, p. 202.

43 The line 'así el fuego, al revés de la ceniza, alisa sus rumiantes ateridos' remains obscure to me, though fire is one of the dominant images. See Zilio, *Stile e poesia de CV*.

10. THE INVENTION OF VALLEJO

1 *OPC*, p. 375. Dated 12 October 1937.
2 *OPC*, p. 373.
3 'Piedra negra sobre una piedra blanca', *OPC*, p. 341. Many critics have spoken of Vallejo's premonitions of death, notably Larrea, *CV o Hispanoamérica en la cruz de su razón*.
4 *OC*, I, 76.
5 'En suma, no poseo para expresar mi vida sino mi muerte', *OPC*, p. 379. Dated 25 November 1937.
6 Xavier Abril, 'La influencia de Quevedo' and 'La tradición estoica', in *Vallejo, ensayo de aproximación crítica* (Buenos Aires, 1958), pp. 166–90.
7 *OPC*, p. 345.
8 *OPC*, p. 429. Dated 20 November 1937. For other comments on this poem, see Higgins, *op. cit.* pp. 318–19. He regards it as an allegory on the world political situation. The notion of 'trenzar' (also 'tejer') recurs in the *Poemas humanos*. The poet often refers to 'mi trenza', e.g. 'Terremoto', *OPC*, p. 285, 'Razonando (callo) mi trenza, mi corona de carne?' Like 'combing', 'trenzando' is essentially a civilizing process, that which signals culture over nature (the 'manes' of the colts).
8 For his view of Whitman, see, 'La nueva poesía norteamericana', *El Comercio* (30 July 1929); included in *Aula Vallejo*, no. 3, pp. 67–70.
10 *OC*, II, 157–8.
11 *Aproximaciones*, I, 122.

12   Georgette de Vallejo, from an interview included in *Aproxima-ciones*, I, 123 and originally published in *El Diario de Hoy* (San Salvador, 24 April 1955).

13   *Aproximaciones*, I, 123. Abril, *Vallejo*, pp. 225–31, does not regard this as authentic.

14   *Aproximaciones*, I, 124.

15   According to Gonzalo More in a well-known letter on the death of Vallejo, he said, 'Me voy a España'; the letter is in Ernesto More, *Huellas humanas* (Lima, 1954), pp. 24–6. Sra de Oyarzún, who heard these words, also declared that Vallejo had called out for his mother. Georgette de Vallejo denies that he made any mention of his family at this time and states that his last words were: 'Palais-Royal' ('Apuntes', p. 185).

16   *Aproximaciones*, I, 125. See also Gonzalo More's letter in *Huellas humanas*, pp. 24–6, *reprinted in Aproximaciones*, I, 125–8.

17   Georgette de Vallejo, 'Apuntes', p. 186, criticizes these words.

18   See his letter, *Aproximaciones*, I, 128.

19   Asturrizaga, *CV. Itinerario del hombre*, pp. 140–1.

20   Larrea, *CV o Hispanoamérica en la cruz de su razón*, p. 72. For critical comments in the same sense as my own see Salomon, in *Aproximaciones*, II, 197. Good work has been done by those who take a stylistic approach, and obviously my own work has greatly benefited from that of Monguió, Coyné, Higgins, Meo Zilio and others mentioned in the Guide. For a discusion of the controversies that surround Vallejo after his death, see Juan Carlos Ghiano, 'Desacuerdos sobre Vallejo', *Aproximaciones*, I, 13–22.

21   *OC*, I, 18.

INDEX

Abril, Pablo, 145
Abril, Xavier, 262
Acuña, Manuel, 7
Adorno, Theodore W., viii, 183, 244
Aguirre, Enrique Ballón, 262
Alberti, Rafael: and anti-Fascist activity, 224, 225; and Congress for Defence of Culture, 228; as friend of Vallejo, 154, 159; poetry readings of, 227; war poetry of, 231, 232, 234, 236
Alegría, Ciro, 4, 13
Aleixandre, Vicente, 227
Alienation: and absurdity, 184; and capitalism, 178–83; and nature, 82, 109; end of, 241; intellectual, 172; of existence, 32, 41, 42, 49, 50–1, 112–13, 163; of one-dimensional man, 56; of poet, 21, 39; of world, 179–80; Romantic, 27–56, 103, 117
Alonso, Rodolfo, 259
Alphabet, the, viii, 3, 73, 135
Altoaguirre, Manuel, 227
Amauta, 139, 144, 148, 157
Anachronism, 1, 12; and modernism, 6–9
Anti-Fascist movement, 140, 224–6
Apocalypse, ix, 165, 192
Apocalyptic: poems, 183–91; vision, 165, 187–91
Apollinaire, 16
Apra movement, 11, 12, 140, 147, 148
Aragon, Louis, 16, 224, 225, 226,

229; on Vallejo, vii, 256–7
Arcos, René, 15
'Aristocracy of the best', 8, 18
Aristophanes, 115
Artaud, 142
Art: abstract, 155; and life, 149–50; and revolution, ix, 138–60; aristocracy of, 17; Bolshevik, 155; bourgeois, 144, 150; collective, 140, 144; committed, ix, 8; Herrera y Reissig on, 15; materialist, 156–60; proletarian, 155; socialist, 144–5, 155–6; Soviet, 151–2, 153; 'that ceases to be Art', 141
Artist, the: and political commitment, 18–19, 140, 150; and revolution, 138–60; as Christ, 17–18; Vallejo on, 149–50
Assens, Rafael Cansinos, 16
Asturias, Miguel, 25
Asturrizaga, Juan Espéjo, 259, 261
Aub, Max, 228
Auden, 230, 233
Avant-garde, 16, 17; Vallejo and, 139–42, 155
Azaña, Manuel, 226
Azul, Mosca, 260

Baca, Juan Mejia, 259
Banville, 15
Barbusse, Henri, 81; and anti-Fascism, 225; and commitment, 140, 145, 225–6; and thematic revolution, 150; funeral of, 256; *Jesus* of, 157; Zaldumbide on, 79–80
Barcia, José Rubio, 261
Baty, Gaston, 158

285

Communism, 150, 167, 224–5
Communist party: and literary
activity, 232; anti-Fascist activity of, 224–6, 229; French,
224; Peruvian, and Socialist
Party, 148–9; Vallejo's membership of, ix, 139, 150, 154,
159, 224, 256
Conceptualization, 11; and consciousness, 176; and experience,
145; and feeling, 33; and
labour, 173; distrust of, 205;
limit of, 177
Consciousness, 33; and capitalism,
179–80, 187; and conceptualization, 176; and 'malicia',
162–3; and religion, 157; and
the body, 187–91, 198, 215;
'babble' of, 78, 207; beginning
of, 3, 64, 68, 74–6, 145, 238;
Bolshevik, 166; child's, 64–6,
74–6; class- 158, 181; divided,
34; false, vii, 57, 76, 121–7;
human, 84, 86, 101; individual-
(istic), 69, 73, 116, 167, 179,
208, 212; language and, 3, 45,
83, 137, 180–1; of 'I', 106,
163; of non-essentiality, 49; of
organic man, 168, 170–8,
180–1; personification and,
100, 102; poet's, 42; proletarian, 160; rejection of, 53;
self-, 162, 163, 205; spatial
configurations of, 58
Cooper, Fenimore, 15
Corbière, 15
Coyné, André, 261
Cuadro, Zoila Rosa, 12
Culture, International Congress of
Writers in Defence of, 223,
228–30, 231

Dada, Dadaists, 16, 141
D'Annunzio, 21
Darío, Rubén, 8, 14, 29, 92
Darwinism, 47
De Berceo, Gonzalo, 15
De Dios Pieza, Juan, 7

De la Torre, Macedonio, 7
Del Riego, Juan Parra, 12
Derrida, Jacques, 263
Descartes, 187, 205
Dickens, 15
Diego, Gerardo, 141, 154
Diego Rivera, 144, 150
Diez-Canedo, Enrique, 15
Dorn, Ed, 261
Dostoievsky, 15
Duhamel, Georges, 15
Dullin, Charles, 158
Dumont, Santos, 132
Duncan, Isadora, 141

Eça de Queiroz, 12
Eguren, José María, 13, 19
Ehrenburg, Ilya, 226, 228
Eisenstein, 158, 169
Élitism, 139; see also Aristocracy
Éluard, 225
Emerson, 11
Escalas melografiadas, 25, 143
Escobar, Alberto, 262
Eshleman, Clayton, 261
España, aparta de mí este cáliz,
vii, 257, 258; and Bergamín,
229, 239; battlefront poems in,
227–8; Christian symbolism in,
233; message of, 233–9; on
volunteers, 239–45; on war
victims, 245–9; Utopian vision
in, 242, 243–4
Espinoza, Antenor Orrego, 260,
261, 262; and Bohemians, 11,
12–13; friendship with Vallejo,
23, 147; on Trilce, 24–5; on
Vallejo's early poems, 15
Espronceda, José, 7
Evolution, evolutionary theory,
57, 59, 79; see also Haeckel

Fabla salvaje, 25–6, 143
Falcón, César, 20
Fascism, 223, 254; intellectuals
against, 224–6
Favorables-Paris-Poema, 139,
141, 161, 162